Crime and Accountability:

Victim/Offender Mediation in Practice

Written and collated by Tony F Marshall and Susan Merry

Published by Coventry Lord Mayor's Committee for Peace and Reconciliation

Crime and Accountability:
Victim/Offender Mediation in Practice
Written and collated by Tony F Marshall and Susan Merry
Contributions from Harry Blagg, Jacky Boucherat, Lydia Callaway, Gwyn
Davis, Ann Garton, Anna Leeming, David Smith, Judith Unell, David Watson,
Paul Wiles and Clifford Williams.

Published by
Coventry Lord Mayor's Committee for Peace and Reconciliation
http://coventrycityofpeace.uk
covlmpc@gmail.com, 176 Greendale Road, Coventry CV5 8AY
on behalf of the Coventry Restorative Justice Forum
http://www.covrj.uk

OGL

Publication History
Originally published for HOME OFFICE by HMSO © Crown copyright 1990
Published by Coventry Lord Mayor's Committee for Peace and Reconciliation
2018

ISBN
Paperback   9781717830241
Hardback   9781871281484
EBook   9781871281491

Foreword

This report describes the first substantial empirical research carried out in the country on mediation and reparation. Its immediate occasion was the decision by the then Home Secretary, Mr Leon Brittan, in 1984 and 1985, to fund four experimental mediation and reparation schemes in the United Kingdom. Arrangements were set in hand by the Home Office Research and Planning Unit to monitor those experimental projects. According to a plan devised by the senior author of this report, Mr Tony Marshall, they were studied by groups of independent researchers, based in each of the four areas, and it fell to Mr Marshall (then of the Home Office Research and Planning Unit) to, supervise, supplement and pull together their work. In addition, as Mr Marshall explains in his acknowledgments, a team of researchers based at Bristol University carried out further studies.

Individual reports on the progress of various schemes have been available within the Home Office for some time. One study has already been published (Research and Planning Unit Paper 42). But only now has it proved possible for all the wealth of material gathered during the experimental period to be brought together in one single coherent report. During the preparation of the report, Mr Marshall, the senior author, took leave of absence from the Research and Planning Unit to become Executive Director of the Forum for Initiatives in Reparation and Mediation (FIRM), thus pursuing in a practical way the academic interest so well evidenced in this study.

This report has gained greatly from Mr Marshall's deep interest in and practical commitment to the concepts of reparation and mediation. It has grown into much more than a simple account of the progress of the four experimental schemes, to become a full and eloquent analysis of the concepts and promise of reparation and mediation. This fuller analysis is inevitably to a large extent personal to the senior author. A new area is being opened up for analysis and discussion. This report therefore cannot be taken as expressing 'a Home Office view'. But nonetheless it clearly should be available in the public domain. It is a fully documented, carefully argued account by a scholar, with considerable personal commitment, of some important innovatory work.

M TUCK

Acknowledgements

This research could not have taken place at all without the full cooperation of every one of the schemes involved. That they suffered the imposition of detailed record-forms on every case, numerous enquiries and demands from a variety of researchers, and the pressure of knowing they were under scrutiny, without anything more than occasional good-natured groans of exasperation, says a lot for the forbearance and understanding of everyone involved in the schemes. In the opinion of the authors it should be adduced as further evidence of the essential worthiness of the projects that those who operated them were so genuinely pleasant to work with, and so imbued with a desire to help the parties — whether victim, offender, policeman, social worker, magistrate, or researcher — with whom they came into contact, that it was difficult to conceive that the motivations and ideals to which they adhered were not of some importance. Behind all the ideologies and justifications that are bandied about, the basic idea that the necessarily bureaucratic and routinised organisation of justice institutions in large-scale modern societies needs to be tempered by humanitarian concerns and opportunities for personal involvement is surely indisputable.

The ideas of the senior author have been influenced by interaction with a great number of people involved in some way with victim/offender mediation, but most especially by John Harding, Chief Probation Officer in Hampshire, and Martin Wright, currently working for the National Association of Victims Support Schemes, who were both influential in originally introducing many of the ideas concerning reparation into this country; by Rose Ruddick, Peter Dixon and John Blinston, with whom we have enjoyed many fruitful and intensive conversations about mediation, and who have all been responsible for running reparation schemes themselves; by Howard Zehr, who set up one of the first victim/offender mediation schemes in the United States and who has inspired many by his realistic brand of idealism; by Jonathan Gosling, coordinator of the Newham Conflict and Change Project, who was a constant reminder that there is a world outside of criminal justice; by Professor Paul Rock of the London School of Economics, who provided a standard of academic detachment in innumerable discussions of the development of mediation; and by all members of the Executive Committee of the Forum for Initiatives in Reparation and Mediation (FIRM), some of whom are also mentioned above in other capacities, who have been both supportive and inspiring in their devotion to the 'cause' of promoting humanitarian conflict-settlement. There have also been many anonymous individuals who have raised awkward and penetrating questions whenever the senior author has had the pleasure of giving talks on the subject of mediation, and who no doubt received less than satisfactory answers at the time, but who caused in the longer term a re-examination of assumptions and ideas that might otherwise have obstructed the path of objectivity and perspicacity.

This research has also been made possible only by the combination of efforts by a large number of researchers working separately but in coordination with each other. The Research and Planning Unit took direct responsibility for the more mundane task of analysing well over a thousand sets of forms pertaining to particular cases, and took the lead in keeping in touch with developments in each project and in coordinating the research. It also compiled a series of case-studies from detailed records kept by schemes and from interviews with the mediators. In carrying this out, the authors were assisted at various times by students temporarily employed at the Home Office: Lydia Callaway, Nigel Mankerty and Vic Hayes. Lydia in particular carried out a great deal of the coding and early analyses and composed many of the case-studies used in the report.

The four Home Office funded projects were studied more intensively by field teams of independent researchers financed on a part-time basis by the Home Office. The Cumbria scheme was the focus of the work of Harry Blagg and David Smith of Lancaster University, who had previously had experience of reparation schemes when studying the Northants Juvenile Liaison Bureaux and the South Yorkshire scheme. The Leeds scheme was the subject of research directed by Paul Wiles of Sheffield University, initially by Ann Garton, who, to the distress of all who knew her, was killed in a car crash just after completion of an excellent interim report. Ann's place was taken eventually by Clifford Williams, of Bradford University, who had previously succeeded Harry Blagg and David Smith in studying the South Yorkshire project. The responsibility for both Coventry and Wolverhampton projects was shared by Judith Unell and Anna Leeming. All of these fieldwork teams have produced separate reports which it is hoped will be published in their entirety, but their findings are summarised here and are integral to the report, which would have been very much impoverished without the data they could provide, particularly from their interviews with victims and offenders who had had experience of the schemes.

Lastly, the Research and Planning Unit funded a team of researchers at Bristol University — Gwynn Davis, David Watson and Jacky Boucherat — to carry out two studies, one (published already as Research and Planning Unit Paper 42) surveying all schemes in England and Wales, especially in relation to their aims and mode of operation, and the other, by direct observation, studying what actually went on in the course of mediation and other negotiations. This research has also had a great influence on the findings of this report, especially through its insights into what actually happens in the course of victim/offender mediation. It has not been possible, in the interests of legibility, to recognise the authorship of every phrase or paragraph taken from the reports of the various researchers. Only major passages are credited to individuals. Even these extracts have usually been subject to editorial amendment. The report, therefore, is a joint effort, but responsibility for the final wording, interpretation and overall conclusions lies solely with Tony Marshall and Susan Merry.

TONY F MARSHALL
SUSAN MERRY

April 1988

Definitions

The words 'mediation' and 'reparation' are used frequently throughout this report. The reader may appreciate at the outset some explanation of how these terms are being used, given the looseness with which they have tended to be employed generally.

(i) *Mediation*   Mediation is the intervention of a third party to help two (or more) parties in conflict to resolve their differences and come to some kind of settlement.

(ii) *Reparation*   Reparation, as used here, is the 'paying back' by the offender to the victim of that which has been taken away — which may be material (money/property/physical well-being) or non-material (feelings of confidence or safety, for instance). The reparation may be 'in kind' (eg repayment of cash stolen, mending the damage) or take some other material form (compensation for injury). Reparation is one form of settlement as a result of victim/offender mediation. Reparation may also be used more generally to include non-material forms of settlement (eg apology), but is used in this report to refer to the material only.

(iii) *Reparation Scheme*   This was the popular term for referring to the projects set up to provide mediation between victims and offenders, which were expected to lead to some kind of reparation. The projects are also referred to as 'victim-offender mediation schemes'. The two terms are used interchangeably here. Other means of arranging reparation (eg compensation orders or community service orders) are not included in the term 'reparation scheme' as used here and are not the subject-matter of this report. Compensation orders were the subject of another recent Home Office Research Study (Newburn, 1988).

Contents

CHAPTER 1

Origins

Imaginations

Whether or not they ever meet, offenders and their victims are locked into a relationship. Without knowing each other in reality, they know one another intimately in their imaginations.

Matza (1964) was one of the first criminologists to recognise formally that a major mental component in the commission of crime was what he called the 'technique' of *neutralization*. In essence, neutralization is a denial of harm — 'he'll never miss it', of responsibility — 'I'd had a few pints', of injustice — 'they always overcharge anyway', or of intent — 'we were only mucking about'. Such denials of the criminality of their action were supposed to enable an offender to overcome the moral constraints against criminal behaviour. While it has been difficult to measure the degree to which such neutralization is a *causal* factor in crime, as distinct from a *post hoc* rationalisation, there has been a wealth of subsequent research evidence in favour of the frequency and universality of neutralizing statements by offenders, over a variety of offence-types, including, most recently, Cressey's (1986) study of white-collar fraud. Whether or not neutralization is a causal factor, it is certainly a barrier preventing the offender from acceptance of guilt and from taking a realistic view of the consequences of his/her behaviour. This may obstruct that learning from past mistakes that probation officers or social workers are trying to achieve in their endeavours to 'reform' their charges.

One important element in neutralization is the fact that the offender may never have to deal directly, either during the commission of the offence or subsequently, with the victim, never having to face up to their individuality or the harm they have suffered. The victim can therefore be seen in terms of conventional stereotypes that reinforce the denial of harm. That is, they can be seen as members of that society against which offenders see themselves rebelling — the rich and heartless, the authoritarian, the hypocritical conformist, the sententious snob, or whatever the favourite imagined target may be. The reality is seldom so simple and generally confounds the naive rationalisations of the stereotypes. Even the self-image as a rebel may itself be yet another technique of neutralization, as a more acceptable motive than that of, say, greed or laziness. Even if rebellion is a genuine motive, its expression against individually blameless victims, indiscriminately chosen, is likely to be a particularly unconstructive expression of such emotions that brings down social retribution without any contribution to social reform, often indeed inviting the opposite reaction of rejection and resistance to change.

While neutralization may be the commonest reaction of an offender to his/her own behaviour, there are individuals who have committed offences for which they feel afterwards genuine contrition. For them an encounter with the victim would not serve to break down neutralizing self-justifications, which do not exist, but might serve the quite separate purpose of being able to relieve their feelings through atonement and 'putting things to rights' that would enable them to regularise once more their relationship to society (cf. Wright, 1982). One must particularly bear in mind that not all crimes are committed for cynical motives. Some offending, especially non-property crimes but not exclusively so, constitutes a cry for help — a desperate attempt to force others to take notice of one's plight. Marx (1976) found that this was a common motive for the more 'emotional' sorts of crime like vandalism and assault. In such cases, the 'offender' is usually more than ready to regularise relationships: that may have been the ultimate aim of the original outburst anyway.

One might, in line with these thoughts, divide offenders up into three groups — the contrite, the neutralizers, and, by elimination, the antisocial. The salience of an encounter with their victims for each of the groups would be quite different. For the contrite — reparation; for the neutralizers — realisation, with reparation logically in train; but for the antisocial, who realise the harm done and have no regrets, it is difficult to see any advantage in terms of reform. This distinction is purely 'idealistic', however. Any particular offender will almost certainly reveal aspects of all three conditions. Meeting the victim will be of variable effect according to the degree to which contrition, neutralization and antisociality are each components of the offender's make-up.

Not only do offenders have stereotypes of society and therefore of their victims as members of that society, but all members of society, most or all of whom will at some time be a victim, have stereotypes of offenders that may be more or less realistic. When we are victimised, especially by someone who remains unknown to us, these stereotypes come to the fore in how we imagine the miscreant. Amongst these stereotypes at such a time, there is no doubt, the 'antisocial' will tend to predominate as the most likely conception of the assailant. Victims support volunteers meet time after time the victims who wait in fear of the return of the supposed ogre who previously invaded their privacy, the victims who cannot walk down the street without suspecting every neighbour they meet, or the victims who fume with impotent anger over the wickedness of people who cannot possibly 'have any thought for others'.

Such stereotypes, along with the anger, the upset, the hurt, the self-doubt, mourning over the loss, the persistent memory like a bad dream, the loss of confidence in one's safety, and, most of all, the impotence of inaction, make the struggle back to normality much more difficult for the victim. (Cf. Shapland et al., 1985; Maguire and Corbett, 1987.) Merely to know who the offender was, what he/she was like, may allay some fears. The reality is seldom as awesome as the imagined. To meet that offender (under safe conditions) is also to be given an opportunity to express one's hurt and anger directly to the one who caused it, to gain understanding of that person's motivation and circumstances, to receive that contrition that serves symbolically to restore the social balance, and perhaps to receive reparation that restores the material balance. On top of that, it gives the victim a chance, if the contrition is accepted as genuine, and if the loss is not too severe, both to censure and to forgive, and it is the act of forgiving, Zehr (1985) submits, that allows the victim to put a closure on the 'whole unfortunate experience, to draw a line under the balance-sheet, and to start to lead a normal life again.

Both victims and offenders may, therefore, stand to gain in different ways from directly encountering one another, in the right circumstances, after the offence. 'Society', too, may gain from such transactions which hold offenders accountable and expect them to play an active part in making good, which may serve the ends of victims, and which may help break down the crude stereotypes of 'good' and 'evil' that often lead to precipitate rejection of the potentially redeemable. Indeed, it is society which produces crime and society ultimately that must control it. That society is not some abstract notion of 'the State' or 'the authorities', but living communities of individual citizens. The law may draw the bottom line, the minimal standard of social behaviour, but, Shanholtz (1986) argues:

This standard is far less than that with which most communities are familiar, or would want to embrace. Individuals and neighbourhood entities have the ability to adopt the behaviour of excellence, provided that they exercise the necessary responsibility to make this expected standard a reality. The greater the reliance on police and agency coercion and fear mechanisms, the more likely that neighbourhoods will suffer a decrease in social responsibility (ie. neighbourhood atrophy), and an increase in the levels of fear and insecurity (ie. unacceptable behaviour).

One of the conditions for a community to be able to control its own members is the capacity to see deviance in a realistic light and its perpetrators as individuals and not as stigmatised social types. Only then can it take positive steps towards reintegration and avoid that polarisation between the law-abiding and the antisocial that creates and reinforces the stereotypes that breed escalating crime. (Several criminological theories — eg. Hirschi, 1969 — are based on the disintegrative nature of modern society and the importance of social ties in the prevention of crime. The converse of these theories is that if ties with conventional citizens are limited, people will be prone to the influence of deviant individuals who do offer a relationship, as is argued by such theories as differential association (Sutherland, 1939) or those evoking subcultural causes (eg.

4

Cohen, 1955; Wolfgang and Ferracuti, 1967). These ideas have recently been synthesised in a paper by Krohn, 1986, which focuses on social ties as the key feature in the explanation of delinquent behaviour. Another recent attempt at integrating criminological theory — Groves and Sampson, 1987 — is critical of such individual-level explanations, but still stresses relationships between groups, classes, and other sub-sections of society that constitute a sociological equivalent of interpersonal relationships.)

The criminal justice system — for good reasons of its own — works by and large to avoid just such contact between the offender and the public that the above arguments would lead one to support. It tries to avoid the trouble that may erupt in the wake of unresolved crime (desires for revenge, for instance) by taking the matter entirely out of the hands of the initial parties. This saves victims a great deal of time and trouble, and also provides them with considerable reassurance. Unfortunately, it may also leave them with a feeling of impotence, a feeling that their concerns are not considered important or relevant, and a desire to know more about what is going on. Surveys of victims and of their involvement in criminal justice (Shapland et al. 1985; Shapland and Cohen, 1987) indicate strongly that their lack of involvement is a frequent and serious concern. Even when they are awarded compensation in court, they may not know of this before the first cheque arrives out of the blue, and are often alienated by the length of time taken for it to be paid, perhaps in small infrequent instalments (Newburn, 1988), so that memories of the crime are continually being resurrected instead of being laid to rest once and for all. (Edelherz, 1978, gives a striking example of a man convicted of murder ordered to pay 40% of his earnings for life to the victim's sons, starting on release from prison. The family had to take legal proceedings to try to quash the order because it would only serve to resurrect painful memories and because it might put the sons in perpetual fear for their lives at the hands of a man who had to bear such an awesome burden.)

The imposing edifice of justice is also meant to exert a profound effect upon the offender. It no doubt does this, but it is difficult to be sure of the lesson that is learnt. Zehr (1985) thinks that the lesson the offender takes away is not that intended:

...our legal process does not encourage...accountability on the part of offenders. Nowhere in the process are offenders given the opportunity to understand the implications of what they have done. Nowhere are they encouraged to question the stereotypes and rationalizations...that made it possible for them to commit their offences. In fact, by focusing on purely legal issues, the criminal process will tend to sidetrack their attention, causing them to focus on legal, technical definitions of guilt, on the possibilities for avoiding punishment, on the injustices they perceive themselves to undergo.

The criminal process, then, not only fails to encourage a real understanding of what they have done; it actively discourages such a realization. And it does nothing to encourage offenders to take responsibility to right the wrong they have committed.

The criminal justice system avoids the active involvement of victim and offender for another reason, too. Legal justice is based on equity — equal treatment for equal wrongs — and the uniformity of decision-making this calls for is supported by a high degree of professionalisation and specialisation among the personnel involved. It is difficult to reconcile this with the concept of individual parties bargaining over reparation. The uniformity achieved by the formal process, however, has considerable limitations (cf. Tarling, 1979) and, more importantly, this legal concept of justice is not the only way of defining it, as one of the authors has explored elsewhere (Marshall, 1 988a). If a more effective way of dealing with offenders and helping victims presents itself, the issue of justice (as legally defined) is not necessarily to be seen as an insurmountable objection. It does raise questions, however, of ensuring fairness and guaranteeing individual rights that alternative arrangements will have to answer convincingly.

This preamble has introduced the essential ideas behind victim/offender mediation to which the achievements documented here must be related. To summarise these basic ideas:

(a) Offenders should be held accountable for the harm they have caused and should be expected, whenever possible, to do as much as they can personally to assuage that harm and to put matters right with the victim.

(b) Victims should be empowered to take an active part in the criminal process.

(c) Citizens generally ('the community') should be encouraged to play an active role in crime prevention and local social control.

It should be stressed that these ideas, as far as the movement towards victim/offender mediation goes, are essentially pragmatic and derived from individuals' personal experience (eg as social workers) or their beliefs (eg, *infra*, the role played by the Mennonites in North America in developing victim/offender schemes). These same concepts also play an important role in some criminological theories, most notably those of the self-styled 'abolitionists' (see Bianchi and Van Swaaningen, 1986), especially Nils Christie (1977, 1982) who stresses the need for the parties concerned to keep hold of 'their' problems or conflicts and to take an active part in their solution, and for the criminal system to focus more on reparative justice (that reintegrates victim and offender into the society from which, because of the crime, they have become alienated) than on punitive justice (that merely reinforces that alienation). An argument for a restitution-based process in terms of 'justice for victims' has also been made by Barnett (1978). Nevertheless, there is next to no empirical evidence as to the efficacy of such ideas — indeed the experience of those reparation schemes that attempt to put them into operation is one of the first practical tests, albeit rudimentary and unsystematic, of the worth of these theories.

The Rise of VORP

We therefore move on from the ideas of the innovators to what they have actually set in motion. Umbreit (1985) has documented the origins of victim/offender mediation in practice in America. The first schemes, in the early 1970s, used such mediation for specific purposes. In such schemes as the Minneapolis Reparation Center, which sought primarily to provide a residential alternative to custody for property offenders, face-to-face meetings with victims were used in order to determine compensation by the offender, such compensation being seen as part of the package of measures that the offender should meet in order for courts to see the scheme as a viable disposal.

In Oklahoma juvenile offenders who were assigned reparative responsibility as part of their sentence might write a letter of apology to the victims or meet briefly with them in order to convey such apology directly.

When all juvenile custodial institutions were closed down in Massachusetts in 1972, there quickly grew up a profusion of community-based facilities, many of which employed restitution programmes. These were organised into a state-wide Youth Services Restitution Program in 1979, taking offenders committed to the Department of Youth Services by the court, or on direct referral from the court. It concentrated on economically disadvantaged youth in an attempt to overcome delinquency that was seen as a product of the social alienation brought on by unemployment. Whenever possible, offenders are brought face to face with their victims to work out a reparative programme, often involving community service jobs found for the offenders to enable them to earn the money to pay compensation. As quoted by Alper and Nichols (1981), they were *"designed so that the juvenile offenders will repay society in a constructive, tangible manner...[and] to involve the youth, their victims and the relevant communities."* The restitution was only one component in a whole programme of counselling, education and training. Similar schemes are also described in Harding (1982) and Wright (1982).

The main rationale for such schemes was the expected impact such responsibility would have on the offender, and the Oklahoma schemes claimed lower recidivism rates. A secondary rationale for those schemes that arranged compensation was the benefit to the victim, in material terms, a benefit which at that time was not generally available through the courts in America, as it was, via the compensation order, in Great Britain. Where direct reparation was not possible such schemes were also able to arrange some kind of community service for the offender whereby amends could be made to society in general. Again this was made more significant by the fact that a Community Service Order, as exists in Britain, was not available to American courts as a disposal.

It was out of one of the ad hoc instances of victim/offender mediation to arrange reparation, in Kitchener, Ontario (Canada), that the first of the **Victim Offender Reconciliation Projects (VORP)** arose in 1974. The judge was so impressed by what happened in this particular case that he encouraged the use of such mediation on a more regular basis. The VORP, however, assumed much more general aims than any previous scheme had done. As its title suggests, it was not concerned solely with reparation, although this remained an important part, but also with the psychological impact the meeting might have on both offender and victim, and the opportunity it gave for both of them, through personal reconciliation, to be reconciled with the wider community as well, becoming normal citizens again as opposed to remaining classed as 'offender' and 'victim'. Such aims were particularly fostered by the beliefs of the local Mennonite community that favoured dealing with trouble within that community rather than disclaiming responsibility by leaving it entirely in the hands of the legal system. Their religious beliefs also stressed the need for the individual to be able to 'atone' for misdeeds, which could be achieved by making reparation materially and symbolically (cf. Umbreit, 1985).

The first VORP in the United States was set up in 1978 at Elkhart, Indiana, also through the agency of the Mennonites, and the idea was soon copied in many communities across the United States, originally in smaller towns that retained a greater sense of community, but latterly, too, in large urban areas. A similar religious group, the Quakers, who espoused the same beliefs in reconciliation and community integration, were also responsible for setting up community mediation schemes that were seen as alternative fora for settling disputes to those provided by the formal courts. Both types of scheme have spread beyond their religious origins as the advantages of social reintegration that they promised were recognised by other social groups.

Now, across North America, there are over 70 schemes employing the VORP model or something similar. For the most part such schemes intervene at the court stage of legal proceedings, sometimes between conviction and sentence (66 per cent, according to Umbreit, 1985), in which case the outcome may be taken into account by the judge in sentencing, but more often post-sentence (76 per cent of schemes had dealt with cases at this stage), in conjunction with a probation order. Nearly half of all programmes had also taken some pre-trial referrals on diversion from prosecution. Although most projects therefore seem to range over a wide range of points in the criminal justice process, research by Coates and Gehm (1985) on a sample of cases from five schemes showed a great preponderance of post-sentence referrals (80 per cent), with 19 per cent pre-court and only one out of 70 between conviction and sentence. One of the major Canadian projects, in Ontario, is entirely post-sentence (Dittenhoffer and Ericson, 1983). In less serious cases the time-interval between conviction and sentence will usually be very short or non-existent, so that intervention at that stage is often impossible. Referrals to the American VORPs come usually through the probation service, particularly from specially designated Restitution Officers (thus emphasising victims' interests at least as much as offenders').

At least one project operates completely between conviction and sentence, however. The Minnesota VORP deals with juvenile burglary offenders at this stage (see Galaway, 1985, 1986). Probation staff refer those offenders who wish to take part and the VORP contacts the victim to attempt to arrange mediation. The project emphasises benefits to the victim above any other aim, and dropped the original joint goal of trying to mitigate sentence on the basis that it conflicted with the major aim.

Some European countries were also introducing similar ideas within a few years of these beginnings. Norway established its first Conflict Council (using victim/offender mediation for juvenile offenders) in Lier in 1981 (Hovden, 1987). By October 1987, some 48 such Councils were in operation, with 29 more about to begin. These schemes operate as an alternative to prosecution, if both victim and offender agree to meet in this way, prosecution being deferred pending their coming to an agreement and the completion of any reparation. Although there was some hope that such schemes would provide an alternative to legal processing altogether, by means of direct referrals from the public instead of reporting to the police, 80 per cent of referrals come from the police and few from the general public. However, with such innovative schemes in their early years, it is perhaps not surprising that they have not been able to compete in the public eye with more traditional agencies.

Finland introduced their first scheme, the Vantaa Mediation Project, in 1984 (Iivari, 1985). It operates for all ages, although three quarters of cases so far have involved offenders aged under 21. It is intended both as an alternative to prosecution for minor offences, and as a means of settling compensation in association with prosecution for more serious crimes. Sixty per cent of referrals are said to come from the parties themselves (Iivari, 1987), but these are probably at the suggestion of the police after reporting of the crime.

There are schemes also in West Germany, such as the Brunswick Victim-Offender Mediation and Restitution Project, which began in 1979 as an attempt to impress upon the offender the distress and fear caused to victims. One of the most recent schemes in that country is Die Waage ('balance'), set up in Cologne in 1986 by a juvenile court judge Dr Ruth Herz. The project is formally independent, with charitable and local government funds, but receives referrals of juvenile offenders from the public prosecutor or from the court. On completion of the reparation the case may be closed without a formal hearing, unless it was referred after conviction under a court order for reparation as a disposal. The aim "*is to find practical strategies for resolving conflicts and at the same time to test whether sanctioning in the juvenile criminal court of Cologne changes when provided with a mediation programme*" (Herz, 1988). A similar project Handschlag ('handshake') exists in Reutlingen, near Stuttgart (Bussmann, 1987).

In France, one victim/offender mediation scheme is in operation in Bordeaux, under the auspices of the *Association de Readaptation Sociale et de Controle Judiciaire*. It began in September 1986 to take referrals of offenders on bail awaiting trial who wished to meet their victims and perhaps make reparation. The outcome of the meeting is notified in writing to the court and may affect sentence (Knapper, 1987).

The Criminal Justice Act 1985 in New Zealand makes provision for compensation/reparation to be assessed by a probation officer at the request of the court, including an assessment of the offender's ability to pay. In the context of this assessment, the offender and the victim may meet with the probation officer to come to a mutually acceptable agreement. The emphasis in this case is entirely on material compensation for the victim.

Prospective new legislation on juvenile offenders in Austria also institutionalises the concept of reparation. It is intended that the public prosecutor will be bound to take into consideration attempts by accused youths to make reparation (material and/or symbolic) to the victims of their offences. If deemed sufficient, such reparation would be acknowledged as a reason for renouncing any further prosecution of the offence. The offence would, moreover, not be entered on the youth's criminal record. Currently, the public prosecutor is legally bound to prosecute every offence and has no powers to divert. The Institut fur Rechts- und Kriminalsoziologie in Vienna has carried out a pilot victim/offender mediation project (Tater-Opfer-Ausgleich) employing probation officers. (Personal communication from Christa Pelikan.)

Mention should also be made of another context in which victims and offenders may meet. This involves schemes such as the American Neighborhood Justice Centers and allied ideas that had their origin in 1971. Where the VORP focuses on the past offence, neighbourhood justice focuses on the *dispute* that exists between victim and offender in many of those cases where they were already acquainted. They are akin to the community mediation schemes that take referrals of disputes from the local neighbourhood, but they concentrate on diverting from prosecution offences involving related parties, on the assumption that conflict-resolution may be more important for preventing future trouble in such cases than prosecution and the punishment of one party for a single misdemeanour. The 'crime' is seen, in other words, as a symptom of a relationship problem between individuals, rather than a reflection of antisocial tendencies on the part of one. In actual fact, the distinction between a dispute and a crime is not so clear-cut (see Marshall, 1988a) and diversion of such cases can be contentious: for instance, in the case of domestic violence which involves both a need for some kind of conflict-resolution and tor social disapprobation. (But see Case Study I in the Appendix.)

Schemes of this type have also been established in many other countries. In Australia the Community Justice Centres of New South wales (begun 1980) have thrived and now serve as a model for the expansion of this kind of scheme to other states in the country, although the experimental scheme in Christchurch, New Zealand, met with less favour and was abandoned. Various other schemes of this kind are discussed in Marshall (1985), the situation and organisation of each project varying considerably with the idiosyncrasies of the cultural traditions of different countries.

One of the most recent innovations is based on the rapidly growing victim support movement in France, where schemes in Paris and Valence do not just offer a counselling and advice service to victims but have also set up a service for mediating between victims and offenders who are in dispute as an alternative to litigation (*S.O.S Aggressions-Conflicts*, information from its director, Jacqueline Marineau). Another scheme in Strasbourg (ACCORD) mediates. victim/offender conflict in complete independence of the court process, with the emphasis not on an 'alternative justice' system, but on helping both the victim and the offender through the experience of a 'second, more psychologically helpful encounter than that experienced in the original moment of aggression, theft or abusive exchange' (Knapper, 1987). Cases are brought by the victim (usually at the suggestion of a victims support scheme), by the offender, or by lawyers and others involved in the justice system, but there is no direct formal link with the courts.

Although we are not directly concerned with these types of scheme in this report, there is no absolute distinction between those offences which involve a conflict and those which do not, as is demonstrated by the ACCORD scheme, for whom the past occurrence of a crime itself creates a conflict (cf. Marshall, 1988a). The VORP-type schemes examined here dealt with many cases involving related parties, and the question whether these need special attention is one that will have to be addressed.

Many of the above experiments are reflected in Britain. Although there are at present no mediation schemes that divert 'disputes' from the legal process, there are a few community mediation projects obtaining such referrals from other agencies or directly from the parties themselves. These have been studied by us alongside the main research into victim/offender mediation, and occasional reference will be made to them here. This report, then, is concerned with all those schemes that were connected with the criminal justice process at some stage or another.

Those most like the North American VORPs are referred to here as the court-based schemes. Most of these at present operate between the point of conviction and that of sentence: the offenders have been proclaimed guilty of the offence, but their disposals have yet to be settled. Two of them pick up cases before a court hearing from among offenders who admit guilt and are willing to participate, this providing more time to carry out the mediation and any subsequent reparation and also minimising the time between the occurrence of the crime and the mediation. One of these (Totton, in Hampshire) works with the Magistrates' Court; the other (Leeds, West Yorkshire) largely with the Crown Court (where the time before a court hearing may be particularly long). Otherwise these two schemes operate in a very similar manner to the other court-based reparation projects. One further scheme, however, operates in a distinct manner, its intervention being entirely post-sentence (Rochdale and Bury, Greater Manchester). As the only one of its type so far, and having had few cases, it was not possible to incorporate it in this research. All these schemes tend to be called 'reparation' schemes, which draws particular attention to the aim of arranging some form of compensation, but in practice, as we shall see, they were all concerned with wider interests than just the material, subsequent schemes thus replicating the experience of the first experiment of this kind in Britain (run by the South Yorkshire Probation Service, firstly in Sheffield and then in Rotherham and Barnsley — see Marshall and Walpole, 1985).

Other schemes in England and Wales that are connected with the criminal process are more like the other American reparation schemes, and are much more focused on reforming offenders (or on diverting them from the presumed harmful effects of prosecution or custody) than on any other aims, including the aim of compensating victims. Intermediate

Treatment schemes (IT), which receive, at the order of the court, juveniles who show signs of incipient criminal careers and who are in danger of incarceration, and which employ varied packages of intensive social work, counselling, educational and other techniques, may on occasion use a meeting with the victim, if this can be arranged, in order to help impress on the offender the real harm done. Some IT schemes use such meetings quite regularly, one of the earliest being the Woodlands Centre in Basingstoke, Hampshire, described in Rutherford (1986). However, all these schemes deal only with small numbers of offenders, and it has not been possible to collect a sufficient number of cases for this research. Nevertheless, the process is probably not far removed from that typically involved in the other schemes that use victim/offender mediation, those based on **police juvenile liaison panels**.

These panels are composed of representatives of a number of agencies, typically the police, probation and social services, but sometimes involving others as well. These panels review most cases involving juvenile offenders, with a view to deciding whether or not to prosecute (or what disposal to recommend to the police). They have the resources normally to make investigations into an offender's background and circumstances, and may propose social work intervention or some other measure that may tip the balance in the decision to caution for marginally serious offences. Such panels may use a victim/offender meeting or negotiated reparation as one of such measures, and some use such an approach quite frequently. Given that the overall aims of such panels are to minimise the prosecution of juvenile offenders, the principal aim of their use of reparation is to be able to demonstrate offenders' remorse and willingness to put things right, and as a demonstration that they have not 'got off scot free', that may help reinforce a caution as a positive disposal and satisfy police demands for something more than just a 'telling off'. Such schemes also have the potential for arranging compensation for victims in cases which do not proceed to court, and where the victim will not therefore receive a court order for compensation. The earliest use of reparation by such panels was in Exeter, Devon, and in several areas of Northamptonshire (see Marshall and Walpole, 1985; Blagg, 1985).

The Crown Prosecution Service was too recent an introduction in England and Wales for any reparation schemes to have become associated with it, but the potential is there for the service to be an important referral point for victim/offender mediation. This has been tried experimentally in Scotland in connection with the Procurator Fiscal's Office, which has been long established as an independent prosecution agency separate both from the police and the courts. Mackay (1986) describes the initial pilot study in Lothian, which was carried out by the author, a social worker, under the auspices of SACRO (Scottish Association for Care and Resettlement of Offenders). He selected cases as their records were received by the Procurator Fiscal on the basis of what appeared to be their 'reparation potential'. When the Senior Depute Fiscal agreed, these cases were marked as 'deferred prosecution', pending Mr Mackay's negotiations with victim and offender. A satisfactory outcome — agreement achieved and kept — would result in the dropping of charges. The explicit aims tried to maintain a balance between victim's and offender's interests. The pilot was deemed sufficiently encouraging for the project to be extended.

CHAPTER 2

Evaluation

"It is both wasteful and irresponsible to set experiments in motion and to omit to record and analyse what happens" (Committee on Local Authority and Allied Personal Social Services, 1968).

However much a burden it might seem to be, and however much an apparent distraction from what seems to the practitioner to be the main task, it is the duty of all concerned with introducing innovatory schemes to document closely the progress made. With its value yet to be established — and independent research studies were slow in developing in North America, despite their earlier experimentation — victim/offender mediation was especially needful of fair and careful scrutiny. Research was therefore built in from the very beginning of the Home Office funding.

Stages of Development and Research

At the time of this research, victim/offender mediation in Britain was still in an early stage of development. There were no settled techniques or methods of organisation. A number of separately managed projects, with varying degrees of inter-communication, were trying out diverse schemes whose only common feature lay in the attempt to negotiate with both victims and offenders and to arrange some kind of exchange (not necessarily involving a direct meeting) between the two.

Although such pilot schemes are regarded as 'experimental', that term is really too grand to describe the kind of exploratory work which is going on. The phase of evolution reached in any kind of social intervention affects the kind of research that is appropriate. Such phases can be summarised as follows:—

Action	Research
Developmental — exploration of techniques, gaining cooperation of other bodies.	Monitoring action; feedback of results to aid development (action-research).
Experimental — extended trials of one or more settled models of operation for a predetermined period.	Evaluation — assessment of outcomes and resource requirements of different models.
Established — continuous operation of an accepted model.	Monitoring effects (and side effects).

Evaluation cannot take place before a more or less settled procedure has been adopted, for one would learn little from a demonstration that such and such had been achieved as a result of practice that had been continually evolving and could not therefore be identified. At the developmental stage research needs to be related to the needs of the practitioner to enable him/her to select the more promising innovations. Much of it will be descriptive, small-scale and short-term.

By the time the experimental stage is reached, practitioners are likely to be committed to a particular way of working — although other practitioners may have developed different models. Change in operation may still occur, but more rarely, and the question arises of what different techniques achieve, qualitatively and quantitatively. At this stage, other interests than those of the practitioner become more central — potential funders, government departments, and the informed public generally. As each interested party will have their own predilections in terms of what they hope to see achieved, this phase is much more complicated from a research point of view, because it must accommodate a great variety of aims and measures. One will also, by this stage, be looking for much firmer and better established results than the tentative findings of the action research phase. Questions of economy and cost-effectiveness, or efficiency, are also prominent at this stage.

Finally, even when a mode of intervention has become accepted, whether or not because there had been positive evaluation results, the role of research has not ended, as it is possible that early research findings become less relevant as the work at issue becomes routinised. Outcomes may also be affected by changing social circumstances, or other effects may only be apparent after a longer time. All social interventions therefore need to be monitored, either continually or from time to time, to assess whether early indications still hold.

Reparation projects being in their infancy, research should predominantly be in the action/research phase, concerned to enhance proficiency rather than to assess the basic worth of the idea. The situation is, however, complicated by the fact that developmental work that goes beyond existing resources of individuals or organizations requires external support or funding which generates an interest in more substantial evaluation. For this reason evaluative research tends to begin at too early a stage, when action is still evolving, and the field of reparation is no exception. While it is useful to ensure that good research procedures are set in train from the earliest moment, because much can be learnt from the way an innovation is influenced by its social setting, the pressure towards addressing evaluative issues prematurely can itself be an extraneous influence that may cramp practitioners' style and force them to persist with procedures that are, in their experience, outmoded, thus preventing the proper development of effective action. Developmental work should take place in an atmosphere of positive reinforcement and maximum flexibility in order to make the most practical use of the original idea, while experimental evaluation requires settled action and rigid control.

It is pointless, however, trying to be puritanical when carrying out applied research of this kind. Potential funding bodies will continue to insist on some measure of success or failure at a reasonably early stage, which is almost always well short of the time needed to develop firm and efficient strategies of work. For the sake of maintaining the confidence of other agencies or of the general public, practitioners (even if there are no doubts in their own minds) will also need to supply some evidence that worthwhile progress towards ultimate goals is being made. Rather than insisting on rigid academic conditions for 'proper' evaluation, researchers are forced to develop modes of investigation that address success while accommodating to the motile reality of what they are assessing. Where social action is concerned, in any case, it is rarely if ever possible to maintain rigid experimentally controlled conditions such that findings are utterly incontrovertible. However much effort is put into trying to construct 'correct' experimental conditions, it is always possible to question findings by pointing to flaws in the controlling features — extraneous influences, for instance, that could account for positive results or for apparent failure. Lacking all else one can question whether the overtly experimental, and hence 'special', nature of the project skewed the findings in some significant way. There has therefore been a tendency in the theory of evaluative methodology to abandon total reliance on 'scientific' definitions that rely on rigid experimental and control groups, and quantitative before-and-after measurements, as not only impracticable in sociological practice, but also as failing to address many important qualitative factors (see Marshall et al. 1978, James et al. 1983).

Evaluation research has therefore been forced to become much more eclectic, and to seek other ways of producing 'convincing' evidence relevant to assessment of social action than the simple comparison of experimental and control groups which, involving people and not inanimate objects, cannot be controlled by the experimenter in the social sciences as they can in their physical counterparts. One result of this has been to break down the rigidity of the distinction between action-research and evaluative methodologies. The techniques involved in the two tend to be very similar, although the difference still remains in terms of the principal customer — action-research being mainly for the practitioner, evaluation for the external assessor. It does mean, therefore, that researchers can address both sets of interests at one and the same time.

There are, however, dangers inherent in this situation, of which it is incumbent upon researchers (and users of research) to be aware. Lacking the firm proof of the experimental model, evaluative findings become less certain, indicative rather than prescriptive. Rather than a statement that a particular idea 'works' for specified conditions for all time — as is possible to attain in the construction of physical scientific laws — one ends up, more realistically, with an account that offers a range of possibilities relating to a variety of possible conditions and costs, and of the interrelationship between the two, such that informed decisions about future action can be taken. A rigorous statement of success or failure would be inappropriate because social or psychological processes will vary according to future environmental conditions that cannot be entirely predicted or controlled. Virtually any idea may work for some persons, under certain conditions, at some place, at some time. The most the researcher can be expected to offer is sufficient understanding of the phenomena involved, especially of the mechanisms by which effects are achieved, so that these can be generalised to conditions that will be encountered beyond the few that it has been possible to observe during the research exercise.

Current British Research

Current research into reparation schemes in this country partakes fully of this hybrid nature. It has had the advantage, compared to research into similar phenomena in the United States, for instance, of beginning at the very early stages of action-development, with the concomitant disadvantage, of course, that action has been changeable and uncertain in nature. The earliest research projects were conducted by a University of Lancaster team in connection with the Juvenile Bureaux in Northamptonshire (a police-based diversion model) and the South Yorkshire Probation Service experimental court-based schemes in Barnsley and Rotherham, both pioneering projects of their kind (see Blagg, 1985, and Smith, Blagg and Derricourt, 1985, respectively). Both were 'generalists' research designs, with an emphasis on descriptive approaches appropriate to the type of intervention and its stage of development. Further, as yet unpublished, research of a similar kind into the South Yorkshire scheme has been carried out by Clifford Williams (Bradford University).

The present research employed local teams on a part-time basis to monitor the development of the projects and describe their mode of operation; to assess their impact upon victims and offenders (using interviews with samples of both); to assess qualitatively and quantitatively the effects on agencies and processes of criminal justice; to document the use made by the courts of reparation agreements; to assess the reactions of other agencies and of the public to the schemes; to assess the fairness and quality of reparation agreements; and to provide an account of the costs or resources involved. This field research was backed up by systematic recording of all cases referred to these schemes, using standard summary forms developed by the Home Office Research & Planning Unit, and filled in by project staff. These forms provided basic details of the types of case referred and the progress of negotiations and mediation. Sent in quarterly, they provided a gradually expanding statistical base which was useful for descriptive purposes, although limited in terms of evaluation, because it depended entirely on information available to the schemes and on their view of matters. The work of the field researchers was therefore crucial in the provision of an independent view, especially through interviews with victims and offenders involved.

The same record forms were also used, voluntarily, by a number of other projects around the country, and thus expanded the range of types of scheme covered, even though most of these were not involved in more intensive field research. The scope of the research was further extended by a team of researchers at Bristol University (Gwynn Davis, David Watson and Jacky Boucherat) who carried out two projects, one recently completed on the aims and philosophies of all schemes in Britain (Davis, Boucherat and Watson, 1987), the other on the actual processes of mediation, and the role of the mediator, in selected schemes.

Problems of Evaluation (1) Change over Time

Evaluation has traditionally been seen as the response to the question, "What works?" This question, however, is not helpful, despite the fact that it would be extremely convenient to get straight answers to it. What works is virtually anything in the appropriate conditions, so the answer is less than useful. A better question is, "What exactly happened (in certain specific instances)?" This orientation emphasises the historical nature of any social action, and the fact that what has happened or is happening is not necessarily what will continue to happen. It also enables the researcher to take a more objective stance to the essential evaluative issue of what "working" entails, for success will be defined in different terms by different parties. The researcher's role is not to choose among such different aims but to recognise each and to collate information relevant to them all. The policy decision whether to continue with such action, to extend it or not, is a political one involving moral and ideological factors that the researcher may attempt to clarify but cannot decide. The emphasis upon collecting information relevant to all the identifiable aims that different parties may have also provides some safeguard against the views of the researchers biasing evaluation towards specific aims. Although it would be a brave (and foolish) social researcher who pretended to complete objectivity, techniques such as these do at least ensure that the research will have some credibility with other people.

While the traditional question, "What works?", leads to an unfortunate tendency to concentrate on such techniques as the controlled trial, the more neutral "'What happened?" allows a more eclectic methodological orientation, adapting research techniques to the exigencies of different kinds of information. While comparisons, if feasible, with broadly similar groups not receiving the 'treatment' in question are likely to be valuable, they should not be allowed to dominate the research design. There will always be some limits to the rigour of such comparisons, and they will be persuasive only in combination with other kinds of evidence that tend to confirm the findings. "Before" and "after" measurements are also relevant to the assessment of change over time, although again they are only partial indicators of success, in that general trends over time may be occurring in the same direction, a factor that has particularly bedevilled research on those schemes employing reparation as a means of increasing rates of diversion from criminal justice for juveniles, given that there is currently a strong trend across all police forces in England and Wales to caution more juveniles rather than prosecuting.

Another way of approaching change over time due to the experimental action is more descriptive — an intensive analysis of what occurs in particular cases from start to finish. This may be carried out for groups of cases of particular types, or for individual cases. Although this approach lacks the valuable external reference points of "control groups" or measurements at particular points in time, it compensates for this by providing a detailed picture of the complexity of interactions in actual cases that enables one to understand the dynamics that achieve whatever results there are. The other, more statistical methods, may help make one surer that the change that has occurred is due to the experimental work, but are too abstract and generalised to show how the change was brought about, and thus to enable one to distinguish the circumstances in which this work is more or less successful. The individual case-study approach is especially appropriate for those kinds of intervention where the objective is liable to vary from case to case. Clients present social workers with a vast variety of problems, each needing different techniques (practical help, counselling, therapy, etc) dedicated to quite different ends. The same is true of mediation, and perhaps even more so, for there it is one of the underlying principles that the desired outcome should be defined collaboratively by the parties and not by the mediator, so that even those running the project do not control the definition of aims, as distinct from certain aspects of the process. (They may well influence the aims adopted and the form of resolution, however, and such intrusion is a subject for research assessment.) In processes like social work and conflict-resolution, moreover, there occurs a vast range of starting-points in terms of the severity of the problems, or of the conflicts, present at referral. A slight increase in tolerance in one case, where antagonisms had been spiralling into violence, may be a greater achievement than total agreement and reconciliation in another where the dispute was a limited one. Unfortunately, it is difficult to obtain any standard measure of the severity of a conflict, and such disparities only emerge from a descriptive case-by-case account.

Problems of Evaluation (2) Ends and Means

Change over time in the cases dealt with is not the only consideration for the evaluation researcher, although it tends to be the main index for those who attempt to answer the traditional question of what works. A more complete picture is needed if such indicators of change are to be incorporated into realistic policy decision-making. A crucial feature is the description of the experimental work itself — what was done, by whom, in what order, according to what system, both qualitatively and quantitatively. If success is shown, one will need to know exactly what kind of action it was that should be replicated in future. There is a tendency in much evaluation work to ignore this rather too obvious feature, under the misapprehension that having named the experimental action, say "mediation", that one has described what it was. However, mediation can be carried out, in an almost infinite variety of ways. Even if practitioners imagine they are all doing the same thing, observation may well reveal that in practice they go about it in significantly different ways, such that it may even be difficult to identify a common core of practice. Moreover, even when the methods are ostensibly similar, in terms of formal characteristics, they may be applied more or less sensitively, more or less persuasively, etc, such that different practitioners obtain different results. If this is true, research will need to study the effect of personal styles as well as formal methods. One suspects that often it is the practitioner rather than the practice that is the crucial determinant. It is especially important to know if this is true when contemplating the extension of experimental work in a few locations (usually being carried out by particularly committed, or experienced, or enthusiastic, workers) to more general application (where it is likely to become more routinised and the average quality and intensity of intervention to decline). Close examination of the work carried out, especially in relation to the relative success of the outcome, will not only be essential for the purposes of replication but also for training new practitioners. (One recent paper, Morash et al. 1986, bemoans the fact that evaluations do tend to focus on success to the exclusion of the dynamics of implementation, providing little guidance for those who wish to replicate the programmes.)

Social intervention does not take place in a vacuum, in the way a controlled scientific experiment might. What occurs in each case will depend not only on the value of the work applied, and on the quality of the worker, but also on the strength of other influences, positive or negative. The researcher must here be prepared to look beyond the experimental scheme itself, and its cases, to the context in which both are set. Are other agencies uncooperative, thus limiting the scheme's effectiveness? Are the right kinds of cases referred? Are the clients subject to strong social pressures — family or peer influence, local difficulties in obtaining employment, etc — that outbalance the contribution of the scheme? Is the local culture amenable to the approach adopted? Are important liaison groups, or the clients themselves, enthusiastic for the new approach or resistant to outside 'interference'?

Schemes themselves may also vary organisationally, even if methods of case-processing are the same. Staff or volunteers may be allocated more or less appropriately, resources employed more or less efficiently, procedures for referral, supervision etc be more or less chaotic, the scheme's public image more or less convincing, morale may be high or low. Research should be able to assess all of these.

A further problem caused by traditional evaluation is its emphasis on experimental work as a means to an end, rather than an end in itself. For some activities the dominance of further ends in evaluation is quite reasonable — whether crime prevention schemes prevent crime, for instance — because their whole rationale resides in such an outcome. Other forms of social intervention, however, are seen as good in themselves — improved housing or environmental standards, for instance. Such action may produce beneficial results in other ways — improved safety, higher social morale, etc — but it would be worthwhile even if it did not affect anything else. The main criterion for evaluating reforms of this kind resides in whether the reforms are implemented according to plan and to the satisfaction of the parties affected. Most social intervention is a mixture of the two kinds — it is seen as 'good' in itself by those promoting it, but it is also expected to lead to improvements in other ways as well. The balance between the two in emphasis may well vary between observers — practitioners or initiators will often tend towards the former, funders and governments towards the latter. Protagonists over the worth of a particular policy are often not arguing so much about the facts as about the aims they espouse or whether they see the policy as good in itself or merely as a means to an end. The arguments about capital punishment are often between groups that oppose it as something unacceptable 'in itself', and groups that see it as a necessary evil towards the protection of society.

Mediation and reparation schemes are no exception to this clash of expectations. Apart from the many kinds of objectives that such schemes may be thought to serve (which we shall come to shortly), there are many advocates who feel that mediation as a means of resolving conflicts is inherently preferable to the use of adversarial methods as enshrined in the law. They would prefer some kind of conciliation even if it were less successful in settling disputes than the law (as long as it were not too abject a failure), because the settlements might themselves be of better 'quality' or because it would be preferable to try the 'civilised' way first, and use the law only when there is no alternative. Other advocates do see mediation as merely a technique towards a particular end, which among the schemes considered in this book would be the objective of reparation by the offender on behalf of the victim. Many again, however, will see such a resolution as sufficiently beneficial in itself, as a better principle of justice than that based on retributive ideals (cf. Zehr, 1985), while others not persuaded to this point of view will demand that reparation schemes be justified in terms of further ends — whether they reduce the propensity of offenders to break the law again, for instance.

These differences in opinion may be represented to some extent as differences of aims, but a substantial divergence in terms of evaluation remains, in that success for one party will reside mainly in the ability to implement the idea and to gain acceptance for it, and success for the other party will reside almost entirely in the achievement of something further. Evaluation based wholly on the first will be decisive only for those already persuaded of the worth of the idea and only worried about its practicability. It will not be persuasive for potential funders or policy-makers who do not share the faith in, say, mediation or conciliation; at least, not immediately. As a new approach becomes accepted and is seen to be welcomed by those who come into contact with it, its worth 'in itself', for its own sake, may establish itself more widely in the public consciousness. Given the empirical difficulties in actually demonstrating convincingly that a species of action does have an effect on some other social variable, it is this process of gradual familiarisation that probably accounts for the establishment of more social policies than is often realised. Where, for instance, is the definitive demonstration of the effectiveness of social work?

While in theory, then, the measurement of outcomes is important to evaluation, in practice their importance is over-stressed. It may lead to the debunking of good ideas merely because they have not had time to establish themselves and because they were tested against unrealistic aims. In the struggle for shares in limited budgets, advocates of particular innovations are liable to be forced into claiming more for their ideas than, in the face of other inimical social forces, can be attained, especially in small-scale trials. It is important that research should be able to address both sides of this debate and to provide information both on outcomes and on those features that may reflect on its quality and on the inherent worth of the scheme (for instance, measures of local enthusiasm for it). Measures of quality will depend on the nature of the intervention.

Problems of Evaluation (3) Measuring Quality

In the case of mediation, there are four principal aspects of quality upon which research should undoubtedly focus. One is the 'fairness' of the process, especially if it is being used in some way as an alternative to the law and its due process safeguards. Are complainants being denied access to legal rights? Are offenders being pressured into acceptance of heavier burdens than the law would have imposed? Are victims being exploited for the sake of reforming the offender, or, even worse, in order to divert him/her from prosecution entirely? Do schemes tend to favour one or other party? As a supplement to the last question, one must ask whether the location and organisation of most current reparation schemes in this country, closely allied to the criminal justice process, dependent on the agents of this process for referral, and almost all run by criminal justice agencies (probation, IT schemes, police juvenile panels), inevitably leads to the dominance of traditional criminal justice aims and a focus upon the offender. Given the lack of information available on victims and their wishes within the criminal justice process, selection of cases for reparation is entirely in terms either of the offence (a legal criterion) or the characteristics of the offender. The anxieties of Helen Reeves (1984), Director of the National Association of Victims Support Schemes, about the ability of such schemes to serve victims' needs adequately or to deal with them sensitively must be central to any research evaluation.

Secondly, the quality of reparation schemes depends on equality of involvement. If parties themselves are, cooperatively, to arrive at some kind of decision, then they must have full opportunity to voice their opinions, freedom to develop the encounter in the direction which best suits their interests, and control over the outcome. This means that not only must participation in the meeting or the negotiation process be unrestricted, but also that the process should be independent of extraneous influences, such as pressures from overhanging threats of legal action that may force a settlement to avoid such consequences rather than because it is valued in its own right. This would argue again for the independence of such schemes from criminal justice processes, at least insofar as judicial decisions should not depend on the outcome of the mediation (and should not be perceived as doing so). Another source of extraneous pressure may come from the mediators themselves, if they have preconceived ideas of the form of resolution they would like to see, or know that certain kinds of agreement will be more convincing to influential outsiders. This is especially likely where schemes are dependent on the goodwill of other agencies — as those court-based reparation schemes that seek to influence sentencing decisions may be, when material commitments by the offender to make reparation seem more persuasive to judges than mere expressions of regret, even if the victim may not really desire the first and may find more genuine meaning in the second, or in the encounter itself. Even without such extraneous pressures, parties do not necessarily come as equals to the bargaining table. There may be differences of status, power, communication skills and commitment that may skew the process in favour of one or other. In the context of reparation schemes, such differences are most prevalent where an individual offender is faced with a corporate victim, a situation which Blagg (1985) found could be quite problematic. The way the mediator handles such situations so as to provide balance could be important here, although it seems unlikely that a mediator would have the means of overcoming gross differences of power based on social or economic circumstances (as against psychological skills). This has certainly worried many people in relation to husband-wife mediation (cf. Lefcourt, 1984). The law, by translating conflicts into contests between lawyers of approximately equal skills and power, at least provides some safeguard against gross inequality — although at the expense of taking matters entirely out of the hands of the parties. The role of the mediator in the negotiation process therefore is a vital one for research examination, by means of direct observation and by interviews with parties after the event. The ideology of the 'neutral' mediator has had to be revised in the face of a reality where parties new to the ideas involved have necessarily to be given some guidance as to how to make use of the process, and where directed intervention is so often necessary both to maintain the required conditions (eg to exclude violence or threats of violence, to prevent disruptive interruptions) and to counteract inequalities. Research has hardly yet started to provide criteria for identifying reasonable and unreasonable mediator behaviour. Indeed, there is as yet, even from those countries such as America where schemes have existed for much longer, virtually no research which shows what actually goes on within the mediation process itself, as distinct from who goes in and what comes out.

A third aspect of quality is the extent to which a scheme is able to maintain those characteristics essential to the ideas on which the new intervention is based. The move towards the employment of mediation in relation to what would otherwise be treated as entirely a legal process has been informed by a general ideology which favours personal involvement in settling one's own dispute or problem, community empowerment, creativity in devising solutions, and the promotion of cooperation in place of confrontation. The ideal is non-professional, non-bureaucratic, empowering the parties rather than the staff of the project. Particularly difficult problems may require a more professional or quasi-professional third party (eg highly trained specialist volunteers), as in divorce conciliation, but such skills should be at the disposal of the parties rather than used to take control out of their hands. The maintenance of these conditions is extremely problematic. Mediation in the United States is becoming increasingly professionalised (cf, Wahrhaftig, 1984), and parallels can be found in virtually any innovation originally intended to hand control over to local communities (cf. Cohen, 1985). The locus of control and whose ends are served are both important topics for research evaluation.

The last criterion of quality to be discussed here is that of efficiency in the use of resources or cost-effectiveness. Although 'inputs' can usually be measured more or less in monetary terms, it is distinctly more difficult in most cases to rate 'outputs' in the same way. For one thing, the outcomes may not be clearly attributable to the intervention, or not wholly so. For another, these outcomes may not be convertible into costs or cost-savings. Furthermore, the considerations of 'quality' outlined above need to be taken into account: these would be impossible to quantify. It is therefore not possible to construct a financial input and output equation. This does not, however, release researchers from the onus of assessing the economic aspects of a scheme. Funding bodies will still be looking for value for money. This can be analysed into two components: whether the results of the scheme seem to be worth the money invested (a slightly weaker version of cost-effectiveness), and whether the resources available (or potentially available) are exploited efficiently. The second is distinct in that outcomes may justify the expenditure incurred but that expenditure might still be greater than it need be to achieve those ends.

In terms of the first of these components, failing a completely quantified equation, the judgement involved is obviously a subjective or political one. The researchers can contribute by supplying details of the costs incurred and the fullest description they can of the type, size, range and quality of the outcomes. Beyond that, except in extreme cases where there is, say, only trivial achievement at vast cost, the researchers must leave others to make their own judgements on whether it is worth it, judgements that will vary according to individual ratings of the importance of different achievements. This illustrates the limits of research as a decision-making tool: in most cases assessment will depend on non-objective criteria that take one beyond the data provided by the research. All research has done is to make that assessment better informed and allow others to progress beyond first impressions and prejudices to a more soundly-based judgement of whether the innovation in question is in line with their interests or not.

The second component can be more fully addressed by researchers. How is staff time used? Do staff spend long periods waiting for referrals or for others to respond, so that their work is compressed into relatively short periods? If volunteer help is required, how well does the project manage to recruit volunteers? Are they the right kind of people? Are there enough of them? Are there too many relative to the workload, so that they get disaffected waiting for cases? How well is morale maintained? Is turnover kept to reasonable levels? Many more such questions will arise, and answers will be useful to project managements as well as those outside who wish to judge the scheme. Comparative research, using a number of different projects of the same kind, is particularly useful for highlighting differences of organisational or managerial efficiency, and for indicating how such problems may be solved.

Problems of Evaluation (4) Intermediate Outcomes

All that has been said above has emphasised that there is much more to evaluation than the achievement of aims. However, these cannot be dismissed, even if such achievement, in strict cause-and-effect terms, will be next to impossible to prove outright. The variety of aims imputed to a particular social intervention at least tells the researcher what major outcomes to look out for, although other, unanticipated, outcomes should also be identified as far as possible.

Before listing the aims that have been ascribed to reparation schemes, the problem of timing needs to be addressed. Certain outcomes are more closely and immediately linked to the experimental intervention than others. The closer this link, the more easily one can ascribe the outcome to the effect of the intervention. It is an unfortunate social fact that the more important the aim to outside observers, the more distant the outcome tends to be from the action taken! Almost any scheme associated with criminal justice will invite the majority of observers to identify the reduction of crime as the prime aim, for instance. The dominance of this criterion has probably led to the demise of many promising ideas. Given the strength of social forces encouraging conformity, including the devastating effect of informal disapproval and shame as well as the more physical threat of the criminal justice apparatus, the strength of the social and/or personal forces conducive to crime among those who do offend, at the risk of a quite unenviable career of punishment, discrimination and rejection, must be considerable. One must therefore remain sanguine about the potential effect of any limited intervention on the propensity to offend. Whatever may be achieved is likely to be merely a drop in the ocean. Such effects may only be perceptible when the intervention becomes widespread and immanent in the social structure.

These problems will not prevent people hoping for the 'miracle cure', but while research must take into account such longer-term aims, it is important also to identify measures of more immediate applicability, more within the capacity of experimental schemes to achieve in a limited period of time. Good performance in terms of these may provide grounds for persistence with the innovation for a much longer period in the hope eventually of establishing more profound effects.

Reparation schemes are characterised by a temporal process marked by a series of stages of achievement, each of which provides an intermediate index of success. The first, and most basic, criterion is the ability to obtain cases — or indeed to survive at all. The project must be able to demonstrate sufficient demand for its services. This depends not only on obtaining referrals from other agencies (which may be problematic if those agencies do not see any value in the new idea) but also on obtaining the agreement of the parties referred. Failure at this stage will unfortunately mean that the essential idea will not have been tried at all. It may mean that there are too few relevant cases to make it worthwhile; on the other hand, it may merely reflect general reluctance to accept innovation, or a failure in implementation.

If a number of cases are achieved, their suitability for the experimental process relative to those not received should also be assessed, although this may not be possible, if there are no predetermined criteria of suitability, until outcomes of different types of case can be compared. If one of the aims of a scheme, for instance, is to help victims to cope with the aftermath of crime, one would hope that the scheme will have picked up a good number of victims who are still suffering to a significant extent and thus 'need' the help offered.

Agreement to participate in the scheme may not, however, imply willingness to take part in a direct face-to-face meeting. Many victims and offenders are happier with the mediator acting as a 'go-between'. The salience of this depends on the rationale behind the mediation process. If the main intention is to obtain some mutually agreeable settlement, indirect mediation may be quite sufficient. It does, however, signally fail to achieve many objectives that mediators tend to hold dear — the handing over of power to the parties to resolve their own problems or disputes, the possibly cathartic experience of a direct interchange of views and feelings, and so on. If these kinds of aim are relevant, then an important index of successful implementation is the percentage of cases dealt with by direct mediation.

If mediation (direct or indirect) is carried forward, the next criterion of achievement will be the ability to reach an agreement. The percentage of mediations leading to an agreement is, in fact, the most widely quoted measure of success. For one thing, it is usually readily available to schemes themselves; for another, it is usually a very favourable figure. The latter is not surprising. Once both parties have agreed to a meeting, they will both be motivated to get something out of it. On the other hand, what is held to constitute an agreement may vary from an apology to substantial compensation plus a signed pledge to carry out certain tasks according to a defined schedule. Almost any meeting that has not ended prematurely by one party walking out may be seen as ending successfully, even if the outcome is only an agreement to differ, or to have nothing to do with one another henceforth. The problem is that these last examples can, in certain circumstances, be real achievements. Lacking any measure of the state of either party, or of their relationship, before mediation, it is impossible to say whether the final agreement is a significant achievement or not. Moreover, it can be quite reasonably objected that 'agreement' is not a measure of the achievement of mediation at all. It may or may not be honoured; it may be more or less meaningful. The essence of the mediation, according to most who engage in it, is the achievement of understanding, sympathy, catharsis, and the exchange of atonement, on one side, and forgiveness, on the other. The achievement may lie much more in the emotional than in the material, and any hope that the effect may be lasting — for either the offender or the victim — is likely to depend on such achievement of 'deeper' meaning in the experience, as against a more or less commercial transaction (which may be no more significant than a fine or compensation order imposed by a court). The extent to which agreement can be achieved is likely to be a much more significant measure for dispute-settlement schemes than for reparation schemes, involving victims and offenders who were previously strangers. In those cases where victim and offender knew one another in advance, especially where the offence arose out of difficulties in their relationship, reparation schemes might be assessed in terms of their capacity to resolve conflict; but in other cases the 'conflict', insofar as it can be said to exist or to be a potential outcome of the crime, is too vague to be used as a material criterion.

These problems with agreements as measures of outcome lead one on to consider less direct assessments of the value of the mediation. One possibility is whether the report on what occurred in mediation was influential in decision-making — whether of the police or of the court. Although this may be an index of how other agencies perceive value in the process, it may not be a true measure of the mediation in its own terms. Sentencers, for instance, may be more easily persuaded to take account of material outcomes — compensation paid, reparative work carried out — than the metaphysics of empathy and forgiveness; but this may not accord with what the parties' desire from the encounter, and may lead a scheme to place undue emphasis on the material agreement. It may only serve to reinforce in offenders a cynical approach centred on financial negotiation and thus fail to impress on them their social responsibility, which the face-to-face encounter with a harmed victim was meant to engender.

Another measure of the outcome of mediation lies in the subsequent attitudes of the participants. What did they believe they got out of the experience? Given that the process, if it is successful, depends so much on personal experience, this is probably the most important of all the short-term measures. Indeed, it is so crucial to the evaluation of mediation that schemes should not leave such assessment to the occasional research exercise, but should incorporate it in regular procedure. Although mediators may have gained some impression of the value of the meeting to the participants at the time, or shortly afterwards, it is vital for any real self-assessment to contact parties, say, a month later, not only to check on how well any agreement has stood up, but to establish how each party still feels about the experience.

Problems of Evaluation (5) Ultimate Objectives

If the immediate purpose of mediation is to facilitate an experience of value to the parties concerned, their views about whether it was worthwhile should be one of the prime considerations for evaluators. Nevertheless, if an innovation is to be acceptable as a social policy, there must not only be benefits to individual participants, but either the results must also be generally beneficial in social and economic terms, or there must be a feeling that the provision of such services is obligatory upon society. In the former of these instances, research should show whether there appear, or not, to be general improvements (reduced levels of crime, more economic justice, better community morale, etc). In the latter, it would have to be able to demonstrate that the gains to victims from meeting their offenders were sufficiently substantial to encourage the growth of public feeling that such opportunities must be provided as of right. Even material compensation for victims occupies an uncertain position in respect of such obligation on the part of the government, and other aims such as reconciliation and the experience of forgiveness are far from being acknowledged at present as fundamental rights.

Turning, then, to the main objectives of reparation schemes, beyond the more immediate operational ones above, they may be divided into those aims that pertain to individual cases and those that relate to more general social benefits. Of the former, there are benefits to victims, to offenders, and to disputants to be considered.

Victims may be helped materially or psychologically. Material compensation is catered for to some extent within the present justice system in Britain, at least as far as offenders are identified and brought to trial (via compensation orders of the court) or as far as the loss is due to injury and exceeds a minimum value (via the Criminal Injuries Compensation Scheme). Mediation schemes are also limited to those cases where an offender is apprehended and admits responsibility — although they can apply where the offender is cautioned and not brought to court. Given the recent extension in the use of police powers to caution rather than prosecute (at least with respect to juveniles) the possibility of extending compensation, even on a voluntary basis, beyond the confines of the court may be of some general benefit to victims.

The growth of victims support schemes in this country has shown that the needs of victims are as often emotional as practical, and that the former may be more important and almost certainly longer-lasting (cf. Shapland et al., 1985; Maguire and Corbett, 1987). Given the chance of releasing psychological pressures emanating from the impact of crime, victims may well value this over any more established right to restitution. Indeed, the calculating and commercial nature of negotiating compensation may well inhibit the kind of exchange that could produce catharsis and satisfactory mutual understanding. To what degree such psychological benefits are actually realised in an encounter with the offender, and in what circumstances, is therefore a crucial subject for research.

Another problem, particularly where emotional benefits are concerned, although it may affect the relevance of compensation also, is the timing of mediation. Where this must wait on a case reaching court, the optimum time for intervention may have passed as far as the victim is concerned. It is difficult to generalise, however, as the optimum time will vary so greatly from case to case. A meeting with the offender could come too soon in some instances, before the victim was prepared to cope with the emotions this would unleash.

The benefit to the offender in reparation schemes is less easy to distinguish from wider social ends. One tends to assume, for instance that the offender benefits from 'rehabilitation' and 'diversion' ~ although these are really more general social ends. The offender may find the process of mediation more 'meaningful' than that of court adjudication, although it may also prove more taxing (cf. Smith! 1986). The principal reason, however, why virtually all offenders offered the opportunity of meeting the victim are willing to accept it must be that they imagine that it may be of practical benefit to them subsequently in the criminal justice process, whether by avoiding prosecution or achieving a lighter sentence. This is reinforced by the fact that post-sentence reparation schemes find it hard to obtain cases, as the offenders see little advantage in mediation at this stage. Even those juveniles for whom a caution has already been decided before they are offered the chance of mediation — and who are nevertheless generally found willing to take part —— may comprise no exception, for they may not realise that they have complete freedom of choice (or distrust that notion), or may be pressured by their parents and other figures of authority. The new reparation scheme in Kettering, Northants, that will deal with cautioned adults rather than juveniles, may be a better test of the idea that offenders may have something to gain from mediation with the victim. Even then, what appears to be eagerness to make amends may be no more than one expression of the general anxiety and desire to appease engendered by the fact of being caught by the police. Nevertheless, experience of mediation with the victim may create feelings of regret and of accountability lacking beforehand.

In the case of those offenders who previously knew their victims, where the 'crime' arose from problems in relationships, here mediation may have something more concrete to offer participants, in helping them resolve such problems sufficiently to avoid further trouble. In such cases the reparation schemes become more akin to the community mediation schemes, in Britain, America, Australia and elsewhere, that take referrals of disputes directly from the community, without recourse to criminal justice agencies at all. The American Neighbourhood Justice Centres and the similar Australian centres also take disputes out of the criminal justice process itself, as an alternative to adjudication for those parties who prefer the idea of mediation. None of the British schemes are focussed on the diversion of such disputes, and this seems to be an unexplored area in this country. To what extent are related parties who enter the present reparation schemes helped to a resolution of underlying conflicts? How many, indeed, of the schemes' caseloads, involve such cases at all?

Mediation may also pass beyond purely reparative concerns in other cases where the victim and offender were not previously acquainted. If they live in the same neighbourhood, as they frequently do, there is a chance of a later encounter, which might be a continuing source of fear for either the victim or the offender (possibilities of revenge). Reconciliation between the two parties and the establishment of a stable basis for future relationships may therefore be an important product of mediation. Research should be concerned to identify these other mediation roles beside those of material reparation or catharsis.

The other aims associated with reparation schemes concern their wider social impact. Some of them are not new objectives at all, but traditional criminal justice ends that the schemes might help promote. These include the rehabilitation of offenders (including, of course, the reduction of recidivism rates), the diversion of cases from courts or from custodial disposals, the prevention of further 'trouble' (as might result from revenge for unsettled grievances or from unresolved interpersonal relationship problems), and economy of resources (if mediation is a cheaper mode of resolution than adjudication — although this only applies to those schemes whose caseload is diverted from normal justice channels). While such effects will obviously be the subject of research scrutiny, it is also important to investigate the effect of these aims, which are to some extent imposed upon mediation schemes for extrinsic reasons, upon the efficiency with which the more central purposes of victim/offender mediation are achieved. The essential characteristic of mediation, empowering individuals to participate in the handling of their own disputes or problems, may be endangered by these demands, which emanate from those agencies on which reparation schemes depend for referrals and for general support. While diversion has considerable support these days, for reasons both of parsimony and of avoiding disproportionate reaction to minor offending, there could be concomitant disadvantage of 'net-widening' (as far as offenders are concerned) or of restricted access to justice (as far as victims are concerned). These indirect effects need also to be assessed.

Other social aims associated with reparation schemes are more intrinsic to their central ideology: how far is personal involvement furthered? Is there genuine empowerment of the individuals concerned, or is professional control maintained? How far is the local community involved, eg as specially trained volunteer mediators? Is maximum flexibility encouraged to allow the appropriate creativity between the participants? If so, how is 'fairness' maintained — if, indeed, this is a conscious concern of the mediator at all? (In theory, any agreement is entirely voluntary on the part of either party, so that the issue of fairness should not arise, but various factors may interfere with the freedom of parties in the mediation — pressure from the mediator towards particular kinds of settlement, an imbalance of power between the parties for economic, physical or social reasons, or an overshadowing threat of prosecution, for example.)

Further social aims are so long-range and nebulous as to lend themselves hardly at all to evaluation, at least over the feasible length of a single research project. These include such ideals as the promotion of constructive conflict management, the inculcation of cooperative methods of problem-solving or peace-making attitudes, and the furthering of reparative justice (Christie, 1981; Zehr, 1985). At the most research will, in the short term, be able to comment on whether such ends might be feasibly served by the precise action they document on the ground.

While this report seeks to indicate how well the schemes have worked so far, its value lies equally in the overall description of what occurred in each case, the problems encountered, the successes and the disasters. It attempts to provide the uninvolved reader with a rounder picture by means of which the schemes can be understood rather than accepted or dismissed on some simple figure of 'success-rate' or 'cost-effectiveness' abstracted from the daily process. There are matters of quality of service, fairness and justice that cannot be subsumed by quantitative equations, important as the latter may also be. We cannot, for instance, put a figure on the benefits/costs to the victims who are involved, but we can present what they said they felt about the experience. It is partly in the nature of victim/offender mediation, as indeed of many other kinds of intervention like social work or psychiatry, that the human experience is as important as any objective measure of achievement. Those who would judge have a duty to try to understand the 'essential nature' (Merry, 1982) of the phenomena they are judging, and not to accept or dismiss them on the basis of superficial evidence or too brief and inadequate implementation. There is certainly a danger otherwise that good ideas will never be given the chance to show their true benefits, as Kressel (1987) fears with respect to divorce mediation: *"Much of the evidence on divorce mediation's effectiveness comes from studies of relatively inexperienced mediators, given the hastiest of training, working under severe constraints of time…and significant ambiguities of practice."*

The methodology employed in this research is accordingly varied and wide-ranging, ranging between direct observation, interviews, analysis of case-records, statistical comparisons, and illustrative case-studies. We have also tried to study all the major schemes and different varieties of organisation extant in Britain over the last couple of years. Such a multi-pronged approach is in line with recommendations only just now emerging from experience in such research on the other side of the Atlantic (Kressel, 1987; Irving and Benjamin, 1987) — what the latter authors describe as 'triangulation'. The danger is, of course, that such an approach will be closer to strangulation than triangulation, and at times the research presence may have become a little intrusive (one project was being studied at different times by four different teams of researchers). To compensate, the research was not intensive, nor did it demand rigid 'controlled experimental' conditions: the projects were allowed complete freedom to find their own ways and the researcher's role was mainly to observe developments as they occurred. This freedom from rigid conditions enables researchers to feedback information as and when they think it important or when the projects request it. Given the brevity of the experimental period of two years, however, such feedback was not substantial: only at the end of this period have enough data been accrued to start commenting sensibly on relative successes and failures.

Given this orientation, it was not possible to follow one of the recommendations made by both Kressel and by Irving and Benjamin. Both are in favour of 'true experimental designs', with random assignment and comparison of experimental and control groups. For several reasons little attempt was made in this research to use such designs, although the Leeds fieldwork team did use a modified form of comparison between project clients and offenders/victims who had not had a chance of mediation, prior to the setting up of the project. The reasons were manifold: most importantly, a desire not to interfere with natural processes, the difficulties always encountered in maintaining the purity of control groups (especially where participation is voluntary on the part of both offender and victim), and the fact that the organisation and methods of work of all the schemes studied were influx. Random assignment of offenders to experimental and control groups was attempted in one piece of American research, but could not be maintained for practical reasons (Hudson and Chesney, 1978), and this is by no means an unusual experience in the use of controlled trials (cf. Clarke and Cornish, 1972).

This is not to say that we have not been able to make any assessments of effect, or any comparisons between schemes or with the normal legal process, but that such comparisons are always capable of several interpretations, and the ultimate conclusions come from a multiplicity of evidence rather than any one watertight measure, a situation familiar to any court sentencer! Insofar as we lack data, it is not so much in relation to the experimental schemes as in relation to the normal criminal processes: we asked clients of the projects for their reactions to mediation and their subsequent feelings, but we did not ask such questions, for the most part, of those who had only had experience of the normal court process. It is not what happens in victim/offender mediation that is a mystery as what happens when victim and offender are not involved in this way. Kressel (1987) strongly makes this point himself — that we now need just as systematic and intensive studies of legal process and its results: these cannot be taken for granted. If alternatives appear a mixed blessing, is the traditional criminal justice system itself perfect?

The freedom from a rigid comparative design has, on the other hand, substantial advantages. It gives the research flexibility to follow up issues as they arise — the activities of each of the fieldwork teams were, in fact, significantly different, responding to the particular experiences and problems of their subject projects. It shifted the focus from simple quantitative measures of 'success' to more qualitative investigations of advantages and disadvantages that give a more rounded, if more equivocal, picture. It allowed a search, apart from any overall assessment, for the kinds of case with which mediation might be more successful, for the possibility that different approaches will work in different circumstances, or for a precise description of what happens in practice compared with the process in theory — "what mediators say they do and what they actually do may or may not coincide" (Irving and Benjamin, 1987).

It also permits an approach which took into account the vast multiplicity of aims and goals with which victim/offender mediation has become surrounded (see, eg. Davis et al. 1987; Marshall, 1988b). *"There exist a number of different possible beneficiaries of the victim/offender mediation process. Because of this, programs...may attempt to simultaneously achieve multiple, if not conflicting, goals. The results of this occurring can be both confusing and dysfunctional..."* (Umbreit, 1985). Particularly interesting is how projects sought to resolve such a variety of intentions and how priorities were assigned. It is not the job of the researcher to assign such priorities, but to provide comprehensive information that may help others to assess the schemes in terms of whichever ends they choose. There is a tendency for research to concentrate on the easily measurable or on simple definitions of success, which attention to the multiplicity of aims may help overcome. It is often too easy to assume that mediation is about resolving problems — coming to an agreement, but, as Albert and Howard (1985) aptly say, *"The need to be heard is often as important as the need to resolve the problem."*

The research reported in subsequent chapters is organised in terms of the different kinds of aim. The next two chapters address the implementation of mediation: the organisation of the schemes, their procedures, from whom cases were referred, what work they did with them. Chapter 5 deals with the intermediate measures of achievement — how many cases did they manage to obtain, of what type, what proportion resulted in mediation, how many came to an agreement, were criminal justice decisions affected, and how did participants rate what happened? Chapter 6 deals with the ultimate objectives — often too diffuse or too remote to assess rigorously, but relating more strongly, nonetheless, to what most see the schemes as being for. These aims range over the help given to victims, the impact on the offender, the resolution of conflict, the impact on traditional criminal justice aims, and the wider social impact. Chapter 6 also deals with aspects of 'quality' — fairness, equality of the parties, cost-effectiveness, and maintenance of the essential conditions. In all these chapters the results are an amalgam of the findings of all the different research teams funded by the Home Office listed in the acknowledgements (page vi).

One technical point should be mentioned here. There is a problem in connection with mediation schemes in counting the number of 'cases'. Insofar as a referral pertains to an offence by a single offender upon a single victim there is no ambiguity, but when multiple offenders or multiple victims (or both) occur, the number of potential mediations may exceed the number of referrals. Many schemes reporting their own figures count the-number of victim/offender pairs as the number of 'cases' they have dealt with. Others may quote separately the number of offenders contacted and the number of victims. In the following report we have followed the convention of counting each referral as a separate case, except where several offenders who committed the same offence together were referred separately to the scheme, when we recombined these as a single case. This means that many cases in our sample involve several victims and/or offenders, and total figures are often less than the number of cases that a scheme may have provided in its own annual reports. It also means that, on some variables, percentages may add up to more than 100% because of the possibility of multiple outcomes. This convention was employed in order to give what seemed to be the most realistic idea of the number of cases dealt with, and in order not to over-emphasise the few cases that involved several offenders and several victims, thereby involving a very large number of potential pairs.

CHAPTER 3

The Schemes: I. Police-related

This group of schemes employs victim/offender mediation in the context of offences for which the offender has been cautioned instead of prosecuted, or where such a course of action is being contemplated. All such schemes in Britain have, until recently, been concerned with juvenile offenders only. An Adult Reparation Bureau has recently been started at Kettering, Northamptonshire, to deal with older offenders.

The main schemes studied as part of this research were Exeter Youth Support Team, one of the earliest reparation schemes in this country, established since 1979; the Cumbria Reparation Scheme, funded experimentally by the Home Office for two years from 1985 to 1987, although it had already been running for a year on the basis of existing agency resources, and is continuing to operate since the end of public funding; and the Sandwell Mediation and Reparation Project, which is primarily a community mediation scheme set up in 1984 as a West Midlands Probation Service initiative funded through the Sandwell Urban Programme. The latter scheme takes a small number of referrals from the local police juvenile liaison panel, and it is only these cases that are discussed here, not the more numerous non-criminal neighbourhood dispute cases.

All three schemes filled in case-record summaries on standard forms. The Exeter scheme was also observed in operation by the Bristol-based fieldwork team (Jacky Baueherat, Gwynn Davis, and David Watson), who carried out similar research at the Northampton Juvenile Bureau, a scheme which was not involved in the case-records study. In addition, the Cumbria scheme was the subject of a wide-ranging study by Harry Blagg and David Smith of Lancaster University. For the purposes of analysis the Cumbria scheme has been divided into four samples corresponding to the regional panels (North, South, East and West) that operated in a significantly different manner in many respects. All these sources have been drawn upon for this chapter. The Sandwell scheme has been independently studied by Richard Young (1987) at the Institute of Judicial Administration, Birmingham University.

Exeter

The Exeter Joint Services Youth Support Team aims to pool the resources of police, probation and local authority social services to provide a range of support services for young people and a co-ordinated response to juvenile crime. According to their own literature, a central purpose is "*to encourage through inter-agency co-operation the diversion of young offenders from prosecution*": Their support for diversion is based on two arguments: first, that most juvenile offending is 'minor and transient'; secondly, that prosecution can be positively harmful by 'labelling' young people as 'criminals'. They particularly wish to avoid using criminal justice processes as a route to welfare intervention, as this tends to relate the severity of the disposal to the seriousness of a child's problems instead of the gravity of the offence. By offering welfare support outside the context of prosecution, the team hope to limit prosecution to that group of offenders whose behaviour is sufficiently serious and persistent to warrant strong sanctions. One of the alternatives offered is the Reparation Scheme, started in 1980 "*with a view to assisting the young person to integrate with his (or her) community in a positive way, through taking steps to put wrong things right by methods which will hopefully benefit the offender, victim and community as a whole*".

The team is run on the basis of existing resources of the co-operating agencies, staffed by one senior and three other social workers, one probation officer, a police inspector, two sergeants and a constable, along with clerical assistance. All of them have additional responsibilities within their own departments. Although they share premises, they are less a 'team' than a collaborative enterprise between three separate agencies, and staff identity and accountability is with their parent agency rather than the team.

Juvenile offences are referred on a special form completed by the arresting officer, relating basic details, the offender's attitude at the time of arrest, previous record, and the officer's opinion as to the appropriate disposal. The form is followed in due course by a full police file with fuller information, including statements, but this may take several weeks to come through. The police representatives in the team are responsible for reading this file before discussing it with the other staff at a 'liaison meeting'. This meeting either determines the offence disposal (prosecution, or one of a variety of alternatives) or defers this decision in order for a social worker to undertake a visit to the offender and his or her family, when this additional report will be considered at a later liaison meeting.

A range of formal alternatives is available to the police — 'no further action', an informal warning, or a formal caution. The latter may be repeated several times, but there is a reluctance on the part of the police to repeat a caution for a similar type of offence. In such a case, the team may look for some reinforcement of the repeat caution, which may involve the offender in group-work, in making reparation to the victim, or both. Thus reparation would not usually be considered for a first-time offender receiving a first caution. Such 'reinforcements' are voluntary in that they are undertaken after the caution has been administered. There is no sanction against an offender who declines to do as suggested, at least in relation to that offence, although his/her willingness to take part will have been assessed before the decision to caution. Of course, an offender who does rescind such a promise may have this taken into account if caught re-offending and may therefore be more liable to prosecution next time.

The reparation scheme itself is run by a police sergeant and constable. They make the arrangements for whatever form of reparation has been agreed at the liaison meeting. This includes asking the victim whether he or she is agreeable to the idea. The officer seldom attempts to mediate in the sense of resolving a dispute, enabling both parties to obtain a better understanding of one another's position, and so on, although this was contemplated in early plans "in cases of assaults where the victim and the offender each have a percentage of the responsibility". The object in practice is normally to negotiate some form of reparation which is seen to be sufficiently punitive and likely to make an impact upon the offender. It may be no more than a written apology, but compensation or work for the victim (or for the community) may be involved. A meeting between the offender and the victim is unlikely to occur until the form of reparation has been negotiated by the officer talking separately with both parties. Such a meeting, if it occurs, is solely for the purpose of delivering a personal apology or for confronting the offender with the upset caused to the victim. In their own literature they state:

Each programme is carefully planned to try and ensure victims will feel adequately compensated and the offender will consider he/she has contributed constructively and been fairly treated. The Reparation Scheme is planned with a view to assisting the young person to integrate within his community in a positive way and to be mutually beneficial.

The Youth Support Team operates only in relation to Exeter itself, but the Reparation Scheme has recently been expanded to take in the whole of East Devon. Outside Exeter the police negotiate directly with the relevant social services department rather than working through an established inter-agency team, as the number of cases for any one area outside Exeter would not warrant such standing arrangements.

Northampton Juvenile Liaison Bureau

The Northampton Juvenile Liaison Bureau is a multi-agency project, begun in 1984, along similar lines to earlier bureaux in the same county at Corby and Wellingborough. Like them it intends "*to make juvenile court appearances the exception rather than the rule*" or "*to divert young people wherever possible away from the penal and welfare systems into informal networks of control, support and care*". This aim is underlain by a well-articulated argument that most juvenile crime is minor; that most juvenile offenders will grow out of such behaviour in time without intervention of any sort; and that being exposed to the justice system will do more harm than good, partly by negative labelling, partly by removing informal networks of care and control. They apply the same arguments even to 'welfare' intervention, particularly if delivered via the justice system, because it is of limited value and may also have labelling effects, and because the employment of the justice system to provide help can lead to 'net-widening'. The Bureau prefers to encourage *"more low-key, community-orientated responses which concentrate on putting things 'straight' in a way that is direct and understandable to the child's age and ability"*, and to encourage families and schools *"to respond constructively to adolescent behaviour"*.

The Bureau recommends various alternatives to prosecution, aiming at a response proportional to the offence while taking into account the child's previous record and current circumstances, previous sanctions applied, and the potential for reparation. Unlike Exeter, it does not operate a 'Reparation Scheme', but it does view 'offence resolution' as an important part of their work. This entails *"arranging and supervising written apologies, direct and indirect reparation, payment of compensation and victim/offender liaison"*. They also say that *"the Bureau always seeks to examine ways that offences can be resolved in a constructive way for victim and offender...the Bureau [has] concern for victim and offender alike...In simple terms, if any offence is resulting in loss to a victim, then that loss will always be a priority in the resolution of the matter."*

This is not what happens in practice, however. Bureau staff themselves, in November 1986 at the time of the research, admitted that their written policy on reparation, from which the above quotes were taken, was out of date. They said that juveniles are rarely in a position to offer financial compensation; that victims tend to be corporate, so that a meeting is less relevant; and that due to the power imbalance between a juvenile offender and an adult victim the exercise may be experienced as further punishment (which the Bureau was keen to minimise). The prevalent view now would appear to be that the Bureau is primarily concerned to achieve 'minimum intervention', which was not compatible with an equal concern for the victim. They might approach a victim if they thought it would improve the offender's prospect of 'diversion' — for example, to establish that the victim did not wish to pursue compensation — but would otherwise rarely consider doing so, unless the offender had expressed a wish to apologise.

The Bureau is formally independent of any agency and jointly funded by five agencies concerned with juveniles. Staff consist of a director, social worker, probation officer, two police constables, a youth worker and a teacher, along with an administrator and a secretary. Although seconded from their parent agencies, staff are responsible to the director, in turn accountable to an inter-agency management committee. The bulk of the team's work lies in making recommendations as to the appropriate response in all juvenile offences referred to them. They also participate in training events and offer short-term work with young offenders of an 'offence-analysis' kind.

Referrals are taken only from the police and are of all juvenile offenders in the city who have admitted guilt. Referrals are only received when the police file on the offence is complete. This can at times mean considerable delay, so that one of the presumed advantages of police-based as against court-based schemes, that they can intervene earlier in the course of events, is substantially eroded.

Bureau meetings are the core activity and they take place twice weekly, attended by all the professional staff who take it in turns to chair. The team will decide either that it is necessary to carry out an assessment visit to gain more information, or they will make an immediate recommendation. Decisions on the assessment cases are made at a subsequent meeting. If a recommendation has been returned by the police, requesting further consultation, the team may also discuss how to strengthen the case for diversion before consultation takes place. Discussion tends to move more slowly than at Exeter and everyone is encouraged to express an opinion. Although more openly 'democratic', the resulting argumentation may sometimes prove unsatisfactory to the participants and the director is called on to exercise his mediating skills in a context very different from that between victim and offender.

It is agreed policy within the police force "*that no juvenile should be prosecuted until every alternative has been considered*" and the Chief Constable had ordered that "*the recommendation of the Bureau shall be accepted in all cases unless there are powerful arguments against*". Finally the decision does rest with the police, but during the phase of observation by the researchers all recommendations were accepted with one exception in which a caution rather than informal action was eventually agreed. However, several cases were referred for further consultation.

Possible disposals, short of prosecution, include:-

(a) *No Further Action* for more trivial cases, even if the juvenile has a crime record already.

(b) *Informal Action/Informal Warning*, which is what the Bureau will generally aim for unless the offence is particularly serious or the offender is 17. This response is not citable in any subsequent court proceedings, so it does not add to the juvenile's criminal record. A member of the police or of the Bureau will administer an informal warning, if this has not already occurred during the process of arrest, during the assessment visit, or as a result of sanctions applied by the child's own family.

(c) *Police Caution*, regarded as a serious response, citable in court and more formally administered. It is a response the Bureau would seek to avoid whenever possible, especially for first-time offenders. On occasion, a caution may be supplemented by further action, such as 'offence analysis work' by the Bureau.

Prosecution is only recommended when all other alternatives are exhausted, the child has a long record, the offence is serious, and there seem to be few mitigating circumstances. The police may decide to proceed with prosecution in very serious crimes without referring to the Bureau, passing the file for 'information only'. Such offenders will have been remanded in custody and are likely to receive a custodial sentence.

Assessment visits are carried out when prosecution seems likely, in order to find further reasons for diversion and to see if the offender will agree to participate in alternatives such as 'offence analysis'. They are primarily offence-focused; any apparent long-term welfare needs are referred on to other agencies, in line with Bureau policy of minimal intervention. Although reparation work is rare, there have been cases when this might clearly have been appropriate. One such case is given as an example at the end of this chapter.

Since the research was carried out there have been a number of staff changes at the Bureau, and the nature of the work carried out there may have changed somewhat, although mediation still forms a very minor part of it.

Cumbria

As in Exeter, a system of juvenile liaison panels intended to divert juveniles from the criminal justice system whenever feasible has been constructed as a joint exercise between the police, social services and probation. On the part of the latter two agencies at least the scheme is underpinned by a belief that, at least for the majority of petty offenders, the judicial process is unnecessary and even harmful, and that a system of cautioning and diversion would be preferable. An important difference between this scheme and those at Exeter and Northampton, however, is the lack of systematic recourse to 'lower-level' disposals such as 'no further action' or 'informal warning'. The decision to be taken is essentially between a caution and prosecution. There is thus no way of avoiding an official criminal record for the offender.

Reparation and mediation are seen as useful learning experiences for young offenders that the courts fail to provide, while serving the needs and interests of victims. The probation service, with the assistance of Home Office funding of £15,000 p.a, for two years from 1985 to 1987, employs four ancillary staff as 'reparation workers'. Following initial enquiries by a probation officer, these ancillaries are responsible for negotiations between victims and offenders arid for the supervision of any agreed practical tasks. With rare exceptions, however, victim/offender meetings were in practice a fairly perfunctory business, with an apology (and sometimes compensation) being inarticulately offered by an apprehensive juvenile, and received by a well-intentioned victim who might use the occasion for some moral reflections or impromptu social work.

The scheme covers the whole county (identical to the police force area) and is divided into four panels representing the police divisions based in Barrow (South), Whitehaven (West), Carlisle (North), and Kendal (East). All cases of juvenile offending are, in principle, referred to the appropriate panel, generally with a police recommendation for either a caution or a prosecution. The panel consists of a police Chief Inspector, the police juvenile liaison officer, the probation officer attached to the scheme, the divisional Intermediate Treatment Officer (representing the Social Services Department), and an Education Welfare Officer. The local reparation worker normally also attends, the panels meet on police premises and are chaired by the Chief Inspector.

Although the panel meetings have some features in common, striking differences have emerged, so that separate accounts of each have to be given. The two most prominent common features, however, are:-

(1) In all the panels the police are clearly the dominant agency. Unlike the Juvenile Bureaux in Northamptonshire, in which the agencies involved in diversion second full time workers, the police retain the right to make the initial recommendation, set the agenda and chair the meetings. Although the police force has produced their own document, 'Cautioning — Policy and Criteria', which is largely in line with Home Office guidelines on cautioning, their practice in this regard has been far less ambitious in scope than in Devon and Cornwall, or in Northants. A cautioning 'ceiling' has been established of about two cautions. Third and subsequent cautions are very rare, unlike the other two forces. Whatever the nature of the current offence, the police are usually very reluctant to caution a juvenile quite soon after a previous caution (because it might make the police 'look foolish'), if the offence involved the taking of a motor vehicle (because of issues of motor insurance), or if the person was the subject of a conditional discharge or had recently been in court for some completely different kind of offence.

(2) The social services representative in each panel will only rarely have any direct knowledge of the cases being considered, as they do not carry caseloads of their own or conduct pre-panel enquiries. They are generally dependent entirely on written reports from social workers, whereas the probation officer and the EWO will either have conducted enquiries themselves or have discussed the case with a colleague in the same office.

54

Kendal Panel (East Division)

Geographically by far the largest area, this division is overwhelmingly rural, the main centres of population being Penrith and Kendal. The area also includes the best-known tourist centres of the Lake District. Offences committed by visitors to the area pose particular problems to the panel, and the size of the area has led to administrative problems which have sometimes caused delay and missing reports, especially given that the other services involved are not organised according to the same divisional boundaries as the police.

The police representatives effectively controlled the initial agenda by virtue of their more detailed knowledge of individual cases. They expressed reservations about the value of the panel meetings, which they saw as tending to slow down the process of decision-making. They were therefore generally unsympathetic to social services and probation suggestions that decisions might be deferred on some cases until reports had been prepared. There is inherent conflict in the situation where one agency values speed and efficiency and the other agencies value more highly the provision of adequate information as a basis for discussion.

The members of the panel who were more committed to diversion wherever possible were often hampered in their attempts to argue against prosecution by reports prepared by schools or social workers who were unfamiliar with the context for which they are writing (especially when the offender came from outside Cumbria, a particular problem for this panel).

In practice, reparation has been very little used by this panel, for which the two main reasons appear to be, in the first instance, the attitude of the police representatives, who appear to have seen little in the idea, and secondly, general uncertainty about the purpose of reparation in the context of the panel's decision-making. Should it be a means of enhancing a caution, to persuade the police that a particular case need not be prosecuted? And if so, should the caution be conditional on the completion of an agreed form of reparation? Or should reparation be added to a caution (already decided upon) in cases deemed suitable? The first approach was seen by the probation officer as raising problematic justice issues, the second as involving excessive and unnecessary intervention. While this uncertainty was general throughout the divisions, its resolution seems to have been more protracted in Kendal.

While some diversion seems to have been achieved by this panel, mainly as a result of positive school and family background reports, or some evidence of remorse on the offender's part, the reparation worker's under-employment was causing her frustration and disappointment. If there were a difference of opinion the police representatives would effectively operate a veto. This occurred in one case involving the theft of a carton of apple juice from a milk lorry by a 13-year-old. The other panel members seemed to consider this a straightforward case for a caution, but the boy had been cautioned only a month earlier and the local police inspector took the view that he was *"holding up two fingers to everyone"* by re-offending so quickly. Despite a recommendation for a caution from the boy's social worker, who was attempting reparation work, the panel chairman decided to *"fall in line with the wishes of the inspector...who knows him, and prosecute"*.

In the last few months a change in police personnel resulted in an initial upsurge, at least, in the number of cases where a caution was recommended, so that at the pragmatic level there seemed more willingness to accommodate to the rest of the panel.

Whitehaven Panel (West Division)
This panel covers a fairly extensive area which includes the towns of Whitehaven and Workington. It had a moderate workload, and consistently produced the highest proportion of cautions of any of the four divisions. From observation and the accounts of participants, it would seem that the discrepancy between this panel and the rest was largely attributable to the views and style of the Chairman. Unlike the others, he was firmly predisposed in favour of cautioning whenever possible. He himself had close knowledge of most of the cases and remained firmly in control of the panel's transactions.

It was said, by one of the probation officers who attends the panel, that although the chairman was predisposed to caution, he preferred to be able to justify this decision to the arresting officer, so that the practice developed of offering some 'enhancement' of cautions, either by means of reparation, or by some commitment to action by the EWO or the Social Services Department. Initially, the decision whether to prosecute or not was deferred until it had been established whether the offender was willing to agree to reparation, or whatever else was proposed, cautions thus being made conditional on the offender's agreement to cooperate. This practice, however, was soon reviewed, especially by the probation service, and it was agreed that cautions should not be made conditional in this way in future. An offer to explore the feasibility of reparation is now used solely as a means of encouraging agreement to a caution. It is still not seen as an addition to an already agreed caution, but as a way of increasing the proportion of cases diverted.

The practice of reparation itself has changed as well. The main move has been away from a conception of reparation as literal compensation, involving sometimes substantial sums of money, to a more symbolic conception which might entail the payment of a small sum or some form of indirect reparation. The reparation worker herself was strongly committed to this change, feeling that assessment of compensation is more properly a matter for a court.

This panel has therefore shown potential for development on the basis of active self-criticism and discussion about its purposes. Its participants viewed it positively, and the probation members were in a less obviously subordinate position than in the other panels. Bargaining was able to take place meaningfully without having to struggle against a strong predisposition to prosecute on the part of the police representatives. A new police representative was assigned here too, about half way through the project. He initially saw his role as 'goalkeeping', since the region was getting a reputation (in the police force) for excessive liberalism, but seemed quite quickly to be persuaded of the value of the panel discussions. He was generally felt in the end to have allowed a more participative, less authoritarian style to emerge. In the last few months of the project there was agreement at chief officer level to rotate the chairmanship among the panel members, a policy that was more readily implemented in this division, although without obviously altering the degree of police domination of the proceedings.

Carlisle Panel (North Division)

This panel suffered from the usual problems of inadequate reports from schools or social workers. The probation contribution was normally the most constructive. They appeared to use the option of reparation to bolster a decision to caution rather than in cases where a caution was likely anyway. There was, however, a tendency to become involved in fixing precise levels of compensation in complex cases, rather than concentrating on the symbolic dimensions of reparation, a feature that seemed to be due to the stance taken by the probation ancillary in this area, who regarded reparation in traditional terms as a form of punishment.

Barrow Panel (South Division)

This division was dominated by the industrial, working-class town of Barrow, and was reputed to be the most punitive of the four police divisions. Particular offences of concern tended to be illicit BMX rides and litter, and in these cases the social work agencies would have difficulty obtaining cautions. Nevertheless, it seemed that reparation was pursued selectively, when it might affect the decision whether to prosecute or not. The police generally agreed to reparation and a caution when a well thought out case was presented, even though they would clearly have prosecuted in normal circumstances.

Both the probation officer and ancillary responsible for the reparation work believed in the value of reparation as a symbolic act, part of a process of genuine reconciliation between victims and offenders. Unlike those in some of the other districts, they stressed the needs of victims that the criminal justice system left unsatisfied. Even so, in practice they became disillusioned with a scheme that did not work out as they intended. Interviewed afterwards, the ancillary expressed doubts about whether things had been made any better for victims because the panel as a whole did not share the same views and tended to take a material view of reparation. He did not even see the scheme as having been successful in terms of diversion, as most cases were very minor.

Sandwell

The Sandwell Mediation and Reparation Scheme was established in 1984 with Urban Aid funding, sponsored by the West Midlands Probation Service who formally manage the scheme. The scheme is, however, relatively autonomous in practice, the probation service exercising little day-to-day control, while an advisory group of community representatives does not wield a great deal of influence. This places a substantial burden of responsibility — and a great deal of liaison work — on the staff's lone co-ordinator and part-time clerical assistant.

The scheme is primarily a community mediation service, training and employing local volunteers to help resolve conflicts, usually between neighbours. Cases are referred by other agencies, of which the Citizens Advice Bureau is the most prominent. Victim/offender mediation was developed later (although it was always the intention to do so), taking referrals from the local police Juvenile Liaison Panel, an inter-agency group advising the police on the disposition of juvenile offenders. As with such panels generally, their main aim is to divert as many juveniles from prosecution as possible by encouraging more frequent use of cautioning. The panel's recommendations are forwarded by the police representative to his superiors, who generally ratify them. The mediation scheme's co-ordinator attends the fortnightly meetings of the panel and deals with any referrals there might be for arranging reparation. The co-ordinator handles this mediation personally, without involving the volunteers trained for community mediation cases (who were usually resistant to the idea of extending their work to victim/offender meetings). Very few cases have been referred to the scheme, however (only 1% of all those reviewed by the panel in 1985 — according to Young, 1987), so that the overall impact of the scheme on police force practice is minimal.

It was originally envisaged that mediation would be offered before the panel made its recommendation, but objections have been raised on justice grounds to a caution being made conditional on participation in the scheme. This means that mediation can only be attempted after a decision to caution has been made and that the initial diversionary aims have had to be modified. There is still some doubt, in practice, about the relative timing of the mediator's intervention and of the decision to caution, and this could benefit from clarification. The scheme still aims, ultimately, to be diversionary, in that as its credibility grows more cases will hopefully be cautioned in anticipation of a successful outcome to mediation. The aim of the mediation itself, however, is restricted to the facilitation of negotiations between victims and offenders leading to a mutually satisfactory resolution of outstanding issues.

Procedures as Reflected in the Case-records

Intentions and actual practice do not necessarily correspond. Many factors may make it difficult to translate the first directly into the second. Resources in terms of personnel and time may restrict what is possible. The fact that staff in some of the schemes — eg. Exeter, Cumbria — had other departmental duties may have restricted their input, a fact which may be vital in the development of innovatory work (see Davis, Boucherat and Watson, 1987). Organisation may be more or less inefficient. Staff and volunteers may have their own personal conceptions of what they want to achieve that are not the official aims. The intentions themselves may turn out to have been based on false assumptions. Other agencies may not lend sufficient support, or may even be obstructive. Inadequate preparation may lead to misunderstandings in such relationships (cf. criticisms of the planning of the Sandwell scheme by Young, 1987). Davis et al (1987) found that police were reluctant to refer cases to some schemes because *"They saw it as something for offenders and likely, therefore, to prove an additional burden for victims."* Given that reparation would normally be seen as primarily for victims, this may be a surprising anomaly that might have been sorted out through better preparatory liaison. At the same time, in those schemes that used the reparation idea primarily in order to divert offenders, the suspicions of the police may have been a matter of seeing through the social work rhetoric.

It is important, then, to examine what did happen in the schemes studied compared with what was intended. Data are available on 326 referrals to these schemes: 97 from Exeter covering the period May 1985 to October 1986; 218 from the four Cumbrian panels, June 1985 to May

1987; and 11 from Sandwell, December 1984 to March 1986. Numbers from the Cumbrian panels varied considerably from 95 (Cumbria North) to 21 (Cumbria East). The other two panels averaged about 50. These figures apply only to those cases specifically referred for reparation, not all juvenile cases considered by the referring panels.

All but two of the referrals came ultimately from the police (via juvenile liaison panels or the Exeter Youth Support Team), as was to be expected, but Cumbria North and Sandwell each received one referral from the probation service. Ninety per cent of cases referred had already received a formal caution for the offence, but 6% were still under threat of prosecution, while the remaining 4% were not subject to legal action at all, but had been referred by the police on an informal basis. In those cases where the defendant was still under threat of prosecution, cautioning was delayed in order to ensure that reparation was satisfactorily completed. Most of these occurred at Cumbria North (thirteen cases, 15% of total caseload) and Sandwell (three cases, 27% of cases studied), but were mainly in the early months of the schemes.

The schemes proceeded with virtually all of these cases. Five were dropped for miscellaneous practical reasons, such as the death of one of the victims.

The amount of time spent in negotiation of reparation agreements was usually very small, averaging about 2.7 hours per case. Cumbria North and Sandwell were higher than the other schemes in terms of number of meetings and other contacts, averaging about 3.5 hours per case. Exeter was the most economical at just over 2 hours per case. (Schemes recorded numbers of meetings and letter/telephone contacts, which were converted into 'times' by coding meetings as 1 hour and the other contacts as 10 minutes.) Across all the schemes directly based on police liaison panels (Exeter and Cumbria) the number of contacts with the victim (averaging 1.5 per case) was not much more than half the number of contacts with the offender (2.7 per case). The independent mediation project (Sandwell) showed less bias towards the offender, and spent more time on negotiations overall (averaging 3.2 contacts with the victim, 4.1 with the offender). The ratio of victim contacts to offender contacts was very similar across all the schemes other than Sandwell, although

Cumbria North and East panels spent more time in absolute terms with both parties than other panels (averaging over 2 contacts per victim, about 4 contacts per offender). That the projects other than Sandwell concentrated on working with the offender seems to be in line with their main objectives described above. This is reaffirmed on the whole by the relative preponderance of victims among the first party contacted by the scheme. At Exeter the victim was contacted first in only 10% of all cases, whereas at Sandwell the figure was 50%. In Cumbria there was variation between the panels, with East and West tending to contact the victim first slightly more than the offender, while North and South contacted the victim first substantially less often.

A meeting between victim and offender was not always offered by the scheme. In fact, in only 68% of cases were the parties given this opportunity. Three of the Cumbria panels offered such a meeting in three-quarters or more of cases, but Cumbria South offered it in less than half (43%). Exeter and Sandwell were close to the average rate. When a meeting is arranged 89% take place within a month of referral to the scheme. In only 8 cases was the interval 3 or 4 months, and 7 of these cases were at Exeter (13% of all their cases taking this long). The date of referral to the schemes, however, may be some time after the commission of the offence, so that the time elapsed between offence and victim/offender meeting can be quite lengthy.

Virtually all the meetings were managed by a single member of the scheme's staff. The fact that usually one of the parties was a schoolchild seems to have been taken into account by the fact that the meeting was more often than not arranged for some time after four o'clock in the afternoon (60% of all meetings in the sample). In Cumbria North this applied to 80% of all meetings. Few meetings were held, however, at the weekend (generally about 5%, although 20% were held at that time in Cumbria East).

When the victim was an individual or a private household, 61% of all meetings took place at the victim's own residence. Only one meeting was held at the offender's address: the rest were evenly divided between the scheme's own premises and some other venue sometimes the victim's place of work). In the case of 'corporate' victims (shops, firms, schools, various agencies etc), almost all meetings were held at their own premises with one or more representative of the organisation. Typically, a meeting would occur between a single victim and a single offender, but in 19% of all cases analysed there was more than one victim involved (the largest reported number being 7), and in 26% more than one offender (at the most four). Generally when there were multiple parties separate meetings would be held between pairs of individuals. Occasionally some other individual(s) than the immediate parties and the mediator would also take part, eg the mother of the offender, or a relative of the victim, but this only applied to 16 meetings altogether. 78 per cent of the meetings lasted for less than half an hour, 38% less than quarter of an hour, with only 8% lasting an hour or more. A written record of any agreement reached was rarely kept; only 14 such cases were recorded in the sample, almost all of them from the Cumbria West panel.

Chapters 5 and 6 will give much more information about the types of case and outcome involved in these schemes, but the best way of providing a picture of the operation of victim/offender mediation is to look at a few specific cases in detail. The three cases below are not 'typical', as there is no such case — the individual variations are legion — but they do give a flavour of what can occur. They were chosen largely on the basis of sufficient available information and on their inherent interest. They are slightly more involved and substantial than would ordinarily be so. The first and third are cases from the Exeter and Northampton schemes respectively, compiled by Jacky Boucherat, Gwynn Davis and David Watson; the second is from Sandwell, compiled by Lydia Callaway. The accounts have been adapted for this report by the collators. All names are pseudonymous. (Other cases will be mentioned more briefly in the course of the later text when discussing particular issues.)

Case-study A

Mark (15 years old) had three months previously stolen a wallet from the car of a teacher at his school, Mr Symes. £12 cash was taken and a window of the car was smashed. As it was the culmination of a series of transgressions, Mark was suspended from school and thrown out of his home by his father. He was admitted into Local Authority care under a voluntary care order.

At a liaison meeting it was agreed that Mark be cautioned and asked to make a personal apology to the teacher, which he agreed to do. Mark was already attending a voluntary group run by the project because of committing previous thefts and burglaries. Through this group he already knew Michael, the social worker who organised the apology in this case. Normally the reparation would be managed by the police representatives on the team, and this was the social worker's first essay at organising a victim/offender meeting.

Michael discussed the offence and the events surrounding it with Mark, and helped him plan an apology. He did not discuss the possibility of compensation, being aware of the fact that Mark already had many fines and debts outstanding. Michael also contacted Mr Symes, telling him that Mark had been cautioned for the offence because of 'problems at home'. Mr Symes agreed to meet Mark.

On the appointed day Michael collected Mark from the Children's Home and accompanied him to the school, once again discussing what might occur and for the first time mentioning the possibility of offering compensation. They met Mr Symes in his room, which was unfortunately part of a thoroughfare leading to other rooms, which occasioned numerous intrusions and interruptions, making a smooth exchange difficult. Michael explained the reason for coming and then asked Mark to make his apologies. Somewhat cowed, Mark made a rushed and awkward statement: "Yeah, well, it was nothing personal, just happened to be your car — and I'm sorry."

Mr Symes thanked him for the apology. The researcher present at this session observed that throughout the interview the teacher directed his remarks to Mark, talking in a straightforward way without being patronising, which appeared to have the effect of giving Mark's apology greater weight. Michael encouraged Mark to relate how he was feeling at the time of the offence, how he was in a miserable mood because of problems at home, but Mark was embarrassed by intrusions of other people into the room, and Michael had to provide this information himself. Finally he raised the issue of compensation. Although the car window was covered by insurance, there was still the question of the stolen cash, which Mark muttered that he was willing to pay back. The conversation became encumbered, however, in the detail of arrangements for repayment, made difficult by Mark's impecunity and the fact that the teacher was leaving his present job at the end of term. Meanwhile knocks at the door were getting increasingly frequent, and Michael suggested winding the meeting up, asking Mr Symes whether he had any questions for Mark.

Mr Symes took this opportunity to ask what Mark had done with the other items in the wallet, which, it turned out, had all been flushed down the toilet. Mr Symes then listed the items — photos, credit cards etc — and indicated the problems involved in getting replacements. The researcher felt that this came over as spontaneous and direct, an expression of annoyance and frustration that seemed to serve to vent the victim's anger. Mr Symes then ended by reiterating his gratitude for the apology, saying "I appreciate that it can't have been easy" and shaking his hand.

After the encounter, Mark appeared relieved and expressed a positive attitude toward the teacher. He said that he had not liked the idea of apologising, but felt he ought to do so and that it turned out well "because it means I can speak to him again",

Mr Symes later talked to the researcher." "Is a caution, and having to come back to say he's sorry, likely to have any effect on him? ...having seen him, I think probably it will — I mean, it's not something that happens easily, after doing that sort of thing, to come back and apologise. And it opened my eyes up a bit to how somebody like that feels...I thought a lot more of him, after having seen him, and I felt a bit better, letting him know about the trouble he'd put me too. Plus there was him making the offer of paying the money back. Whether anything more will come of that, I don't know — it was the offer that was important, rather than the money itself..."

The social worker was impressed by what he saw as the 'power' of a personal apology, even though there were several aspects of this case that were less than perfect — the interruptions, several awkwardnesses that could have been avoided with better planning and more adroit management, and especially the missed opportunity of promoting a fuller exchange between victim and offender because of the preference of the scheme for a mere delivery of an apology.

Case-study B

This case was referred from the Police Juvenile Liaison Panel, on which the scheme co-ordinator regularly sits in attendance, just before Christmas. A caution was being considered. On the face of it, the offence seemed to be a disturbing act of violence; a 13-year-old boy delivering a karate kick to a registered disabled man, who suffered bruising about the chest.

The scheme co-ordinator herself visited the house of Mr Robertson, the victim, who was mobile but suffered from heart trouble. He said he knew the boy, Dan, concerned. Dan had often called him names in the street and used to tease his 13-year-old daughter and her friends when coming out of the local play centre. Dan had told her that he knew she was having sex with her father, and the same rumour was picked up by Mrs Robertson through neighbour gossip.

Mr Robertson had spoken to Dan after that, saying there was no truth in the accusation and warning him that it was dangerous to spread such rumours. A few days later he encountered Dan in the street with a group of friends. Dan came across and kicked him in the chest. Mr Robertson returned home shaken and reported the incident to the police, telling them that he thought Dan had been egged on by his friends.

Mr Robertson told the mediator that he was willing to meet Dan to discuss what had happened. He was concerned to know where the rumours about himself and his daughter had come from, as this had upset him. At this time Mr Robertson said that he believed Dan was already on probation, and that it would do him good to be sent to a detention centre.

The mediator then visited Dan, who was staying with his elder sister, along with his mother, who had recently separated from her husband. His mother said that she would be willing to accompany Dan to a mediation meeting with Mr Robertson. Dan was worried that the police might be present, but the mediator assured him that the meeting would be entirely private.

A meeting was arranged for 12 January at the scheme's premises. When everyone had assembled, the mediator explained that Dan's mother was present only because of his young age, and that it was important that Dan himself did the talking. He was asked to explain what had led to the attack. He said he and his friends thought Mr Robertson was "funny in the head". He had only repeated a rumour that he had heard from others. Mr Robertson explained what a trauma would have been caused if Social Services had followed up such an accusation. Dan admitted that he had not given any thought to the implications of what he had been saying.

Dan also said that his friends had encouraged him to attack Mr Robertson. They had all been sniffing glue, and he could feel himself gradually getting worked up. He ran over and kicked Mr Robertson, then punched him in the face. He related that later, sitting in his room at home, he realised the seriousness of what he had done. He described how he could not sleep for thinking about a grandparent and an uncle both of whom had died of heart attacks. He was worried what would happen to Mr Robertson.

Mr Robertson said that he thought Dan very brave to talk like he did in the meeting. He seemed to be basically a 'decent chap' and that he should come and knock on his door the next time he felt like glue sniffing. Dan admitted he had been frightened of the meeting, but was now glad he had gone through with it. He was surprised that Mr Robertson had listened to him and had been so understanding; he had expected him to be angry. Mr Robertson advised him to keep away from the boys in the area who were trouble-makers, and Dan responded by saying that he truly regretted what he had done and did not want to get into any more trouble.

After Mr Robertson left the meeting, the mediator talked with Dan's mother. She related the problems she was going through with her marriage break-up and that she had not been giving Dan enough attention. The mediation session had opened her eyes, hearing Dan talking. They had now found a place of their own to live and she was hoping to settle back to stable family life again.

The Juvenile Liaison Panel decided to caution Dan once they received the mediator's report on the meeting. When she called at Dan's house to deliver this news, Dan volunteered the information that, when asked recently to join a glue sniffing session, he had instead visited Mr Robertson, telling his friends that he had arranged to go elsewhere.

Case Study C

Simon (16) admitted causing (grievous bodily harm' to Richard. It was his first offence. The two were school friends who fell out when Simon formed the impression that Richard had spent the night with the former's girlfriend. A few days later, Simon threatened Richard with a knife: in the struggle that ensued, Richard sustained a deep wound in his arm, requiring surgery and likely to cause some disablement for up to two years. The arresting officer claimed that the victim's parents "want their pound of flesh" and were seeking prosecution. Simon, on the other hand, was full of remorse. In the opinion of both the arresting officer and his head teacher, the offence was "totally out of character".

The victim maintained that the injury was sustained in trying to defend himself as Simon "lunged at his chest". Simon himself insisted that he did not intend to wound the other, but only wished to threaten him; the wound was accidental as they struggled together. A witness's statement seemed to support the latter version of events.

At the first Bureau meeting the police force members began by stressing the serious nature of the incident, the knife having caused injuries to tendons and nerves, despite expressing some sympathy for the offender's point of view. The fact that the case had been referred to the Bureau gave the panel some hope that the police might consider an alternative to prosecution, but it was apparent that more information would be needed to back up such a suggestion and it was agreed that one of the police constables would make further enquiries of both parties.

In the second panel meeting the constable related his interviews with both families and with Simon's head teacher. He had formed the opinion that Richard had not in fact spent the night with Simon's girlfriend, but had brought her home after an evening together; and that the wound had been caused more by accident than design, when Richard grabbed at Simon's wrists as he was waving the knife at him. He was certain the victim was embellishing his story to impress others. He was also unimpressed by Richard's father's attitude in his insistence on getting compensation and suing Simon's family. Nevertheless the scar was large and unsightly, and the victim still did not have full use of his arm. Even when he left the family after one and a half hours, the father was still extremely angry.

The team were generally in favour of a caution, in recognition of the severity of the offence, but difficulties were caused by the victim's insistence on compensation, and that the case proceed to court. After further discussion, the final decision was to recommend a caution.

They were probably not too surprised when the police informed the Bureau the next day that they would challenge this recommendation, as this, eventuality had been anticipated. The caseworker tried to argue the case with the Chief Inspector whose decision it ultimately was, but with no success. The issue than went to a formal discussion between the Chief Inspector and the Bureau Director, accompanied by the caseworker.

In the course of this meeting, it was questioned what would be gained by prosecution. It was felt that the most likely outcome would be a fine or conditional discharge, which the Chief Inspector accepted would do little for either party. He also accepted that Simon was depressed and that a court case could lead to a breakdown. Interestingly, it was the Chief Inspector who put forward the possibility of mediating between the two boys, especially in view of the fact that they were both members of the same brass band and thus still likely to encounter one another. The victim, however, had categorically refused to meet the offender when approached by the Bureau. Eventually, considering that the victim could still play his musical instrument and could claim compensation whether or not the police prosecute, the Chief Inspector agreed to a caution on certain conditions; that Simon should seek medical advice about his depression; that he should apologise to Richard "if circumstances make this viable"; that steps should be taken to reduce tension in the school orchestra; and that Simon should agree to dispose of the knife. In this way he ensured the Bureau's involvement in the case for a short while to cover the risk of further trouble.

CHAPTER 4

The Schemes II. Court-based

Three of the Home Office funded experimental schemes were court-based — Coventry, Leeds and Wolverhampton. All three participated in the research, both the centrally collated case-records and the intensive fieldwork. Coventry and Wolverhampton were studied by Anna Leeming and Judith Unell, Leeds initially by Anne Garton and then by Clifford Williams of Bradford University under Paul Wiles' direction. Coventry, in addition, was one of the locations for the observational research carried out by the Bristol University team. As well as these three schemes, another independent one, the North-East Essex Victim/Offender Reparation Project, kindly filled in the same case-record forms and enabled the research to extend to a slightly different kind of organisation. On top of this, a further court-based scheme at Totton in Hampshire allowed the Bristol team to carry out an observational study, although we do not have any case-records material. All but Essex are continuing to operate, Tatton and Leeds currently on the basis of probation service resources, Wolverhampton receives charitable trust funding, as does Coventry along with funds from the West Midlands Probation Committee since the end of the two-year central government grant. Most of the cases involve adult offenders (17 years and over). The descriptions of Coventry and Wolverhampton were written by Judith Unell and Anna Leeming, of Totton by Jacky Boucherat, Gwynn Davis and David Watson (who were also the source of a few extra observations on the Coventry scheme).

Coventry

The Coventry Reparation Scheme is administered by the West Midlands Probation Service but managed by an independent committee of representatives of court user groups and local voluntary bodies. It operates from its own premises near the city centre. During its first two years, Home Office funding of £35,000 p.a. was supplemented by a grant from the Monument Trust, enabling the scheme to employ four full-time members of staff, a project leader, two assistants and a secretary. The involvement of volunteer mediators had originally been proposed, but in the event the scheme was operated entirely by the paid staff. At the outset the scheme took referrals of adult offenders from the magistrates' court only, but over the first two years extended its services to the juvenile court and later to the crown court, although the magistrates' court remained the principal source. In addition a system was set up for taking a few referrals from the police, of non-criminal community disputes.

In their Twelve Monthly Report, the scheme defined mediation as *"a method of providing a framework within which a victim and offender can communicate with one another through the involvement of the mediator who has an equal concern for both parties...the primary aim...is to help both Parties come to terms with the aftermath of the crime and discuss issues relating to it. In addition mediation can be a process used by victim and offender in order to reach a personal agreement as to how the offender might make some amends for the harm he has caused."* The wording suggests that good communication is perceived as an end in itself, with the making of amends a secondary and inessential outcome. It also does not commit the scheme to a direct encounter between victim and offender, as communication may be carried out through the agency of the mediator.

With respect to reparation, the same report observes: *"Reparation is a general term meaning 'to make amends'. In this context reparation is direct, with the offender trying to put right some of the harm caused to the victim by way of apology and acknowledgement of the harm caused and in some cases by way of completion of a reparation agreement."* This is a broad definition which includes not only practical reparation but also expressions of remorse by the offender. The idea of a mediation scheme in Coventry originated among senior members of that division of the probation service as a possible answer to the problem of fines. This issue had been raised at a meeting of the Magistrates' Bench in 1982 on the subject of non-payment of fines. They were concerned that the poverty of many offenders and the inadequacy of existing mechanisms for enforcing payment were undermining the efficacy of fines as a disposal. Although the probation staff who promoted the idea of reparation were undoubtedly sympathetic to the plight of victims, they were motivated principally, then, by the need for a new and effective disposal for the offender.

A feasibility study was carried out by Martin Wright in 1983 (Wright, 1983). It drew upon American experience as well as an analysis of local court statistics which provided an estimate of 120-200 offenders a year that might be referred by magistrates. The report was significant in drawing reparation to the attention of groups such as the magistracy whose support would be needed to launch a new scheme. Wright's model, however, was influenced particularly by the Massachusetts 'Earn It' project and directed towards practical restitution by the offender, rather than victim/offender communication as an end in itself. Reparation would have been made either through practical work or financial payments, monitored and enforced by the scheme. Where the offender had no means, short-term job opportunities would be negotiated with local employers so that offenders could earn the money to compensate their victims.

At a time of high unemployment, however, the employment aspects of this proposal were not thought to be feasible, and others in the probation service were not happy with the idea of the scheme being primarily a compensation enforcement agency. Although useful as a baseline model, the specific details were quickly modified and the lower key approach reflected in the above definitions had been adopted by the time the scheme began.

Basic guidelines were offered to the court to help in the selection of referrals. A guilty plea and the presence of an identifiable victim were minimum requirements. In addition, it was suggested that the scheme might be particularly appropriate in cases where offender and victim knew each other before the offence or where a low-paid or unemployed offender faced the prospect of a fine or compensation order. Referrals could come at any point in the sentencing tariff. Although it was hoped that reparation would modify sentence in most cases, the project leader did not want to be manoeuvred into the position of negotiating reparation agreements which were directed towards satisfying the court that 'adequate' restitution had been made, rather fulfilling the wishes of the individual victim and offender. The main disadvantage with this approach was that the courts were left without clear signals for pinpointing suitable referrals, as a result of which the project workers had to maintain an active and continuous presence within the courts in order to prompt referrals and act as a visible reminder of the scheme's existence. Generally speaking, the referral procedure follows these steps:

1. Project staff view court list
2. Defence solicitor or court clerk are approached
3. A recommendation is made by the solicitor or clerk to the magistrates that a referral might be appropriate
4a. Referral from magistrates; this may be for mediation only, but often it is combined with a request for a social enquiry report
4b. Referral from probation (a small number of cases that have bypassed the court)
5. Approach to offender
6. Approach to victim, if the offender consents
7. Mediation and/or reparation occurs
8. A written report is presented at court before the magistrates pass sentence.

The need to complete mediation and reparation within the three week period allowed for a social enquiry report puts considerable pressure on project staff. It is inevitable that in some instances the time restrictions will jeopardise the extent and quality of the mediation which can occur. The magistrates have the option of a direct referral for mediation upon an adjournment for 28 days, which went some way to alleviating this problem, being used in about a quarter of cases.

The preparation for mediation by the Coventry project is, however, careful and principled. The first interview with the offender is used to explain the workings of the scheme, to discuss the offender's version of events, and to set him/her thinking about what they might wish to say to the victim. The offender is then asked to think this over for a few days and then to contact the scheme again in order to give a definite decision whether or not to proceed. The scheme thereby puts the onus firmly on the offender to demonstrate sufficient commitment before the victim is contacted. A second interview is then arranged to consider with the offender just how to go about making amends.

The mediator will then contact the victim and ask to call to discuss the case. At this interview the mediator describes the scheme, explores the victim's perspective on the crime and its aftermath, conveys what the offender is willing to do, discovers what the victim may wish to convey to the offender, and establishes whether they wish to proceed, if at all, by means of a joint meeting or indirectly. The mediator will continue to meet separately with both parties as often as is considered necessary in order to clarify what might be expected of the meeting, which takes place with the mediator, usually at the scheme's own offices. Otherwise, the mediator may pass information between the two or convey a letter of apology from the offender. If the latter has agreed to pay compensation, the mediator will normally ask that this be done independently of the scheme, perhaps through a court order, so that the project avoids being cast in the role of debt collecting agency.

At the time of its launch, the relationship between the scheme and the probation service was confused. The project leader took the view, shared by the other members of the team, that the corporate ownership of the scheme by all court user groups through the management committee was essential to its independence and its acceptance by the court. Also, the capacity of the scheme to meet the needs of the victim and to deal impartially with victim and offender within the mediation process had to be proved and it was felt that this was best done in an independent setting. The ambiguity of the staff's position as employees of the probation service was resolved by an agreement that the scheme would be accountable to the management committee in its day-to-day work. This arrangement worked well in practice in satisfying all concerned that the scheme was able to maintain its independence and impartiality.

The scheme had recognised from the beginning that many victims and offenders would meet their needs by expressing their views and feelings within the mediation process and would not always seek practical reparation. As the scheme progressed, the latter function received decreasing emphasis and few reparation agreements emerged. Where reparation was performed it was increasingly seen as an enhancement of the understanding achieved by victim and offender rather than as a main object. Instead of the supervision of reparation agreements, the main energies of the staff were directed towards the promotion of the scheme within court and managing the mediation process. Almost all the management committee members also came to accept the team's view that successful mediation was the aim and that reparation was only appropriate when it was actively desired by both parties. One member interviewed disagreed with this view, suggesting that a stronger commitment to reparation would have substantially increased its appeal to the court.

Leeds

The Leeds Reparation Project was the result of a probation service working party that finished its deliberations in 1984. Their proposal suggested that reparation *"could challenge offenders, help victims and make a contribution to enabling courts to use non-custodial alternatives in certain cases"* (Myers, 1987). This last consideration led to its targeting a high tariff group of offenders, of which they hoped to deal with over a hundred a year, and therefore the aim of providing an alternative to custody was originally the predominant one.

On being awarded central government funds of just under £35,000 p.a, for two years (with the help of only a nominal sum for rent of office space, and a small contribution from probation service funds to cover a small overspend at the end of two years) the probation service placed the project under the management of a senior probation officer (Terry Myers) responsible for all initiatives involving alternatives to custody and his ACPO (assistant chief probation officer). They convened a steering group of representatives of the local magistracy, court clerks, police, social services and victims support. Although they intended to work by and large with the Crown Court, they were unable to find a barrister or a judge to take part in the group. Although this group performed a useful monitoring and support role, they did not exercise the degree of autonomous control manifest in Coventry's management committee.

Unlike Coventry too, the staff were probation service employees. The project leader was a probation officer, John Blinston, who had already been experimenting with victim/offender mediation as part of his normal work with probationers. One of the former victims involved in this informal exercise was sufficiently enthusiastic about her experience to be taken on by the scheme full-time as a probation service assistant. Both she and the project leader were convinced advocates of the use of mediation, capable of persuading other agencies to take the idea seriously during the difficult early stages faced by all innovative activities. The remaining staff member was a clerk/typist.

The project was always committed to the idea of using volunteers, but decided to recruit a relatively small number and pay them £3 per hour in order to achieve a high level of time commitment, training and standard of practice. The project seems to have been successful thereby in attracting a group of mediators of high quality, although their approach naturally varies according to their individual experience and orientation. Training consisted mainly of role-playing seminars and on-the-job training by pairing experienced and novice mediators.

Mediators met together each month with the project leader and senior probation officer (projects). The mediation meetings usually lasted about two hours, and provided an opportunity for the project leader and senior probation officer (projects) to keep mediators informed of any developments and changes to the project and also provided a forum for discussion of issues arising. Mediators were often asked to relate case studies and share both their 'successes' and 'failures' with the other mediators. There was a sense of unity among the mediators as a group and the monthly meetings appeared to be an important source of moral support for the mediators.

Although taught to be sensitive to victims' needs, mediators are also encouraged to 'sell' mediation, and a refusal by any party to take part is seen as a 'failure'. While being careful not to 'pressure' victims, they tend to be persistent in their arguments. The stress on diverting offenders from custody inevitably makes the project more difficult to sell to victims and therefore leads to internal dilemmas in the practice of mediation which must be seen to be of equal potential value to both parties. The project was, however, very aware of these problems. As their own report stated: "*In fact coercion by whatever means of either victim or offender would be counter-productive. Mediation and reparation only works if the people involved want it to work*" (Myers, 1987).

The project commenced operations in May, 1985. It was prepared to accept referrals from any agency, but expected that most would come from probation officers assigned the preparation of social enquiry reports. Considerable effort was therefore expended early on to inform local officers of the project and to encourage referrals. This approach did not restrict itself to 'high tariff cases. In fact almost all referrals were to come from probation officers and most related to cases before the Crown Court. There were considerable differences of opinion amongst probation officers, however; some took the attitude of the October 1984 NAPO conference resolution that concern with victims and reparation could, in the long term, dilute resources for offenders. Probation officers' reasons for referral were largely, of course, perceived benefit's to their charges (whether psychological, or material by making a reduced sentence more likely) rather than any perception of victims' needs.

The project leader scrutinises all referrals to ensure their suitability, although very few are rejected. It is, of course, difficult at an early stage to determine whether an offender's motivation is genuine or not, although the project report surmises "*that in fact the majority of offenders are less cynical than might be thought and that declining to participate is a difficult and threatening thing to do*" (Myers, 1987).

As to the meetings themselves, the project leader states that it "*has operated on the strict premise that mediators have absolute control of the structure of the mediation session but that the content belongs to the participants. It is their meeting. The structure adopted as a working model was taken from the Friends Suburban Project, Philadelphia, USA*" (a community mediation scheme for neighbour disputes rather than victims and offenders). The structure referred to consists of a process of:

(a) "*opening statement*" (establishment of ground rules by mediators);

(b) *"uninterrupted time"* for each party in turn to speak without interruption;

(c) *"exchange"*;

(d) *"agreement"* (incorporated in a written document);

(e) *"closing statement"* (a review of the experience by the mediators).

They consider that *"Mediators working in pairs at this stage can better facilitate the process"*.

The agreement is incorporated in a written report to the court, which is thereby invited to endorse it. Sometimes the reparation has already been voluntarily carried out by the offender, but the project does not encourage this in case this is seen as pre-empting the court decision. If the court does allow reparation to go ahead (or incorporates it in an order), the project is responsible for its supervision. Such supervision can be very burdensome in terms of time and resources, but it does at least ensure substantial follow-up contact in such cases with the offender and often the victim too, which otherwise would not occur.

The project encountered one serious problem at an early stage working with a Crown Court case (R. v. Clough and Moorhouse). Given the long period of remand before such trials, intervention occurs before the offender makes a formal plea in court. It is possible, therefore, that an offender admits guilt at first and is accepted on the scheme as a result, but decides later to plead 'not-guilty' in court. This is rare, but in the above case this did happen and the case was dismissed by the judge as untriable for this reason. No resolution to this problem has been found — although it has not recurred. One possibility would be to allow for an early plea in those cases where referral was being contemplated. On the other hand, it is not necessarily true that all such cases are indeed 'untriable', and this point needs more legal discussion.

The R. v. Clough and Moorhouse case came before His Honour Judge Hurwitz at Leeds Crown Court on 29th January, 11th March and 8th April, 1986. Briefly, Clough and Moorhouse were charged under sections 18 and 20 of the Offences Against the Person Act 1861. A deal was expected at the 'plea-bargaining' stage to drop the higher section 18 charge on the basis of a guilty plea to the lesser section 20 charge, and mediation went ahead on the basis of this guilty plea. In fact the higher charge was pressed, and the defendants' barristers advised a non-guilty plea. To complicate matters further the mediation session between Clough, Moorhouse and their victim had been filmed by the BBC for a documentary about reparation schemes. Furthermore, it was a part of the defendants' bail conditions that they did not in any way communicate with the complainants.

Judge Hurwitz claimed that the case was untriable, due to interference with the prosecution witnesses. Judge Hurwitz remarked *"In fact it is a well-established principle that where a man is facing prosecution he ought not to be in contact with those who are to give evidence against him, for the most perfectly obvious reasons, and the only reason for introducing a condition prohibiting approaches is because it is thought that in the circumstances of the particular case an additional order of the Court is required to secure what is in any event the accepted practice of keeping them apart. What we have had in this case is a round table conference between defendants and complainants…it seems to me that the whole legal process in this case is corrupted…One wonders whether in itself it is not a criminal offence before a case has come to trial to arrange almost to buy off a complainant with money to be paid by the defendant."* (Transcript of the case R. v. Clough and Moorhouse, 8/4/86). Judge Hurwitz cited the circumstances in which the case could not be stopped. However, he felt that in this case he had every justification for stopping the case.

The prosecution had requested the BBC to allow them to see the recording of the mediation session. The BBC were not prepared to do so without an order of the court. Judge Hurwitz remarked than in any discussion about meeting such an order the court might require the presence of an *amicus curiae* (to argue the issue from the point of view of public policy). Furthermore there was the question to whom the application should be made. Judge Hurwitz suggested that the Divisional Court might be more appropriate. The Judge further stated *"(the television) interview took place without caution, without anyone being told this may be the subject of evidence in the trial and you (prosecution) will know that if a man has been charged, anything said to him or by him in relation to the case will also very likely be inadmissible, and indeed there are Judges' Rules which deal very firmly with such a situation. How on earth do you suggest that there is any conceivable way in which you can argue that anything that happened across the table can be admissible?...*" (Transcript of the case R. v. Clough and Moorhouse, 11/3/86).

The Leeds Reparation Project had a strict policy of not accepting cases where the defendant was not admitting guilt. As the senior probation officer (projects) noted; "*referrals come from Probation Officers who would not generally be writing reports in not guilty pleas and who would not refer such cases.*" In the Clough and Moorhouse case the defendants were quite clearly admitting to assaulting the victims and the notion of a tactical not guilty plea took the project somewhat by surprise. As a result of the ramifications of the case the deputy chief probation officer and the senior probation officer (projects) met with the Crown prosecuting solicitor who was "*reassured about the level of risk in working with pre-plea, and was happy for his department to cooperate with us once more.*"

The issues raised by this case resulted in the case papers being sent to the Director of Public Prosecutions, the Lord Chancellor and the Lord Chief Justice. As a consequence of the remarks made by Judge Hurwitz, the project altered its practice in so far as mediation would not proceed until the defence solicitors had confirmed in writing that a guilty plea would be entered, and agreeing to mediation. If there was any doubt as to the plea, or it was possible that the defendant might plead guilty to one offence and not guilty to an alternative charge the case would not be accepted.

Consideration was given to the possibilities of a post-plea system which would avoid the dilemma found in the Clough and Moorhouse case. Amongst the arguments presented against such a system was that it would delay significantly valuable work with cases, and increase the risk of the voluntarism of the mediation idea being compromised by increasing the pressure on victims to take part. The delay caused by adopting a post-plea system would, the project argued, risk taking cases beyond their 'optimum time' for mediation. The senior probation officer (projects) noted that: "*If the loss experience of victims of crime can be compared with loss through death, divorce or separation then the* *intervention is likely to be most productive after the initial grief experience during the period when the victim is attempting to come to terms with the loss and is beginning to reinvest in the future. In practical terms this is likely to be some weeks after the event. This would suggest that diversion from prosecution schemes or post-sentence work in Crown Court cases is likely to be less effective...To delay until post-plea or sentence means the optimum time for intervention with victims may have passed. The **formal** involvement of the court will also tend to compromise the voluntarism of both the victim and offender. The optimum time, therefore, in our view is during the committal period."*

In fact, cases reaching the Crown Court vary significantly in the number of weeks after the actual offence that they appear. Introducing a post-plea system would not necessarily have a significant effect, nor is there any clear evidence for any such 'optimum time' for mediation.

Another practical problem arose from the fact that the project sought particularly to deal with 'high tariff' offences. A substantial proportion of the offenders referred to the project were remanded in custody and, therefore, the project had to arrange for mediators to visit prisons to explore the possibility of mediation, and also to arrange mediation sessions in prison. Neither HMP Leeds nor HM Remand Centre Thorpe Arch were aware of the Leeds Reparation Scheme until the project leader approached them for permission for victims to meet offenders in their institution. A meeting was held between the probation service and the governor of HMP Leeds and two senior prison officers to discuss the scheme.

The Governor placed certain restrictions on the type of cases which could be mediated in the prison. Violent crimes were to be excluded on the grounds that further violence might occur. It was felt that victims with a criminal record, and elderly or young victims should not attend mediation meetings in prison. These restrictions on mediation meetings in prison meant that some cases which the project regarded as suitable could not be considered for mediation meetings, and this posed a potentially serious restriction on the use of mediation with the project's target group — 'high tariff' offenders.

Where it was possible to arrange mediation in the custodial setting victims and mediators entered the prison on a 'welfare visit' conducted under the auspices of the probation service.

The original criteria established by the governor were provisional, and in fact a victim who had previously been a prison inmate himself did attend a mediation meeting at the prison, along with his wife who had experienced visiting him in prison. As both had already been to the prison before they did not seem to have any qualms about a meeting in the prison. The offender, however, was described by the mediator as very nervous and was only able to say a few words. He had only received fifteen minutes notice of the meeting taking place.

Any future high tariff reparation and mediation schemes will have to consider carefully the difficulties involved when arranging mediation meetings with offenders who are in prison. In fairness to the Leeds scheme the problems were exacerbated by the industrial dispute then ongoing in the prison. The project hopes that some offenders may keep their mediation agreements when released but unfortunately the research period was not long enough to monitor this.

N.E. Essex

This scheme was an initiative of the Essex Probation Service. With the support of the Chief Probation Officer, plans were developed by three Senior Probation Officers with relevant responsibilities (Mr J Parry-Williams, community programmes; Mr J Green, community service; and Mr M Armstrong, victims support coordinator for Colchester, Clacton and Harwich). A steering group was formed of local magistrates, the Clerk to the Justices, policemen, solicitors, and prominent community members. A pilot project was agreed for six months from 1st November 1985, run part-time by another probation officer, Alan Critchley, as Project Development Officer. Without extra funding the scheme has been limited to working within current probation resources, which has kept it small in capacity. Experience was sufficiently encouraging for the scheme to be continued after the pilot phase.

Five local community volunteers were recruited and trained to carry out the mediation, all former Victims Support Scheme volunteers or Probation Voluntary Associates. Mediation occurs between conviction and sentence for offenders whose cases are adjourned at the magistrates' court. A reparation 'package' is prepared for the court, which may take it into account when deciding upon sentence. Among victims the scheme is targeted at individuals, households and certain kinds of corporate institutions (voluntary organisations, local authority departments, etc).

A particular strength of this scheme is its direct link to Victims Support. The coordinator of the project at the time of the research (Dr Fiona Hetherington) also ran the Colchester Victims Support Scheme, as did the previous coordinator, Michael Armstrong. Despite the probation service base and strong representation from criminal justice agencies on the management committee, therefore, the project is capable of holding both victims' and offenders' interests equally to the fore. A leaflet drawn up by the scheme emphasises the emotional rather than the material needs of victims: *"Anyone who has been the victim of a crime may feel hurt, upset and angry. The feelings can last for a considerable time. Experience has shown that those victims who meet the offender often recover more quickly from the trauma. This may be connected with identifying the offender and seeing that he/she is actually a normal person. Traditionally, the victim has been left out of the Court process. This scheme attempts to achieve some involvement for the victim"*. The same leaflet also stresses the importance of making offenders accountable: *"Offenders have not generally been made to face the distress they have caused"*. The stated aims are *"To allow victims of criminal offences to meet with the offenders. To provide an opportunity for an offender to offer an apology for the offence. To enable the offender, if appropriate, to perform some task to remedy the wrong or make recompense for the loss"*.

Totton

Totton is a relatively prosperous outlying district of Southampton. The victim/offender mediation scheme has been in existence since July 1985, having evolved from a working party set up by the Hampshire Probation Service the previous year. The resources committed to it by the service are, however, minimal. Immediate responsibility for the project lies with a probation officer based at the Totton office, but it is heavily dependent in practice on four or five accredited probation service volunteers. They undertake most of the mediation, acting in pairs, although the supervising officer also does some. As the latter is a busy officer with many other responsibilities the scope of the scheme has inevitably been restricted.

The scheme's objectives, as outlined in the supervisor's 1985/86 annual report, are as follows:

(1) to look at the feasibility and value of effecting mediation between offenders and those affected by their offences, pre-trial;

(2) to see whether the Courts, having been made aware of this process, would be prepared to consider and accommodate agreements in their sentences, or at the very least, not to undermine a voluntary resolution;

(3) to continue the mediation process post trial, either on a voluntary basis where appropriate, or for supervising reparation sentences: and

(4) to use volunteers as a primary resource.

In a report prepared by the volunteers' group (September 1986) it was observed that *"the lack of one clearly defined aim has caused concern to some, but the Tatton group seems broadly to agree that an attempt to help resolve the personal conflict between those 'joined' by an offence is worthwhile"*.

The scheme is distinct from all other current court-based projects in the country in that it operates before a court hearing. The supervising officer is granted access to charges and summonses which are to be heard at the magistrates' court (both adult and juvenile) over the next few weeks. Although this allows for earlier intervention than in the other schemes, it has the drawback that it is often unclear whether the person charged intends to plead guilty or not. This places the scheme in the same position as the Leeds project relative to the Crown Court.

If the project deems a case suitable and it has resources available, it is allocated to two members of the group who make preliminary enquiries of the offender. If mediation still appears a possibility, they seek to complete the whole process in time for the hearing, when a report is presented to the magistrates.

The local magistrates and justices' clerk are content that mediation be attempted without securing their agreement in each case, but there appears to have developed an understanding that the scheme will generally operate at the lower end of the tariff. Serious assaults would not, for example, be considered suitable. Typical offences are theft (including shoplifting) and criminal damage. More serious offences would, in any case, be more difficult to take up before a court hearing, given the greater possibilities of a 'not guilty' plea or of adjournment, and given the short time available to carry out mediation (three weeks or less).

The majority of cases accepted are abandoned before reaching a victim/offender meeting, because one party may not keep the appointment, or decline to participate, or because the offender's attitude seems unfavourable. The members of the scheme are concerned that the offender's decision to take part should not be too heavily influenced by anticipation of a lighter sentence, and they feel that their scheme is less coercive than many of those operating on adjournment.

Wolverhampton

The Wolverhampton Mediation and Reparation Project (WOLMARP) is based within the Crypt Association Ltd., a large and prominent voluntary organisation in the town centre. It grew out of a close working association between The Crypt and the local division of the West Midlands Probation Service. The Home Office grant of £17,589 p.a. provided an important element of independent funding over the first two years, but the project was also supported from the Crypt's own resources. A full-time project co-ordinator was employed, later augmented by a full-time assistant and part-time secretary. Both the latter posts were filled by MSC Community Programme workers, and were over and above the funding sought from the Home Office. The project, in fact, was seriously under resourced and there was widespread regret that the request for funding had been pitched at such a low level.

The co-ordinator is accountable through line management to the Board of the Crypt, but independent support is provided both through an advisory committee with representatives from court user groups and other interested bodies and through an informal support group composed of project workers and members of the probation service. The latter group was set up deliberately to counteract earlier failures to consult with and involve front-line probation staff, who showed little interest and enthusiasm in the scheme, a problem exacerbated by a resolution passed at the National Association of Probation Officers (NAPO) annual general meeting in October 1984 opposing the further development of direct reparation and urging officers to withdraw their support from new local initiatives

The original brief enabled it to accept referrals from the magistrates' and juvenile courts; later it extended its scope to include crown court referrals. In practice, most of its business is generated by the magistrates' court. It was originally assumed that the project would receive its referrals directly from the court, but in the early months the level of referrals was extremely low. Magistrates were apparently reluctant to refer out of a fear that the victim would feel pressured to participate. There was also some unwillingness among defence solicitors due to the possibility of increasing delays to the processing of cases. At the same time the number of referrals from probation officers was also low.

After only three referrals were received during the two months of December 1985 and January 1986, there was urgent consultation with the Assistant Chief Probation Officer and the Clerk to the Justices which led to an informal agreement that details of offenders referred for social enquiry reports after conviction would be made available by the probation service and that the project would be able to make an independent selection of suitable cases. Referrals subsequently picked up, but, despite the fact that direct court referrals were still sought, most cases over the next couple of years were selected independently by project staff. A consequent disadvantage of this method of referral was a few days' delay in obtaining details after conviction, effectively reducing the already short three-week period available for mediation. These difficulties were increased by the refusal of prosecuting solicitors to allow the project direct access to prosecution files. As a result less time was available for a considered assessment of each case and for preliminary discussions with victims and offenders. Where practical reparation was agreed, there was sometimes an unseemly haste to find a task which could be completed before the court appearance.

In its 18 months Interim Report, the project defines mediation as *"The provision of opportunity for all parties involved in an incident to converse with each other with the assistance of a trained mediator who has a neutral stance in the operation...The objective is...to achieve some agreement upon common ground, usually for future conduct or payment of compensation, in an effort for the party at fault to make amends to the victim"*. This contrasts with the definition adopted by Coventry, in that it has both parties moving through the mediation process towards an 'objective' which is the reparation agreement.

Reparation, in turn, is described as follows in the project report: *"Reparation is a term used for the operation of 'making amends' by offender to victim for the offence committed. It may take the form of financial recompense directly related to the loss by the victim, or by the repair or replacement of articles damaged or stolen during the commission of the offence. In cases where none of these alternatives are suitable there is a facility for the offender to perform some service to the community as a demonstration of remorse. In all instances the amount or degree of reparation has to be mutually agreeable and in proportion to the offence subject to discussion. Details of the reparation are often included in a document referred to as a reparation agreement"*.

This definition confines reparation to a practical act of making amends, decided upon through mediation but constituting a separate event, unlike the philosophy of the Coventry scheme which does not focus on material reparation in the same way. Nevertheless, it became clear quite soon after the launch of the project that the negotiation of practical reparation agreements was to play a far less significant part in the meeting between victim and offender than had been thought at first: *"The element of reparation, once quite a strong plank in the organisation of the Wolverhampton scheme, has been found to be viewed as unimportant by many victims, who seem quite content with a meeting with the offender and accept that the discussion and apology fulfils their requirements*" (18 months Interim Report). This change of emphasis, as at Coventry, was accepted by almost all the advisory committee members interviewed. One member, however, regretted that reparation had not been more actively pursued, because he felt that it was important for offenders to have the opportunity to make reparation, and that this might carry more weight with the court when considering sentence. Most members did indeed recognise that mediation as an end in itself was difficult to promote since there was no finished product to symbolise the offender's contrition.

Although the impetus for the scheme came from within the probation service, an independent base was desired both in order to attract funding and because it was doubted that mediation could be immediately integrated into probation work. The Crypt's innovative style and its experience of victim support work were considered particularly appropriate for the new venture. The original proposal recognised that mediation could provide reassurance for the victim and promote mutual understanding, but it was unequivocal in its view that the main objective was to facilitate reparation by the offender. There was no attempt to link the project with a particular level of sentence. It was envisaged that mediation would be most appropriate for offences against property and cases of minor violence, especially where the amount of compensation was not likely to be substantial. The presence of an identifiable victim and the voluntary agreement of both parties were emphasised. The project would operate only when a social enquiry report had been requested by the court. A report on the outcome of mediation would be presented to court on behalf of the project and the probation officer involved by the court duty probation officer. When reparation could not be completed within the adjournment period, it was envisaged that the agreement could be attached to a variety of existing sentencing options.

There was from the beginning a firm commitment on all sides to a volunteer model. This stemmed partly from a philosophical position that mediation and reparation provided means for the community to solve its own conflicts and that the involvement of ordinary members of the community was therefore appropriate. It was also related to the Crypt's experience of involving volunteers in victim support work. There have, however, been a number of unanticipated problems in involving volunteers in this project. Recruitment and training needed time, and when volunteers were ready the low rate of referrals meant that they were unoccupied. Nine volunteers were originally recruited, three of whom dropped out soon afterwards. In the second year, another training programme recruited eleven more.

Very few of the volunteers have, unfortunately, become actively involved as mediators. This is partly due to the modest flow of referrals, but perhaps the greatest barrier is the limited time scale within which the project must operate in each case. Volunteers with other commitments during the day have not always been able to pursue new referrals immediately. Also, the volunteers work in pairs and must liaise with each other, another source of delay. Despite the considerable enthusiasm of the volunteers, it has proved difficult to persuade them to work to deadlines or to keep written records. The original plan of transferring responsibility for arranging mediation to volunteers as the project became established has therefore not materialised. As a result the management of volunteers has increased rather than relieved the burden on the project's limited resources.

Junction Project

The Junction Project was established in 1981 as an intermediate treatment scheme by Save the Children fund. It is now managed by Lambeth Council. The project works with young offenders who would otherwise be in custody or residential care because of serious or persistent offending. The mediation and reparation programme is offered to complement the project's Group Work programme (attended full-time as an alternative to a custodial sentence of more than three months).

The project aims to use mediation and reparation with young people who face custody, who are known to the project through previous participation in their programmes, and who are willing to take part. Suitable cases are identified using established 'gatekeeping' practice. Social Services court files are checked for young people over 14, who are within the jurisdiction of the magistrates' court, live in Lambeth and meet the above criteria. Direct referrals may also be made by social workers and probation officers. The programme is explained to the young person and, where possible, his or her parents. If the young person is willing and able to participate, the project's 'reparation coordinator' informs the Police Juvenile Bureau. An officer from this bureau then makes the initial approach to the victim. If the victim is willing to take part negotiation commences between the parties as to the nature of mediation and/or reparation, assisted by the coordinator. The young person may be called to court at any time during this process. Progress is then reported to the magistrates and, if negotiations are on-going, a short adjournment sought. Once agreement has been reached between the parties on some form of reparation, the magistrates are informed and a recommendation for either a Community Service Order or a deferred sentence is made. If the court concur then reparation can proceed, otherwise it is feared there is a danger of 'double sentencing' with the offender carrying out reparation and then being sentenced without regard to his efforts.

The programme encourages reparation specifically related to the offence or, if this is not possible, general reparation to the community. The project co-ordinator counsels the young person and closely supervises any work undertaken.

In defining their orientation to victims and offenders the Junction Project states that it aims *"to create a situation which is less alienating for the victim that their current experience of the juvenile justice system, and which is both a less damaging and a more constructive response to the offender's behaviour."* Whilst endeavouring to occupy the middle ground between victim and offender, they admit their *"point of departure and first responsibility is to the offender."*

Procedures as Reflected in the Case-records

Data are available on 521 referrals, starting with the first referral in each case, to the four schemes: 144 from Coventry over the period September 1985 until August 1987; 218 from Leeds from April 1985 to February

1987; 31 from N.E. Essex, January 1986 to March 1987; and 123 from Wolverhampton, October 1985 to May 1987; and 5 from the Junction Project, April to December 1985. Virtually all these cases were proceeded with by the schemes (97%).

Most cases referred to the two West Midlands schemes, Coventry and Wolverhampton, were derived directly from the court (93% in the former case, 71% in the latter). The other major source of referrals at Wolverhampton was from defence solicitors (13). Fewer than 10% in each of these schemes were referred by the probation service, which is the major source of cases for the other two schemes (98% at Leeds, and 65% at N.E. Essex). The referrals to Leeds were not, however, spread evenly across all local probation teams. 72% came from only three particular teams in the east of Leeds. N. E. Essex received 16% of its caseload from the court, 10% from other agencies (including one from a solicitor), one 'case directly from the police, and two from individual citizens, so that it was less bound to its court base than the other schemes.

Because of the long lead-in time before a court appearance for most of the more serious offenders coming to the Leeds scheme, 95% of its cases were taken before the first court hearing, ie before conviction. The West Midlands cases, on the other hand, were almost entirely referred between conviction and sentence in conjunction with an adjournment for either social enquiry reports, or specifically for mediation. At N.E. Essex the latter also constitute the majority, but only at 45%; the rest are largely court cases before conviction (39%), along with a few that were not being prosecuted (involving civil actions or informal police action). All the schemes also received a very small number of cases after sentence — 5 at Leeds, 2 at Coventry, and 1 at each of the others.

Negotiation prior to mediation was usually carried out by a single member of staff at each scheme (74% of cases), sometimes by two or, very occasionally, more than two. Although Wolverhampton and N.E. Essex had recruited volunteers, these were seldom involved in the prior negotiations at Wolverhampton (only 3% carried out by a volunteer alone, 13% by a volunteer along with a staff member). At the Essex scheme negotiations were most often carried out by a staff member and a volunteer working together (48%), although volunteers acted alone in 31% of cases. The involvement of volunteers in the North American VORPs is also as well developed as in the last scheme — Dittenhoffer and Ericson (1983) report that volunteers also handled 31% of the Ontario VORP cases, with staff only handling 54%, 15% being shared.

There were large differences between schemes in the amount of time devoted to such negotiations. Coventry spent an average of 7.1 hours per case, averaging between 5 and 6 meetings with the parties. Leeds was substantially lower, averaging 4.3 hours per case and nearly 4 meetings with the parties. The other two schemes both averaged just over 3 hours per case. Almost always it was the offender who was first contacted at both the West Midlands schemes (93% or more). Leeds usually contacted the offender first (63%), but N.E. Essex was different from the other three in its tendency to notify the victim first (59%). All schemes but Coventry tended to have more contacts with the victim (usually 3 or 4) than with the offender (2 or 3). Coventry had more contacts with both parties, but spent more time with the offender (over 10 contacts on average) than with the victim (4.3 contacts).

A direct meeting between victim and offender is offered in the great majority of cases (84% overall), with the West Midlands schemes being the most inclined to do so (85% and 95% for Coventry and Wolverhampton respectively; 76% for the other two schemes). Mediation usually took place on a weekday (96%) and during working hours (67%). The Coventry scheme, however, held more of its sessions after four p.m, (45%). In terms of location, both West Midlands schemes were evenly split between the scheme's own offices and the home or workplace of the victim, with very few mediations carried out elsewhere. The Essex scheme carried out mediation at the victim's home in all but two cases. Leeds was more variable, with 38% at victim's home or workplace, 18% at the Probation Office, 32% at another neutral location (eg church hall or community centre). The remaining 11% were either at the offender's home (one case) or in a custodial institution to which he/she had been remanded or sentenced. The tendency for mediation to be carried out at the home or other premises of the victim is shared by American VORPs

— Coates and Gehm (1985) found that two thirds of all meetings took place there.

Mediators worked in pairs (occasionally three together) slightly more often than they worked alone (53% against 47%). At the Essex scheme, they were always volunteers, at the other schemes usually paid (at Coventry wholly so). Usually a single victim and a single offender were present, although more than one victim attended in 24% of mediations, and more than one offender in 11%. Very seldom were any other parties present at the mediation. A session usually lasted between 1 and 2 hours at Leeds, but between half an hour and an hour at the other schemes. Sessions with personal or household victims (as against corporate representatives) tended to take rather longer (50% under one hour, as against 80% for the corporate victims). These results are again not dissimilar to those for North American VORPs. Umbreit (1985) remarks that victim/offender mediation there usually lasts about an hour. In these schemes, too, an agreement will usually be written down and signed by the parties, but such formalities were not always fostered by their British counterparts. The Leeds project usually kept such a record (81% of all cases where there was some kind of agreement), but the other projects did so much less frequently. The Coventry scheme only did so very rarely (5%). It must be remembered, however, that all schemes submitted a written report of the meeting and any agreement to the court.

As in the case of the police-based projects, the best way of obtaining the flavour of victim/offender mediation in these schemes is to examine a few actual cases. The first three, from Coventry, Essex and Wolverhampton respectively, were compiled from the scheme's records and from talking to the mediators involved by Lydia Callaway. The fourth, from Totton, is taken from the report of the Bristol University team by Jacky Boucherat, Gwynn Davis and David Watson. The last, from Leeds, was written by the fieldworker for that scheme, Clifford Williams.

Case-study D

The offender in this case was Mr Colley, aged 26, an exhaust fitter, married with two children. He had been drinking heavily at his niece's wedding reception. His memory was vague after he left, but he was refused a drink at his local public house, went home to fetch a hammer and returned to smash car windscreens at random in the pub car park.

When contacted by the reparation scheme, Mr Colley readily expressed his willingness to take part. The mediator later came to the opinion that he had agreed without really knowing what he was letting himself in for, but he became more enthusiastic and concerned, and more accepting of his responsibilities, as negotiations proceeded.

The landlord of the pub was then visited. He said he would not allow Mr Colley to enter the pub again. Feeling against Mr Colley was running high amongst the customers, as he already had a reputation for violent and irresponsible behaviour. The landlord warned the mediator that one of the two major victims, Mr Taylor, was extremely upset and angry about the offence because his car had sentimental value for him, his wife who had died after a year of marriage having paid towards it.

When she visited Mr Taylor, the mediator did indeed find him to be very distressed by the incident and threatening to retaliate if he saw Mr Colley. He seemed to appreciate having someone with whom to talk about the crime, but the mediator decided that a meeting between him and Mr Colley would not be appropriate at that time. Nevertheless, the information about the significance of the car was relayed to the offender, who was quite upset at the thought, and this started him thinking about his behaviour.

The second major victim was a car hire firm. The managing director, Mr Birch, was very keen on the idea of meeting the offender. It was not possible to set up mediation immediately, however, as Mr Birch needed permission to proceed from his insurance company and Christmas holidays further intervened. Nevertheless, the court decided to adjourn for a further period to allow the mediation to take place.

The meeting eventually occurred at the car hire premises. It lasted an hour and a quarter. There was much discussion about the effects of drink. Mr Birch did not condone Mr Colley's actions but he was understanding and expressed concern that he should learn a lesson without there being any detrimental effect on his family. Mr Colley admitted that he felt very silly and said that he was concerned for both his job prospects and his family. He offered to make amends. It was agreed that he should carry out twenty hours unpaid work for the car hire firm. Both parties seemed to have got a lot out of the meeting.

Mr Colley works long hours, six days on and one day off a week. Consequently it was many weeks before he was able to complete twenty hours for Birch's car hire. The mediator found such an extended period of reparation difficult and embarrassing to supervise, and felt that a smaller amount of work would have been equally beneficial. Mr Birch subsequently agreed with this and also suggested that the work would have meant more to the offender if it had not been so similar to his everyday job. Nevertheless, the victim said that his involvement in the scheme had been both interesting and worthwhile from his own point of view.

Mr Birch attended the court hearing and seemed to derive some satisfaction from being allowed to play some part in the criminal justice process. Mr Colley also seemed to have benefitted enormously. He received two years conditional discharge, but was ordered to pay costs and compensation to the five other victims whose cars had been damaged, totalling £644.

Case-study E

Mark was 20 years old. He had already served three years in custody as a juvenile for burglary, had spent three months in a detention centre, and was currently on probation for taking a motorcycle without consent, possession of a weapon, and two other offences taken into consideration. He was working part-time as a gardener. His present case involved two counts of burglary.

With another person he had burgled his own sister's house and then went on to break into the house of a Ms Turner, an office worker, divorced, with an 18-year-old-son. There they broke a beer stein of sentimental value and carried off a video that Ms Turner had borrowed, *worth £700. This they managed to drop on the way, damaging it beyond repair. It was not covered by insurance.*

Mark himself restored his relationship with his sister, but the scheme was asked by the magistrates' court to try to arrange a meeting with Ms Turner. When approached, she said that she was very keen to meet Mark. Her own son, she explained, had been involved in the past with some petty crime, though not burglary. She said she would be interested to find out from Mark himself what made him intrude into people's homes in this way, and to point out to him that it was not just a matter of the material loss involved but also the violation of her privacy.

A letter was sent to Mark suggesting a date for a mediation meeting. No reply was received, but the scheme eventually managed to contact him through his employers. It emerged that he was practically illiterate. He was, in fact, keen to apologise to Ms Turner, although frightened of his parents hearing about his crime. Over the time of his involvement in the scheme the mediator came to know Mark as a lad of limited intelligence, easily led, but with a pleasant personality.

A meeting was arranged at the home of the victim. The two parties got on well from the beginning. Mark did not have a close relationship with his parents and responded to Ms Turner's willingness to talk to him, the respect with which she treated him, and her apparently selfless attitude. Mark explained he had been drinking on the night in question, while Ms Turner spoke about the way she had suffered as a result of the burglary, questioned his behaviour and said that she hoped he would benefit from taking part in the scheme. The mediator put forward the suggestion that Mark might like to make some payment to Ms Turner as reparation. Mark was agreeable to this, although he earned only a small amount. It was eventually settled that he should pay weekly instalments of £5 to Ms Turner, signing an agreement to this effect. The mediator found the whole event quite 'moving', and she felt that the meeting had been very successful.

As it would have taken Mark nearly three years to pay off the full cost of the video at the agreed rate, the scheme recommended in its report to the magistrates' court that they should make a compensation order to the amount they felt he should be expected to pay. The case was, however, referred to the Crown Court by the magistrates because his co-defendant had a more serious criminal record and was liable for a long period of imprisonment. This meant that the recommendation was never read. Mark received two years probation at the Crown Court, a sentence that was seen as relatively lenient in view of his record and probably due to his involvement in the scheme. No compensation was awarded by the court, which meant that there was still no agreed limit to Mark's payments. Nevertheless, he has continued paying them, delivering the money to Ms Turner in person every week. A good relationship had subsequently developed between the two parties, and there was some hope that this would help Mark behave more responsibly in future.

Case-study F

Elroy Masters, aged 22 and unemployed, had been charged with the theft of motor vehicle parts from a car repair business. According to the scheme's own report,

> The matter was adjourned by the Court for a Social Enquiry Report and an approach from the Project Coordinator to defence solicitor and offender after the Court appearance resulted in a referral to the Mediation/Reparation Project.

> Initially the offender maintained that his name was Malcolm Smith but during the contact with the Mediation staff he has agreed that he is in fact Elroy Masters. This fact was revealed in sufficient time for the prosecutor to be informed and avoid the necessity of producing expert evidence to prove his identity. His reasons for this conduct were related to apprehension about non-payment of a fine, [but] he has come to terms with this and is in a position to resolve that particular problem.

> Elroy is brother to a nationally well-known sportsman, and another reason for his use of an alias was concern about adverse publicity. He was ambitious, too, to follow in his brother's footsteps. He had been convicted of previous offences of theft and fraud.

> Elroy explained to the scheme that he had called at the car repair business to enquire about some spare parts on a car he had seen in the yard. The employees said that he could probably have them, but that he

should call back the following Sunday when the boss, Mr Pacino, would be there. Elroy called as arranged to find the premises unoccupied. He made the decision to take the parts he wanted, but Mr Pacino and his employees returned from their lunchtime at a local pub to catch him in the act of stealing.

Both parties, on being contacted by the scheme, agreed to meet to sort things out, despite a little reluctance on the offender's part at first. The mediation took place in the garage office, amongst a jumble of mechanical equipment, with two mediators present. Given the circumstances and the nature of the parties, there was some apprehension on the part of the mediators as to the likely result. This was enhanced when it quickly emerged that at the time of the original encounter there had been an exchange of blows, a fact that had not emerged in the police report. Elroy, however, apologised to Mr Pacino for the incident and for giving him a thick lip. He further expressed his appreciation that Mr Pacino had restrained him with minimal use of force when he might have retaliated more aggressively. The two parties then had a long discussion about Elroy's work and domestic prospects, Mr Pacino being concerned that Elroy might get a custodial sentence, which he felt would be too severe in view of what Elroy had done and the fact that he was obviously remorseful.

The mediators noticed at this point that an unexpected 'reversal of guilt' took place, with Mr Pacino apparently feeling guilty for reporting the incident to the police in the first place, when the property had been immediately recovered and no damage had been done. He thereupon asked Elroy if he would be interested in a job in the firm should a vacancy arise. Elroy replied with some embarrassment that he appreciated the offer but was too ashamed to work with those who had caught him stealing. The meeting was unhurried, lasting over an hour, and ended with Mr Pacino saying that he would be glad to receive Elroy's custom at any time in the future and that he need not be afraid to call, while Elroy for his part promised to have more respect in future for other people's property. Mr Pacino did not wish Elroy to make any additional reparation, being satisfied with the frank discuss-ion and the apology.

Mr Pacino had been extremely understanding. After the meeting Elroy told the mediators that he felt 'great' and thought it was a 'fantastic scheme'. He was very relieved that there would be no further aggravation between the garage owner and himself, and saw the experience as a fresh start. In court a few days later he was fined £50. He has since won national sporting success just like his elder brother.

Case-study G

This was the most serious offence dealt with by the Totton scheme during the period of the research. Michael Morley (along with another person who was remanded in custody and not referred to the scheme) had attempted, in two separate incidents, to snatch the handbags of two women. They were camouflaged in balaclava helmets etc.

The case was allocated to a probation officer working with a volunteer, who immediately called on both the victims. The younger one was the more upset and declined to meet Michael (18). The other, Mrs Hall, had succeeded in hanging on to her bag and agreed to take part.

A meeting was arranged to take place in a local probation office, both mediators present. Michael (tall, well built, tidily dressed) looked chronically anxious and embarrassed. He could hardly bear to look up as the introductions were made.

Mrs Hall was asked to begin. She had no difficulty. She was very voluble and in control of the situation, her tone reproachful and yet sympathetic. "I know how you feel — you must feel terrible — but what on earth made you do it? How would you feel if my son had done that to your mother?" She asked Michael if he had ever thought how this sort of thing makes a woman feel — "It's only because I'm a woman; it wouldn't have happened to a man." Several times she stressed that "it's a violation". "The first week [after it happened] I could really have strangled you, but I'm over my anger — it's gone now." Throughout Michael looked most contrite and mumbled some words of apology and assent with what she was saying.

Eventually Michael was able to say that he was looking for a job and had no money. He explained that they had not singled Mrs Hall out *specially, and she agreed that knowing it was not a personal thing made her feel a bit better. He offered to do some work for her, such as gardening, but this was laughingly dismissed by Mrs Hall as unnecessary. Michael began to open up. "My mum was devastated. It's the first time I've been in trouble with the police [not strictly true — he had been cautioned for shoplifting three years before]. I don't know what came over me." Mrs Hall mentioned that because of the incident old people from the home in the same street were so nervous that they had to be escorted to the shops. Her line was a successful one in getting through to Michael — critical without being condemning of him as a person: "I should imagine you feel a right idiot. I should hope you feel hurt for your mother's sake and for your own sake. I was imagining, if it was my son, I'd think 'how **dare** you!' You put so much trust in your children, but when they do something wrong, you stand by them. I don't feel angry towards you now — my anger's gone. I wish you well — if there's anything I can do..." The mediator reminded her at this point that in agreeing to come to this meeting it was helpful for Michael. There followed a long discussion about the problem of finding employment, all four of the participants working together to try to solve the offender's problems and thus to establish a role for himself in the community.*

*Michael renewed his offer of doing some gardening for Mrs Hall, but she still did not seem to take this idea very seriously, although she replied that "When the spring comes you can mow my lawn, **willingly**". This was followed by some chat about gardening. The meeting had by now become quite affable. It seemed to have had quite an impact on Michael. He was expecting to be confronted by a vengeful victim, but a meeting with a real person who did not act like that had been a much more powerful challenge to his preconceptions.*

Some time later Michael appeared in the Crown Court for sentence, accompanied by his mother, both of them extremely nervous. It was generally thought likely that he would be sent to prison for such an offence. His co-defendant was dealt with first. He was already in prison for another offence and had a considerable criminal record. He was sentenced to two years imprisonment, partially concurrent with his present term.

Michael's barrister referred to the mediation report in his defence, and the judge acknowledged that he found it "very persuasive". In his summing up he referred again to the encounter with Mrs Hall, as well as the social enquiry report and Michael's age, as reasons why "it is not necessary to send you away". He placed Michael on probation for three years.

Case-study H

Ian struck Bill, a steward at a local working man's club, giving Bill a face wound which required seven stitches above the eye. Ian was charged with assault occasioning actual bodily harm and appeared before the local magistrate's court.

Ian, in his early thirties, had already served a prison sentence and his previous convictions included some violent offences. Ian told the probation officer preparing a social enquiry report on him that he had already apologised to the victim after appearing before the club's committee to explain his behaviour. The case was felt to be suitable for reparation and the probation officer referred the case to the project.

The incident at the club arose when Bill tried to prevent Ian banging his head against a wall. Ian's partner had left him, and a neighbour in the club was making comments about his partner's new boyfriend which upset and angered Ian. He had left the bar and was taking his anger out on himself by banging his head on a corridor wall. Bill, the steward, had tried to stop him and at this point Ian struck Bill. Ian explained to the probation officer that he had no grudge against Bill. He was unfortunately the nearest person when Ian lashed out and he greatly regretted the incident.

A mediator contacted Bill who agreed to meet Ian in a mediation meeting, provided it was held during his lunchbreak and near to his place of work. Arrangements were made, and both Bill and Ian were picked up by separate mediators and taken to a local community centre. With two mediators present Ian apologised to Bill for what he had done, explained his reasons, and said he wished to show his regret in deeds. Bill said he was not seeking any monetary compensation but would accept work by Ian. He suggested a task which Ian had the skills for, namely repointing the outside of Bill's house. Bill stated that he thought this reparation would be more appropriate than sending Ian to prison. The two parties to the dispute and the two mediators then signed a mediation contract. This stated that

1. Ian is sorry for the incident at the club. Bill accepts his apology.
2. Bill is not seeking any form of monetary compensation from Ian.
3. Ian has offered to repaint Bill's house. Bill accepts this offer. Ian will start on Monday...this work will take until...(2 weeks)
4. Bill states that he hopes Ian will not go to jail.

This was presented to the court together with the social enquiry report and reparation project report. The court deferred sentence for three months to see if the reparation work would be carried out. The reparation project monitored the repointing work by routine weekly visits. Twice it was necessary to write to Ian to tell him to get more done, as he was doing the job in rather a dilatory way. When Ian returned to court the project reported that approximately 10% of the work was uncompleted, and that despite the agreement and in the full knowledge of the court's sanctions if the work was not completed, the project has had a difficult task getting Ian to carry out his side of the bargain. The court adjourned the case for a further week to allow Ian to complete the work.

The work was duly completed, and the project arranged for a professional builder to inspect it. The builder confirmed that the work had been completed, saying that it was of an excellent standard and worth approximately £800 in labour.

The court commented on the satisfactory reparation work and put Ian on probation for two years.

Photographs

"MEDIATION BEGINS: Feelings are aired and communication established.
(Photo courtesy of: Leeds. Mediation and Reparation Project.)"

"RECONCILIATION: Victim and offender shake hands to signify a satisfactory
agreement and the successful conclusion to mediation.
(Photo courtesy of: Leeds Mediation and Reparation Project.)"

CHAPTER 5

Intermediate Outcomes

Although many have expressed high aspirations for victim/offender mediation in terms of offender rehabilitation and victim recovery, as well as in terms of impact on the criminal justice process, it is still early days for anyone to be sure of the likely impact in these ways. These ultimate aims will be the subject of the next chapter. Here we consider the more immediate question — is victim/offender mediation practicable? This chapter documents the extent to which projects succeeded in obtaining referrals, the apparent suitability of these cases, the frequency with which they were able to arrange for victims and offenders to meet directly, and how often they were able to facilitate agreements between them. It also looks at the perception of their work held by other important parties — the criminal justice agencies and victims or offenders who went through the schemes.

Rate of referral

The first measure of success listed by Pearson (1982) is the extent to which a scheme is actually utilised by other agencies or parties. Although there is much more to success than this, it is obvious that, however well a process works, if no-one mobilises it there will be no benefits. It is not enough, therefore, for a scheme to work, but it must also be seen to work (or seen to have the potential for success) by those who might make use of it. Beyond the fact that no referrals at all must be accounted a failure, however, it is difficult to say how many referrals would be optimal. This will, of course, depend on the resources available to a scheme and on how big a caseload it can manage without experiencing a decline in the quality of the work done. There is inevitably a pressure from funders and potential funding bodies to produce impressive statistics of caseload and to demonstrate a measureable effect, but this may be an unrealistic demand at an experimental stage when schemes are small and processes tentative. It may even hamper the proper development of successful ways of working and lead to acceptance of many unsuitable cases which fritter away valuable resources. Ultimately one would wish such schemes to be relevant to at least a good minority of offences, but currently it may be better that they restrict numbers so as to be able to pay more attention to good selection and improved standards of operation,

As a comparison to our own figures it is worth noting the rates of referral achieved in other countries, some of which have had longer experience. Coates and Gehm (1985) provide the widest-ranging sample of American VORPs. The average rate of referral in their 1983 sample was 6 cases per month. A more recently established VORP described by Galaway (1985, 1986) reached a rate of 4.7 per month over the first eleven months of operation, but this rate was improving: it had been 3.7 per month over the first six months. Rates can, in any case, be variable — a report on the Tri-County Juvenile Restitution Program in Minnesota (Kigin and Novack, 1980) cites 22 referrals per month, although these were referrals from the court after sentence for the purpose of determining compensation or community service restitution in 'victimless' as well as other crimes. Only 14 of the 22 referrals per month pertained to identifiable victims.

Reports on various European schemes show substantial variation in referral rates, but all apply to newly established enterprises. Vantaa, in Finland, was said to have had 400 referrals over 1984 and 1985, an average of 17 per month (Iivari, 1987), by far the highest rate. The West German projects mentioned in Chapter 1 were receiving 5 to 6 cases per month in 1986 (Bussmann, 1987), and the Bordeaux project was already getting 2 or 3 cases a month in its first quarter of a year (Knapper, 1987). The Norwegian Conflict Councils were receiving fewer than one case a month, however, in 1987, even though the rate had increased from the previous year (Hovden, 1987). These figures applied to 29 projects, however, most of them very recently started, which may have under-represented utilisation of the more established ones.

Police-based Schemes

As the longest-established scheme, it is no surprise that Exeter has achieved the high rate of referral among the projects studied. Over the period examined it received 5.4 referrals per month on average. Nevertheless, one of the Cumbria panels (North) managed to achieve a rate not far below this, at 4.1 referrals per month. This panel covered the more urbanised area of Cumbria — Carlisle — which could explain its higher number of referrals compared to the other panels. A more typical rate for more rural areas might therefore be the rate of 2.2 or 2.3 achieved by the West and South panels respectively. It was not surprising that the Sandwell scheme had a low number of referrals (less than one a month) as its primary activity was devoted to community mediation, but the almost equally low rate at Cumbria East of slightly less than one a month (21 cases in 22 months) is more notable.

Over the period studied, the rate of referral at Exeter increased markedly, from 4.4 over the first half of the period to 6.3 in the second half. This is probably explained mostly by the extension of the area covered by the scheme. Even so it reflects the fact that the Exeter scheme has achieved quite a high degree of acceptance. This may not have been so in Cumbria where, with one exception, figures have declined significantly from the first half of the period to the second, decreasing by between 22% and 33%. The remaining panel, East, was the one with the lowest initial rate of referral, and it managed to attain a 71% increase. Notwithstanding, this panel still remained the lowest in terms of caseload.

Table 1: Average monthly referral rates for Cumbria Panels

	WEST	EAST	SOUTH	NORTH
Overall period	2.2	1.0	2.3	4.1
First half	2.6	0.7	2.6	4.6
Second half	1.7	1.2	2.0	3.6

As the number of cases considered by each panel may have varied significantly, especially given the rural nature of some of them, it is more instructive to compare the percentage referred to mediation out of the total number. With respect to the East Cumbria panel, data were available on 547 cases from the Kendal area and 220 from Penrith. Of the former 26 (4.8%) led to discussion of reparation and of the latter just eight (3.6%). Six of these 34 were eventually prosecuted. In the western region, 619 cases from Workington (Allerdale) and 784 from Whitehaven were examined. Reparation was discussed in relation to 32 (5.2%) at Workington and 73 (9.3%) at Whitehaven. All the former and all but five of the latter were cautioned. In the northern region, 91 cases were involved in reparation out of 780 (11.7%); and in the south, 69 out of 1,150 (6%). At Exeter between 6 and 7 per cent of all juvenile cases reviewed result in some kind of reparation, a quite comparable figure to the Cumbria panels. The low percentages presumably result from attempts to use reparation only when some extra factor is needed to encourage cautioning. The schemes cannot therefore be viewed as offering a service to victims generally.

Court-based projects

On the whole, these projects received more referrals than the police-based schemes. The highest rate pertained at Leeds, which received 9.5 per month, quite adequate for the project's resources of personnel and funding, and more or less to target. The other two major projects, in the West Midlands, also achieved rates of 6 or 7 per month, comparable to the American VORPs. Of the less well-resourced projects, Essex dealt with 2.1 referrals a month, and Totton with one a month over its first year. The Junction Project, as is to be expected in view of its IT base, dealt with a very small number of cases — 5 cases over 9 months.

As happened in most police-based schemes, rates of referral show a slight decline over time. Using just the second half figures from each scheme, the later referral rates would be 9.2 at Leeds, 5.2 at Coventry, 5.8 at Wolverhampton. Essex remained unchanged. Due to changes of staff and other problems the Totton scheme carried out no mediation sessions at all for six months after its initial year, but has achieved its earlier rate of intake since the beginning of 1987.

These rates of referral are generally lower than those anticipated in the original proposals for the projects. Wright's (1983) feasibility study for

Coventry, for instance, anticipated 120-200 referrals a year, or 10 to 17 a month. Indeed, of all indictable offences passing through the relevant courts in one year, these referral rates represent between 4 and 5% at Coventry and Wolverhampton, 3% at Essex and 2% at Leeds (Crown Court only). Given the restricted resources of the schemes, it may be as well that the rate is not higher, but it does indicate that referral agencies could surely be making more use of the facility than they do.

Where schemes did not have full-time staff the problem might not be so much one of other agencies choosing to refer as whether there is adequate time to carry out the sometimes laborious consultations that setting up mediation requires. The Totton scheme, for instance, had only to read the files and start work. The only real problems they faced were uncertainty as to plea and the short period (three weeks or less) available to complete the exercise, a major problem when using volunteers who are not always available at convenient times. Many suitable cases had to be dropped merely because of lack of resources.

Case characteristics: (a) the victim

The question of what sort of victims are most suitable for a meeting with their offenders has been discussed (see, eg, Blagg, 1985; Marshall and Walpole, 1985; Davis et al., 1987) but not resolved outside the practice of individual schemes. To some extent it depends on the prime aims of the scheme. If these are concentrated on reforming offenders by drawing their attention to the personal impact of their depredations, then one would seek victims who had been markedly affected, were articulate, were able to exhibit their feelings, but were not so angry that they alienated the offender altogether. One would also seek those for whom the offender might more readily have sympathy, such as the old or people who were not too evidently wealthy. From this point of view personal victims might be seen as more appropriate than corporate ones (see Blagg, 1985). A scheme might, however, take the view that the salutary effect on the offender comes from the experience of practical reparation rather than the psychodynamics of an encounter with the victim. In such a case a scheme might particularly seek corporate victims, as being better placed to make available opportunities for reparative work, or victims that have suffered material loss which has so far gone uncompensated. On the other hand, if the primary aim of a scheme is to provide a service to victims, one would expect priority to be given to those with the sort of needs that could be met through mediation, whether emotional or material. One would also seek to avoid drawing in those who were too upset or nervous or angry to be able to cope with the emotions of a direct meeting. If schemes seek to serve the interests of victims and offenders equally, they are faced with the difficult task of trying to match both sets of considerations.

Whether or not the complainant is a personal or a corporate victim will markedly affect the nature of a victim/offender meeting, as the emotional aspects of a personal encounter may be entirely absent when an offender faces a representative of a corporate body. The possibilities for carrying our reparative work, however, may be enhanced in relation to a victim who is already used to acting as an employer. Schemes have taken opposing lines on the desirability of corporate victims as parties to mediation. They tend to feature quite strongly in North American schemes (see eg Hudson and Chesney, 1978). Two-thirds of the cases at the Ontario VORP involved corporate victims, generally small businesses (Dittenhoffer and Ericson, 1983), as did nearly half of those at the Minnesota VORP (Galaway, 1986: 11% small businesses, 36% large organisations) and at the Minnesota Tri-County Juvenile Restitution Program (Kigin and Novack, 1980), where 18% were owner-operated businesses, 18% larger business concerns, and 11% governmental and other agencies.

Another practical consideration is whether cases involving several victims (or offenders) should be accepted, given that the arrangements for mediation may be more complex and time-consuming for the mediators, and may in any case impose too great an emotional burden on participants facing several parties, whether together or consecutively. Some schemes avoid taking such cases (cf. Hovden, 1987; Galaway, 1985), but it is a striking fact that the original Canadian VORP at Ontario began as a result of successful mediation in a case involving two offenders and 22 different victims (Dittenhoffer and Ericson, 1983)!

Since it formally began operation the Ontario VORP has dealt with multiple victims in a third of its cases.

Figures for a sample of United States VORPs (Coates and Gehm, 1985) show a greater concentration of victims in the middle age range, with only 14% over 60 and 14% under 30. How far this might represent a deliberate policy of avoiding victims who are too old or too young is not known, although there seems to be no evidence that such people would be any less suitable for mediation purely because of their age. Coates and Gehm's (1985) figures also show a higher proportion of male victims, amounting to two-thirds of the total.

Police-based projects
Most of the victims were corporate bodies (business concerns, local authority departments, and other agencies). Only 34% were individuals, and a further 7% households or informal social groups. These are quite comparable percentages to those pertaining to American schemes.

The majority of the victims were the sole victim in their particular case. 12% of victims were one of a group of victims of the same offender. The greatest number of "multiple victims" was nine.

Most of the personal victims were adults aged 26-59 (43%). 12% were 60 or over, 14% 21 to 25, 9% 17-20, and 29% 16 and under. Compared with census figures (1981), the schemes are receiving fewer aged victims and more young ones than would be expected from their distribution in the population. For instance, the Exeter scheme's caseload included only 6% over-60s, against 26% in the general population of Devon, and 59% aged 25 and under, compared with 33% in the general population. For all the Cumbrian panels, 9% of victims were 60 and over, versus 21% in the general population of the county, while 42% were 25 or under, against 35% generally. This is in line with the usual findings on victimisation, that the old are less likely to be victimised and the young more likely (Gottfredson, 1984).

Victims were more likely to be men than women (58% male). This is also in line with general findings on the gender of crime victims.

About 40% of all victims were employed, split more or less equally between manual and non-manual occupations. Eight per cent were unemployed. The rest were neither employed nor seeking work (students, housewives, retired persons). The latter category may, however be over-represented because of the many younger victims who were still at school.

Court-based Projects

In contrast to the above schemes, the majority of victims were personal rather than corporate — 63% individuals, 6% households and 2% informal social groups (ie 71% 'personal') against 33% corporate (mostly business concerns). [Percentages total to more than 100% because of a few cases where there were several victims falling into different categories.] There were, however, significant differences between schemes. The small number of Junction Project cases all involved personal victims, as did over 80% of those at Leeds and Essex. Wolverhampton was the only project to deal with more corporate than personal victims, 55% of the total caseload (42% businesses, 8% local authority, 5% other agencies).

The majority of corporate victims, across all the schemes, were commercial firms (60% of all corporate victims), among which shops and stores predominated (23%), followed by garages and car sales firms (11%) and major national services (gas, electricity, Post Office, British Telecom) together forming 8%. The major category of non-commercial corporate victims was educational establishments (12%), with other local authority departments making up 9%. The greater proportion of corporate victims a scheme dealt with, the higher the concentration on commercial firms (75% at Wolverhampton, 58% at Coventry, 43% at Leeds and 25% at Essex).

The proportion of multiple victims is higher for these schemes — overall 19% of victims were one of a group of several victims of the same offender, the greatest number of multiple victims being seven.

Personal victims were again mostly adults between the ages of 25 and 60 (56%), with 20% of cases involving older persons and 30% younger ones. These figures are closer to the general age distribution in the population than were those for the police-based schemes. The elderly occur at more or less the expected rate, but the under-25s are substantially under-represented. This presumably reflects the fact that the court-based schemes only involve a minority of juvenile offenders, as well as the fact that many of the under-25s in the general population will be much too young to appear as crime victims. This does seem to show, however, that when offenders are not juveniles there appears to be no particular difference invulnerability according to the age of the victim. The common finding of such differences in victimisation studies may therefore be the result of a preponderance of juvenile offenders, or because of a focus on personal offences, excluding household ones such as burglary.

Once again male victims predominated — 54% of personal victims, against 34% who were female, and 12% involving both sexes.

Sixty per cent of the victims were employed, split about two-thirds non-manual, one-third manual, and 12% were unemployed. The rest were students, housewives, etc. Unlike the figures for the police-based projects, these are approximately what one would expect given the victimisation rates from the British Crime Survey (using data from Gottfredson, 1984).

The fact that virtually all the police-based projects studied were working in more rural areas of the country meant that there were few parties, whether victims or offenders, who were non-white. The court-based schemes, however, are largely situated in urban areas with large numbers of people from different ethnic backgrounds. It is therefore important to examine whether the schemes are serving the different groups to the same extent. Victims dealt with by the schemes were 85% white, 13% non-white, with 2% of cases involving victims from several ethnic groups. The closest estimates one can obtain of the proportion of blacks in the general population is that for persons living in households whose head is of New Commonwealth or Pakistan origin in the 1981 Census. On that basis the proportion of black victims in each of the urban schemes is somewhat higher than their prevalence in the population. At Leeds 11% of victims were black, against an estimate of 4% in the city as a whole. Coventry had the same proportion of black victims, against a city-wide estimate of 9.6%. Wolverhampton had very nearly a quarter of black victims, against an expected 15.5%. These figures may well represent a greater likelihood of criminal victimisation among minority ethnic groups compared with the rest of the population. The figures also demonstrate that the reparation projects were in no way failing to serve minority as well as majority groups in the local areas they covered. In all three of the projects in major urban areas (in Leeds and the West Midlands) Asian victims were much more prominent then West Indian (25 cases and 8 cases respectively).

For the Coventry and Leeds courts we were also able to examine where the victims lived. In Leeds 47% were from the inner city (especially Harehills, Burmantofts and Gipton), and in Coventry 60% were from the inner city or its fringes (notably Hillfields, Radford, City centre, Foleshill and Stoke). The concentration in the inner city is no doubt due to the high crime rates there, and if one adds in less central districts which are also high in terms of crime, then the percentage of victims from high crime districts is 56% at Leeds (with the high crime estate of Seacroft featuring strongly) and 53% at Coventry.

Case Characteristics: (b) the offender

Selecting the appropriate type of offender is subject to similar problems to those discussed above in relation to the victim. There is a general assumption that on the whole the younger offenders will provide more scope for 'learning', so that mediation may have more impact upon them. Such a consideration may, however, be less important if the emphasis is on serving victims' needs — indeed the likelihood of financial compensation may be greater with older, employed offenders. On the other hand, victims may be more comfortable faced with a young offender and may be more inclined to be sympathetic and positive towards them, contributing to a more rewarding experience all round.

A major consideration is the degree of remorse that the offender seems to exhibit when first contacted about the possibility of mediation (see Davis et al., 1987, for a thorough discussion of this issue). Most schemes say that they will not accept an offender who does not show the least sign of regret. The reason for this is evident, that an unremorseful, even belligerent, offender could upset and frighten the victim even more than the original crime had done. On the other hand, if the intention of the schemes, at least in part, is to impress on offenders the personal consequences of their action that have so far gone unremarked, it would seem that the offender who is not so far remorseful has more to learn from meeting the victim. Nevertheless, protection of victims from possibly deleterious experiences would seem to outweigh such considerations, except in cases involving corporate victims or unusually self-possessed individuals.

It is not necessary, however, to think in terms of absolutes. The experience of being caught for an offence and being charged will be sufficient to incite a degree of regret in most offenders (if only out of self-pity). The task of the mediation scheme is then to build on this spark of remorse to encourage even more insightful realisation of the harm caused and thereby to make that remorse deeper, more genuine, and less self-centred. For those offenders on the other hand, who are visibly gripped by great remorse and a desire to make amends, not so rare that any scheme will not have already encountered a number, although the experience of meeting the victim may not be so much of a learning experience, the chance of expiating their guilt will nevertheless be of great benefit in other ways, both to themselves and to the victim.

American VORPs have a caseload which is largely juvenile (78% in Coates and Gehm, 1985). The same authors also quote a figure of 93% male, although the Minnesota Tri-County Restitution Program quoted 15% female (Kigin and Novak, 1980).

First offenders were also seen as the most suitable (because they were not hardened to crime). The Minnesota project had 83% of its caseload as first offenders (Kigin and Novak, 1980). Some European schemes deal with a more substantial number of recidivists, but the highest rate quoted in the literature seems to be 'about half' for the German Handschlag scheme (Bussmann, 1987).

American VORPs dealt mainly with white offenders (92% in Coates and Gehm, 1985), but this is probably explained by the predominance of schemes in rural and other areas with low proportions of black people.

Police-based Projects

In 63% of cases there was a single offender. In the rest more than one offender was involved, up to a maximum of 8 in one case. Given the recency of most of the schemes, very few offenders had been through the scheme before, except at Exeter which had been in operation long enough to be receiving referrals of offenders 41% of whom were already known.

Given that all the police-based schemes were for juvenile offenders only, most of the offenders were aged 12 to 16. Eight cases (2.5%) were under 12 years. Most of the offenders were boys (87%). Cumbria East had more girls (29%), but the other schemes had substantially fewer (down to 4% in Cumbria South). These are substantially lower proportions of girls than normally found among cautioned offenders, where it is 25% (Criminal Statistics, 1986, Table 5: 10). It is, however, comparable to the proportion of girls among those prosecuted and found guilty in a court, which is 9% (ibid.). This finding does not necessarily confirm that the cases dealt with are ones that would otherwise have been likely to go to court, but it is certainly consistent with that interpretation.

Given the emphasis of these schemes on diversion, and the prevalence of cautioning for first-time offenders, one would expect most of the referrals to be offenders who had previously come to the notice of the law. Overall 69% were known to have a record, 55% a caution only, 14% a conviction. Only one scheme had a significantly higher rate of previous offenders — Exeter, with 79%. More first-time offenders were involved when the victim was a person or a household (38% had no known record) than when the victim was a corporate body (27%). Sometimes the criminal record could be quite substantial. Three offenders dealt with by Cumbria West had had three previous convictions (along with one or more caution). Exeter claims to have dealt with one juvenile for whom the current offence was his nineteenth and half of their offenders in 1986 had committed three or more offences, 10% seven or more.

Court-based Projects

Rather more of the cases of these schemes involved a single offender — 88%, as against the 63% found for the police schemes. This may simply reflect the fact that juveniles are more likely to offend in groups. The largest multiple party was five.

The majority of the offenders were quite young — 54% under 21, and 80% no older than 25. 10% were juveniles (aged 12 to 16). According to Criminal Statistics 1986, the proportion of persons found guilty of indictable offences at all courts who were under 21 was 41.7%. Therefore the schemes were tending to take a younger sample of offenders. The only exception was N.E. Essex which only had 31% under 21. Variations among the rest of the projects were entirely due to the extent to which they sought to deal with juvenile court referrals. The Junction Project dealt only with young people. Both the West Midlands projects took between 10 and 15% of their cases from the juvenile court, while Leeds took fewer than 5%, largely of course because of its emphasis on more serious offences. This contrasts with the concentration of American VORPs on juveniles.

Most offenders were male, 91% altogether, with little variation between schemes. This is only slightly higher than the percentage for all those found guilty of indictable offences at all courts (87% in 1986). This is similar to the American VORPs.

Not surprisingly, given that all these cases had been brought to court, most of the offenders (80%) had a previous record (almost all of them a previous conviction). Despite the emphasis at Leeds on offenders in danger of receiving a custodial sentence, the percentage there with a previous record is not significantly higher than at other schemes, with a possible exception of Essex (84% at Leeds, 81% at Coventry, 73% at Wolverhampton, and 68% at Essex). In many cases the previous record of convictions was quite substantial. According to Leeds Reparation Project's (1987) Report on the Experimental Period, 38% of its offenders had seven or more (83 out of 216 for which the record was known), and a further 18% had between 4 and 6 previous convictions. The average number of convictions for the Leeds offenders is therefore considerably higher than the average for the other schemes, Coventry's cases having on average 3 previous convictions and Wolverhampton's 1.7.

There is little comparative data on the social characteristics of offenders before the court, but a study by Bainbridge (1987) of four

Midlands magistrates' courts is recent enough to be of relevance. His sample of offenders contained 31% first offenders, so that the reparation schemes were getting referrals that were average or worse in terms of previous convictions. Only 21% in that study had had four or more such convictions. Here there is a substantial contrast with American VORPs (see above). The British court-based schemes, therefore, appear to be dealing with more serious offenders than those elsewhere.

Of those who were old enough to be employed, 75% did not have a job. Three-quarters of those who were employed were in manual occupations. Bainbridge (1987) found that 76% of offenders brought before magistrates' courts in four Midlands cities were without a job, and of those who did have one, 90% were in a manual occupation. The referrals to these schemes therefore seem fairly typical of the usual court caseload, except that non-manual offenders are slightly over-represented.

Table 2: Actual and expected proportions black by scheme

	LEEDS	COVENTRY	WOLVER-HAMPTON	N.E.ESSEX
Actual %	3.4	9.4	15.3	—
Expected %*	4.0	9.6	15.5	2.2

*Percentage of all persons usually resident in private households, where the head of household is of New Commonwealth and Pakistan origin. (OPCS Census 1981).

In terms of ethnicity, 90% were white, 9% black, and 1% cases involved a mixed group of offenders. The proportions for each scheme were virtually identical to the expected proportions from Census 1981 figures.

Although victims tended to be Asian rather than West Indian, the opposite was the case with the offenders, among whom there were three West Indians for every Asian.

Not surprisingly, offenders tended to be concentrated even more than victims in inner city areas (52% at Leeds, 65% at Coventry) and in high crime districts (67.5% at Leeds, 61% at Coventry), but the differences are not as large as one might expect, indicating that most offenders are not travelling beyond their own immediate neighbourhoods in the commission of their offences.

Case Characteristics: (e) relationship between victim and offender

Apropos of a method of intervention which focuses on the relationship between the victim and the offender, it is obviously a matter of basic importance whether the two knew one another before or not. A good minority of offences arise from conflicts between individuals, families or other social groups. This particularly applies to those offences that involve an assault as against, say, the theft of property. Mediation between the victim and the offender in such cases could involve much more than simply apologising and agreeing appropriate reparation. It could attempt to alleviate the underlying conflict itself in an effort to prevent further outbreaks of trouble.

Such cases may also be particularly suited for diversion from the criminal process altogether, as not reflecting the antisocial tendencies of an individual (which society might feel obliged to condemn) so much as a specific interpersonal situation which does not spell danger for other citizens. This is what happens in those American schemes, such as the Neighborhood Justice Centers, that divert from the police or the courts offences involving related parties, on the basis that resolution of the underlying relationship problem is much more useful than blaming one party solely and sanctioning that person. This is not to say that all offences between related parties can be seen as relevant for diversion on the basis of this argument — some relationship problems get out of hand precisely because one party is inclined to use violence to get their own way, and criminal sanctions may be just as relevant in such a case as one between strangers.

It can also be argued that the occurrence of a crime in itself creates a relationship between the victim and the offender, even if they did not know one another in advance (see Marshall, 1988a). The exploitation of another person that a crime involves can be seen as creating a power imbalance between the exploiter and the exploited that is perceived as unjust and may be one of the difficult after-effects with which a victim has to come to terms. The direct righting of this imbalance through reparation, especially when conducted personally through a victim/offender meeting, may be an important restorative service to victims. On top of this, the crime may have created possibilities of revenge (by the victim or the victim's friends or family — as was brewing in an atypical manslaughter case dealt with post-sentence by the Leeds Reparation Project: or by the offender — because he or she was reported to the police). Mediation may be able to forestall such developments, which are not always prevented by the fact that the criminal justice process takes the matter out of the parties' hands precisely in order to achieve this end.

Despite the theoretical importance of prior relationships for mediation schemes, surprisingly few reports on their operation mention how frequent such cases were. Given this fact, and the predominance of property offences (see next section), one may reasonably conclude that few offences dealt with by VORPs and so on involve a prior dispute. Dittenhoffer and Ericson (1983) mention that only 15% of the Ontario VORP caseload involved related parties. This would seem to indicate that their emphasis is on the service that mediation may provide to the victim, or in reforming the offender, than in resolving disputes per se.

Although advocates of mediation may believe that parties with relationship problems have the most to gain from co-operating in some sort of informal resolution, it may be that the parties themselves view matters differently. The fact of such complicating overtones may inhibit them from wanting to meet directly, or they may not be emotionally prepared for 'reconciliation'. It is certainly true that victims who suffer assault are less likely to be willing to answer affirmatively to the hypothetical possibility of meeting the offender than are those who suffer property offences, as data from the British Crime Survey show. (We are grateful to Mike Hough for this special analysis.) O'Brien (1986) found that victims who knew their offender were also less likely to welcome such a hypothetical suggestion. Whether offenders would show the same reluctance is not known. It may well be that 'victims' have more to lose by agreeing to a mediation session that will 'reduce' their status from one of being the innocent party to one of 'disputant' on more or less equal terms with the offender. It may seem more attractive to the victim to get 'one over' the offender by letting the legal process run its course than to make an effort to resolve the problem. Indeed, it may be that by going beyond the limits of legally or morally acceptable behaviour in the waging of the conflict the offender has obtained an 'unfair' advantage that needs to be redressed before voluntary mediation can be viable.

Police-based Projects
Overall there was some sort of prior relationship between the parties in less than a quarter of the cases (23%). Very few of these relationships were close (only one case involved persons related by kinship or co-residence); most were between neighbours or former friends and acquaintances (15%) or were formal relationships such as those between employer and employee (5%). Excluding corporate victims, the proportion of related parties increases to 38%.

Court-based Projects
The cases referred to these schemes, were much more likely to involve parties who had known one another beforehand. In fact, half had some kind of prior relationship. Predominantly, these were again casual relationships such as neighbours and acquaintances (27% of all cases) or formal relationships such as employer/employee (17%). In addition 5% involved parties who were kin, married or co-resident. As Wolverhampton had an unusually high number of corporate victims, it is not surprising that it also had more than the usual proportion of 'formal' relationships (ie 29%). Both this scheme and Coventry also had lower than average proportions who were casually related (15% in each case).

Case Characteristics: (d) offences
When it comes to deciding how serious offences should be to be suitable for mediation, schemes are faced with a dilemma. A minor offence may be safer, more acceptable for alternative processing as far as the general public is concerned, and less threatening to the victim. On the other hand, a serious offence lends greater scope for mitigation of sentence and

diversion from more costly legal procedures. (See Davis et al., 1987.) Some schemes, as we have seen, are primarily concerned to take more serious offences in order to make more impact on criminal justice dispositions. Others have accepted caution as the byword for their initial efforts and have focused on more minor crime. The police-based projects, by their nature will be concerned with less serious offences than the court-based. The latter can also be expected on the whole to deal with the upper range of the magistrates' court caseload because most of them take referrals on adjournment for social enquiry reports, when less serious offences will have been sentenced immediately.

With respect to whether mediation is more or less likely to be successful, it seems intuitively likely that the personal characteristics of the victim and the offender will be more influential than the level of legal seriousness assigned to the crime. Similarly, it may be that the type of crime is similarly of lesser moment than the attitudes and feelings of the parties, although the American VORPs deal overwhelmingly with property offences rather than those involving violence (3% violence in Coates and Gehm, 1985). Theft (universally), damage and burglary are the principal offences with which schemes in other countries deal, although Bussmann (1987) does say that forty percent of the caseload of the German Die Waage project constitutes cases of violence. Many schemes deliberately avoid such offences, but even when they would accept them, it seems that they seldom receive such referrals.

Police-based Projects
The most prevalent offence involved was theft (53%), followed by criminal damage (32%). The Table below shows the distribution of offences by scheme. When corporate victims are excluded, the only major difference is that violence offences rise from 8% to 21%. They therefore form a significant proportion of all offences against an individual victim. Victim and offender were more likely to have known one another in cases of violence (76%) and fraud (50%). In the case of the other offences the percentage of 'related' parties only ranged between 14% and 21%.

Table 3: Distribution of offences by scheme (Police-based)

	EXETER	CUMBRIA				SANDWELL
		WEST	EAST	SOUTH	NORTH	
%						
Theft	63	46	57	47	54	9
Criminal Damage	17	46	29	37	37	45
Burglary	13	13	—	4	16	27
Violence	12	8	9	10	3	—
Fraud	2	—	—	2	1	—
Sex	2	—	—	—	—	—
Other	4	4	5	4	13	18

*Totals for each scheme do not add up to 100% due to multiple offences.

Over time there is little change in the proportion of different offences in the caseload, except for a slight increase in burglary (from 9% in the first half to 13% in the second half of the period studied) and a corresponding decrease in damage offences (from 31% to 26%) which might indicate a minor trend towards a more serious caseload.

Percentages in the above table often add to more than 100% because some offenders were subject to more than one charge. To compare with national statistics, which record only the major charge, the above figures had to be recalculated on the same basis. When this is done, the most striking difference is the over-representation of criminal damage, which constitutes only 4% of all juvenile convictions and 3% of all juvenile cautions (Criminal Statistics 1986), but accounts for 18% of cases referred to the schemes. This will be partly due to the inclusion of summary offences of damage among the offenders taking part in the reparation schemes, whereas the comparison figures are for indictable only. Nevertheless, there does appear to be some genuine disproportion here, which may be related to a concept of vandalism as being peculiarly suited to reparation. This would certainly tie in with the fact that compensation is awarded by courts more frequently for damage offences than for any other kind (Newburn, 1988).

Burglary is only as frequent in the schemes' caseloads as it is among juveniles cautioned generally and far below the percentage among those convicted (12% across the schemes, 27% of juveniles convicted). Theft, on the other hand, is more comparable in frequency with the court statistics and less frequent than among cautioned juveniles (53% across the schemes, 71% of cautions nationally). All other types of offence occur with more or less the expected frequency. Overall, therefore, the caseload of the police-based schemes has more damage offences and fewer theft and burglary offences than would be expected compared to the national distribution of juvenile crime.

Court-based Projects

On the whole, as is to be expected, serious offences were more often encountered in the caseloads of the court-based schemes. Theft was still the most frequent category at 39%, but burglary (29%) and violence offences (20%) were also quite prominent. Only 17% were cases of damage (including arson). When corporate victims are omitted, the percentage of violence offences rises to 27%. The Leeds project can be expected to have relatively more of the serious types of offence, but the differences are not large (see Table 4). It had the highest rate of burglary offences and the lowest rate of criminal damage (along with Essex). Among the other schemes there seemed to be a tendency for Coventry to be taking more serious offences than the other two. It had the highest rate of violence offences of all the major projects (28%). (The Junction Project, however, had 2 violent offences out of five.) The rate of thefts at Coventry was also the lowest of all the schemes.

Table 4: Distribution of offences by scheme (court-based)

	LEEDS	COVENTRY	WOLVER-HAMPTON	N.E. ESSEX
%				
Theft	41	30	44	48
Burglary	35	31	24	7
Violence	19	28	8	22
Criminal Damage	11	19	29	11
Fraud	5	4	4	4
Sex	2	1	—	—
Other	9	3	2	15

*Totals for each scheme do not add up to 100% due to multiple offences.

Wolverhampton, on the other hand, had a large proportion of damage offences (29%) and Essex had more than the average number of thefts and of regulatory offences (48% and 15% respectively). As noted above, the Totton scheme aimed primarily at the less serious offences and thus mainly dealt with thefts and damage to property. As was found above, victim and offender were more likely to have known one another before in the case of violence offences (64%) and fraud (62%), although higher percentages of 'related' parties occurred for the other offences than occurred in the police-based schemes (ranging from a third to a half).

As for the police-based schemes, there tended to be a slightly greater concentration on burglary offences (up from 23% to 29%) as time progressed, at the expense of theft cases (down from 36% to 31%), again a marginal shift towards a more serious caseload.

Compared with the distribution of offences in Criminal Statistics for offenders found guilty in all courts, the caseloads of the reparation schemes would certainly seem to include a greater proportion of the more serious offences. The general distribution would lead one to expect only 11% violence offences and 15% burglary, but these figures are well exceeded. The proportion of simple thefts is considerably lower, as they account for almost half (49%) of all indictable prosecutions. Given that most of the referrals will have been associated with a request by the court for a social enquiry report, the greater proportion of serious offences is not unexpected.

Figures for the losses involved were not systematically recorded, but from the detail that was available, it was apparent that the offences were not limited to ones of low value. Nearly 60% of all the damage offences were known to involve either losses over £100 or arson. Fourteen percent of thefts and burglaries were known to involve losses of over £100 (which, given the missing data, may at least be equivalent to the average percentage of such losses across four Midlands courts in Bainbridge, 1987, where it is given as 20%). Nor were all the assaults minor cases. Twenty-two percent involved woundings, 10% G.B.H. (grievous bodily harm), and 19% A.B.H. (actual bodily harm), while there was one case of rape and 12 of robbery.

Although in most cases the status of the offender qua offender is quite clear, there were some (9% of all referrals) where the case records showed grievances on their part against the 'victim'. These might be particularly suitable cases for mediation.

Getting to Mediation

The question we ask in this section is whether people are prepared to take part in mediation as it is offered by the schemes. Davis et al. (1987) have already indicated that many projects modified their original aims of face-to-face mediation in the face of fairly widespread disinclination on the part of those approached to meet directly with the other party, although this has been a greater problem for 'community mediation schemes' that take referrals of disputes directly from neighbourhood agencies or parties themselves than for victim/offender mediation schemes. This would seem to indicate that people who already are acquainted are more resistant to the idea of facing up to one another than people who are strangers, as was noted for victims of crime by O'Brien (1986). It sometimes seems surprising at first that people are more inclined to face a stranger who has committed a criminal act against them than an acquaintance who has not behaved illegally. Resistance to mediation therefore appears to stem from an emotional relationship with the other person (and possibly some feeling that they themselves are to some extent responsible for the dispute, or for escalating it), rather than from criminal behaviour, especially as the presence of a mediator in a controlled setting should take away any sense of fear in the encounter. Resistance to mediation might be expected to come from the offender rather than the victim, as the former must face up to issues of personal responsibility and guilt that may be very uncomfortable, but again such expectations are not borne out, largely because the offender, in the context of these schemes, is still under threat of judicial retribution and may consider co-operation the better part of valour. Even if the parties do not desire to meet, it does not mean that mediation cannot go ahead, but it does mean that it must be carried out 'indirectly', the mediator talking separately with each party in negotiating a mutually acceptable settlement. Some schemes seemed even to prefer this mode of operation, especially if they were more interested in material outcomes than the psychological aspects of a direct discussion.

The experience of projects in other countries is fairly uniform. If one excepts those cases still pending and those where the parties had settled before intervention, American VORPs average about 60% of cases reaching direct mediation (Coates and Gehm, 1985; Umbreit, 1985; Dittenhoffer and Ericson, 1983; Galaway, 1986). The main reason for not reaching mediation is usually a rejection of the idea on the part of the victim (70% of cases where there is no direct mediation in Coates and Gehm, 1985). Sometimes, however, the number of offenders refusing to take part is almost as high (5 offenders to 6 victims in Dittenhoffer and Ericson's study of Ontario VORP, and 11 offenders to 13 victims in Galaway's study of the Minnesota VORP).

Of the European projects, figures are available in the literature only for the Finnish Vantaa project, where half of all cases arrived at mediation, most of the failures due to victims' refusals (Iivari, 1987). In addition, the West German 'Die Waage' project claims that 95% of all referrals receive the assent of both parties (personal communication from Ruth Herz, 1987). The South Yorkshire scheme, the first court-based project in this country, is reported to have achieved a rate of 57% in one of its two areas, but fewer in the other (Smith et al 1986), while the small pilot study by Mackay (1986) of a scheme based on the Scottish Procurator-Fiscal's Office found that only one case out of 22 proceeded with involved a meeting, half of them being carried out by indirect mediation and the rest being abandoned because of the victim's (6 cases) or the offender's (4 cases) refusal. As a diversion scheme, however, the latter was concerned generally with less serious incidents than the other projects quoted above, and this may be associated with the fact that a meeting between victim and offender was less often seen to be worthwhile. Another scheme at Nottingham, mediating between juvenile offenders, who had committed more serious offences of burglary and robbery, and their victims, experienced a mediation rate of slightly over 60%, ie 10 out of 16 cases referred (Stansfield, 1988), as is the more usual finding.

The extant literature contains little information about factors affecting whether cases get to mediation. Coates and Gehm (1985) do report that neither age of offender nor seriousness of the offence had any effect on the likelihood of mediation. Smith et al (1986), discussing their research on the South Yorkshire scheme, say that cases involving multiple parties limited the practicability of mediation. From interviews with parties approached by the scheme they found that the most frequent reason for refusal on the part of the victim was a feeling of having been too "let down", by which one presumes they mean that the victims were too upset or did not trust the offender's offer of reparation. Offenders' reasons for not participating, as far as they could discover, were connected with their 'fear' of such an encounter or their anticipation that it would be too humiliating.

Police-based schemes

As mentioned in Chapter 3, in only about two-thirds of cases was a direct victim offender meeting offered. Schemes exercised discretion with respect to such encounters, which might not be productive in certain conditions — if, for instance, the offender's attitude or demeanour was not one that would inspire confidence on the part of the victim, or if the victim were too angry or too fearful. Again, the substance of the offence might be too trivial to be worth pursuing through such an elaborate procedure.

Just as the scheme might exercise such discretion, so too, of course, did both parties, for whom the suggestion of mediation was entirely voluntary. 'Voluntariness', of course, can have variable implications, at least for the offender, in the context of a dramatic social intervention such as occurs when apprehended for a crime. This point will be discussed fully later on. Here it suffices to say that offenders offered the chance to take part in a reparation scheme almost always accepted the opportunity. Of 208 cases on which we have data, in 188 (90%) the offender(s) agreed to participate, in one joint case one offender agreed and the other did not, five offenders could not be contacted, and only 14 (7%) turned the idea down completely.

The decision whether to take part was affected by some of the other variables recorded. The offenders, who were all juvenile in these schemes, were less likely to agree to meet their victims if the latter were of the same age or were members of the same club or school, whereas they were particularly likely to agree if the victim were elderly. This seems to indicate that in some instances a meeting with the victim has peer-status overtones that are too strong even given the other advantages an offender might receive from collaboration with the scheme. In a case in Cumbria, for instance, a schoolboy refused to apologise to another boy he had assaulted, even though he felt bad about it and would have liked to make amends, because he feared he could never face up to his peers at school again if he did so.

Similar reasons were probably involved in the fact that offenders were less likely to agree to meet victims in the case of assault, or where the victim had suffered emotionally, or where the offender was also said to have suffered emotionally (eg in the case of an attack on a former friend who had broken off relations). Offenders were most likely to agree to meet a victim they had not known before the offence. It was apparently more difficult for juvenile offenders to face up to a meeting that would have emotional overtones. Lastly, there were a very small number of cases referred after informal police action, where neither prosecution nor cautioning were in view, and these were less likely to result in the offender's agreement to participate than cases where there had been formal action.

Although an offender might agree to take part, he/she did not do so with a great deal of enthusiasm. Each offender who agreed to take part was rated by the reparation worker according to their apparent enthusiasm: two-thirds were said to be 'moderately' keen, 14% not keen, 17% very keen, with 3% being multiple offenders exhibiting different responses. Although personal involvement seemed to be a factor inhibiting agreement to take part, once having agreed to do so the same factors seemed to promote enthusiasm, perhaps because the offender saw more clearly the advantages to be achieved from sorting out relationships and relieving his/her own feelings. Thus enthusiasm was greater when the victim was a private individual rather than a corporate body, when of similar age or elderly, when formerly a friend, or when the crime was one of violence or nuisance rather than a property offence. Correspondingly, offenders were least keen to meet adults between the age of 25 and 60, and those victims who had suffered purely material loss. In addition, first-time offenders were more likely to be keen than those with a previous record.

Of 211 cases on which we have information, 167 victims agreed to take part (79%), 17% refused, with 4 cases proving uncontactable and 3 involving mixed responses from multiple victims. Exeter achieved the highest rate of victim agreement (91%), while one of the Cumbria panels (West) secured agreement from only two-thirds. The reparation worker in the latter area was felt to underplay the possible benefits of a meeting and was possibly less effective, therefore, in allaying victims' immediate fears of such an unfamiliar idea. In addition, most of her contacts with victims were by telephone, not the most satisfactory form of communication for this purpose. The fact that the victims were scattered over a wide rural area would have made personal visits very time-consuming. (Maguire and Corbett, 1987, similarly found that personal visits were much more fruitful than telephone calls by victims support volunteers.)

Corporate victims were more likely to agree than individuals, perhaps because excessive emotions were less likely to be involved, or because corporate bodies were more likely to see participation as a matter of social responsibility (a major motive for involvement among personal victims as well — see below). Burglary was the most likely offence to meet with agreement, perhaps as the more serious property offence. Women were also more agreeable than men, manual workers more than non-manual, while unemployed victims were especially likely to refuse to take part. All of these characteristics may be a sign that victims who have a greater attachment to the local community are more likely to show compassion towards other residents and to want to work towards reconciliation, a feature of several cases interviewed in the Cumbria project (see below).

A similar proportion of victims were moderately, or very keen, on the idea (86%) to that of offenders, but more were very keen. Again, corporate victims were more enthusiastic than individuals. Those suffering the more 'emotional' offences such as violence or nuisance, or those who had formerly been friends with the offender, were less keen. This finding is in accord with other indications above that both parties are less inclined to get involved if the emotional overtones are greater. Strangely, in view of the fact that women were more likely to take part, men were found to be the more enthusiastic, as also were those who had employment, while the unemployed were again the least keen. Victims generally were keener to meet a male than a female offender.

In actual practice 47% of all cases referred reached the stage of 'direct' mediation, ie a meeting between the victim and the offender. This overall rate, which is substantially below that for American schemes (see above), obscures large differences between individual panels, however. Although four of the schemes achieved a rate of direct mediation between 45% and 50%, Cumbria East, the panel with the fewest referrals in that county, managed to get victims and offenders to meet in 81% of all cases, while Cumbria South only arranged meetings in 18%. In the last scheme, many fewer were even offered direct mediation than in other schemes (see Chapter 3).

Most of the variables affecting whether a case reaches direct mediation are as already described above in relation to obtaining the agreement of the parties, as this is the major factor in being able to arrange a meeting. Of all victims who agreed to take part, 88% in fact did so, as did 79% of all offenders who had agreed.

If the offender is not subject to a criminal charge, mediation is unlikely to occur. Mediation is most likely when the victim is some corporate body (although less so in the case of commercial firms), and least likely when a private individual. Elderly victims are very likely to meet the offender, but twelve to sixteen year olds much less so. Female victims are more likely to become involved than male victims, and the employed than victims who have no job (whether unemployed or not seeking work, such as schoolchildren). Direct mediation was arranged less often when there were more than two offenders involved, presumably because of the practical difficulties. Offenders were more likely to meet the victim if they had previously had dealings with the scheme, or if they were in employment (only a small number, however, as most of this age-group were of course school pupils), but less likely if they had had a past conviction. Theft from shops at which the offender was already known was especially likely to get to direct mediation (92% of such cases did so), but mediation was less frequent between fellow pupils at school. Violence and regulatory offences were the least likely to reach mediation, as were any offences involving emotional suffering or injury to the victim. Mediation was also more frequent when any property stolen had been fully restored beforehand by the offender.

Failure to arrange a meeting between the victim and the offender does not necessarily mean that the scheme is entirely unsuccessful. It may proceed to negotiate with both parties separately and arrange some kind of reparation. In fact 82% of all referrals are mediated in some way by the schemes, while in an additional 3% the scheme continues to work with one of the parties in some other way (traditional social work help or counselling). In the remaining cases (50 altogether) five were not accepted by the scheme (eg outside the relevant area), twelve involved a party who could not be contacted, 29 a party who refused to participate, and four could not proceed for some other reason (eg death of one party). Table 5 shows the outcomes of all referrals by scheme.

Table 5: Outcome by scheme

| | EXETER | CUMBRIA | | | SANDWELL | |
		WEST	EAST	SOUTH	NORTH	
%						
Referral not accepted/not appropriate	—	7.6	—	—	4.2	9.1
One party only contacted/worked with	16.5	22.7	4.8	22.4	7.4	27.3
Negotiated	33.0	24.5	14.3	59.1	37.9	18.2
Mediated	50.5	45.3	80.9	18.4	50.6	45.5

Whether or not a case is mediated, directly or indirectly, by a scheme is subject to much the same kind of influences as described above for a direct encounter only. One of the main differences is that although women are more likely to agree to meet with the offender face-to-face than are men, there is no such difference when it comes to cooperation with the scheme as a 'go-between' mediator. Men, it seems, are not less co-operative but less prepared to face up directly to their assailant. Whether or not any property stolen has been replaced by the offender prior to mediation also does not affect indirect mediation as it does a face-to-face meeting. When property has not been returned or compensated, of course, there remains an important task for reparation schemes to try to achieve, which is presumably why at least indirect negotiation is likely to proceed.

Court-based schemes

Mediation was offered in a greater proportion of cases than it was in the police-based schemes (84%). Most offenders, however, agree to take part in mediation (95%). As they are under a greater threat of judicial action — ie still subject to a court sentence — this rate of compliance is not perhaps surprising. The only project which had a significantly lower rate of offender compliance was N.E. Essex, where 25% did not agree to participate. There was, however, variation in the enthusiasm (as gauged by the mediators) of offenders towards the idea. Fifty-seven percent were thought to be 'very keen', 39% moderately so, and the remaining 4% not keen. The two West Midlands schemes had much larger rates for 'very keen' than the others, but these may have been differences in the way the rating scale was used by different schemes, so that the validity of this finding must be suspect. Nevertheless, certain variables correlated with enthusiasm independently of which scheme was involved, and these associations may be valid. According to this analysis, those offenders who were most keen were those in employment or related by kinship or ex-friendship to the victim (although those who were married to one another were not so enthusiastic). Offenders were also more likely to be keen when the victim was elderly, a manual rather than a non-manual worker, or 'not employed' as against unemployed. Fraud offenders also tended to be keener (perhaps because a large number of these were acquainted with the victim).

Overall, 51% of victims agreed to take part, significantly fewer than in the police-based schemes, perhaps because the latter only dealt with juvenile offenders with whom victims are more likely to show some sympathy. There was a little variation between the different schemes in this respect, Coventry being lower at 40%, and Leeds, N. E. Essex and Junction Project together averaging 59%. Personal offenders at 46% were slightly less likely to participate than corporate ones, among whom local authority and other agencies were particularly cooperative (78% and 75% agreement respectively). Young people (under 25) were more likely to agree, but the elderly less likely. Victims were also more likely to participate when the offender was school-aged, female or black, and when the offence was one of burglary. There was evidence that victims were less happy to meet the offender when they had been involved in a crime which caused them emotional distress (eg those involving racial harassment or violence, or where the offender is related by kinship). They were also less likely to agree if the offender had been an employee.

Victims were generally seen as less enthusiastic than the offenders, with 21% rated as 'not keen' and 41% 'very keen', but still the picture is generally quite positive. Again, however, there is evidence of inter-scheme variability in the ratings, with Wolverhampton rating many more as 'very keen', and Coventry also rating victims' enthusiasm more highly than either Leeds or Essex. Taking these biases into account, there was still evidence that variables similar to those affecting victim agreement to mediate also affected their keenness to do so. In addition, it was found that female victims were less enthusiastic, and non-manual victims more so, along with those who had suffered nuisance offences.

All told, the major reasons for the discontinuance of mediation were connected with the victim. In a third of such cases it was because the victim saw little point to a meeting. In a further fifth, the victim was seen to be too antagonistic or upset to be able fruitfully to take part, while a tenth were disabled by illness or old age. This pattern was broadly true for all schemes except N. E. Essex, where only 18% of cases were discontinued because the victim could see no point to it. In that scheme, the predominant reason was adduced to the victim's emotional state. The Leeds project, which dealt with the most serious cases, and where the offenders were often remanded in custody, also encountered a fair number of legal and practical difficulties which accounted for a fifth of all the cases that did not proceed further.

In the end, 55.5% of all referrals reached either direct or indirect mediation. 34% involved direct victim/offender meetings. The rate of direct mediation did not vary greatly across schemes, from just over a quarter at N. E. Essex to 38% at Coventry, with the Junction Project achieving a meeting in 3 out of its five cases. Both Leeds and Wolverhampton carried out direct mediation in a third of all cases. There was more variation between schemes, however, in the percentage of cases that reached either direct or indirect mediation, as the following table shows. Coventry were clearly higher with 71% negotiated (if one excludes the Junction Project which negotiated each of its five cases), while the other schemes were all close to one half.

Table 6: Outcome by scheme

	LEEDS	COVENTRY	WOLVER-HAMPTON	N.E.ESSEX
%				
Referral not accepted/not appropriate	12.8	2.8	6.5	6.4
One party only contacted/worked with	36.7	26.4	47.1	45.1
Negotiated	17.9	32.7	13.0	22.6
Mediated	32.6	38.2	33.3	25.8

Victims more likely to be involved in mediation were local authority departments and other social agencies, and adults between the ages of 26 and 59. The elderly were less likely to take part at all, and especially unlikely to meet the offender directly. Those cases involving more than one victim were also more likely to result indirect mediation, but this is obviously a statistical artefact, in that the chances of one victim agreeing are higher in direct proportion to the number contacted. Nevertheless, it might be a factor for schemes to keep in mind: an offender is more likely to receive the experience of making amends the more victims there are.

Offenders who had previously been cautioned only were more likely to be involved in mediation, especially direct mediation, as were those who were first-time offenders, but those with previous convictions were the ones least likely to take part. Criminal damage and 'take and drive away' offences were more often mediated directly than other types, while violence offences were more often negotiated indirectly. Fraud offences were the least likely to be negotiated in either way. Where any property loss had already been restored by the offender, direct mediation was more likely.

Getting to Agreement

If the emphasis is placed on the emotional benefits to both participants, the fact of a meeting and a discussion may be significant on its own. It is usually assumed, however, that the point of mediation is to come to some kind of agreement or settlement that enshrines the result of such an exchange. Such an agreement may be achieved whether or not the parties meet directly.

There has been much discussion of the meaningfulness of either measure as an indicator of success. Given the usual arguments for mediation (see Chapter 1), it would at least appear to be a minimal requirement that a significant number of cases reach the stage of a meeting. If 'reparation' is the chief aim, however, this would not be so, and the stress would have to be transferred to the rate of agreement. Even so, as a bare statistic, the rate of agreement is a rather impoverished indicator. As Walker (1987) says, one needs to know how many of these agreements survive (a matter which will be dealt with below), what sort of matters are enshrined in the agreement, and the initial level of conflict or emotional feeling which mediation has had to overcome. In addition, the fact that an agreement has not been achieved does not mean that the mediation has failed — the airing of grievances, the exchange of information, the mere fact of participation may all be gains in themselves, especially in the less straightforward cases like those involving related parties.

Once parties have agreed to meet, the chance of a settlement is usually high. Pearson (1982) says that agreement rates vary anywhere between 40% and 95%, but her survey included community mediation and divorce conciliation projects that tend to have lower agreement rates.

Divorce mediation agreement rates, for instance, are said by Kressel (1987) to vary between 40% and 70%, while Coates and Gehm (1985) say that 87% of all victim/offender pairs in the American VORPs they studied arrived at some contract involving reparation, while a further 11% also came to some agreement that did not involve reparation. In Galaway's (1986) study of the Minnesota VORP, 45 of 47 mediations ended in an agreement (96%). Scandinavian projects also have high rates of agreement — 90% in both Norway (Hovden, 1987) and Finland (Iivari, 1987). Mackay's (1986) Scottish experiment also failed to achieve an agreement in relation to only four out of 18 victims (78% agreement).

Davis et al. (1987) state that, for early British schemes, the aim of material reparation was as likely to be modified as frequently as the original aim of achieving face-to-face mediation in every case. Thus not all agreements involved material reimbursement (in cash or by some kind of work); in many cases the outcome was simply the giving and receiving of an apology (see below). American schemes, however, have placed much greater emphasis on material reparation. The Ontario VORP (Dittenhoffer and Ericson, 1983), for instance, settled one of 29 cases by apology alone, but every other one involved some kind of payment, to the victim or, in two cases, to a charity selected by the victim. Restitution payments averaged $447 (about £300 at the time), and rose as high as $4,000. A fifth of the payments were reimbursements to insurance companies. There were no instances of offenders carrying out work for the victim. Only a ninth of Coates and Gehm's sample of United States VORP cases did not involve compensation. Compensation was monetary in 58% of cases, work for the victim in 32%, work for some other party in 4%, with 6% other forms of reparation. Money payments ranged from $3 to $10,000, half of them being less than or equal to $71 (about £47), while the average hours worked per victim were 31. The agreements were therefore quite substantial in material terms. Even the juvenile restitution projects are quite onerous. According to Schneider and Schneider (1980), 65% of all orders involved monetary repayments, and these averaged $236. 40% involved community service averaging 49 hours work. There were very few instances of work for the victim (less than 1%), but even these averaged 29 hours work. (It must be remembered, however, that these American courts did not have access to a community service order like our own courts. A community service order in Britain involves a minimum of 40 hours work, although it can only be used for offenders aged 16 or above.)

There is very little in the literature on the determinants of success in terms of getting to agreement. Kressel (1987) refers to a number of variables that he considers important in divorce mediation and which he believes would apply to any kind of third party intervention. These are:

(1) The lower the level of conflict, the better the prognosis.

(2) The fewer the economic resources available for division, the less successful mediation will be.

(3) The more receptive the parties are to mediation, the greater the likelihood of success.

(4) High motivation produces settlement.

In terms of victim/offender mediation these hypotheses would lead one to expect a higher rate of success when the parties had not been in conflict before the crime, and the suffering of the victim was less; when the offender is able to afford some compensatory payment or can carry out some reparative task; when both parties are keen to take part; and when the offender is still under threat of judicial action, thus providing motivation to cooperate. On the latter point, it is already well established that those Neighbourhood Justice Centres established in the United States to divert criminal cases involving related parties from prosecution have much higher success rates (measured in terms of getting to some agreement) with such cases than with those they take on direct referral from community agencies or the parties themselves, ie without threat of legal action (see, eg, Harrington, 1985).

Police-based schemes

Some agreement between the victim and the offender was reached in 79% of all referrals. This was claimed to be full agreement in 73%, the remaining 6% being partial agreements. The negotiations, however, focused solely on the achievement of minimal reparation (see below for the types of agreement involved) and not on solving underlying conflicts, so that agreement will not normally have been problematic — it may have amounted to no more than the victim agreeing to receive, at second hand, a letter of apology signed by the offender. There was no change in rates of agreement over time.

Given as an overall rate, however, agreement is a combination of willingness to take part in the scheme and ability to come to a settlement. In order to disentangle the effects of willingness to take part in the scheme, the agreement rates used in the following discussion relate solely to those cases that proceeded to some kind of negotiation, differentiating between those that involved a victim/offender meeting ('mediation') and those that did not ('negotiation' or indirect mediation).

Looking first at the direct mediation cases, we find that 96% came to full agreement, and all of them came to at least a partial agreement (eg acceptance of an apology but no reparative settlement). Given the high success rate in these terms, it is not surprising that there were hardly any significant differences in terms of other variables between the successful and the less successful cases. The only association we could find was with the occupational status of the victim, non-manual workers being less likely to come to a settlement in mediation than manual workers (70% reached full agreement among the non-manual victims, as against 100% of the manual workers).

Cases that were negotiated indirectly were less often successful, 78% reaching total agreement, 14% partial agreement, and 8% failing to agree at all. As the most co-operative parties will have agreed to a direct meeting the lower rates of agreement for the negotiated cases are to be expected. Over time, however, the rate of agreement declined from 89% full agreement in the first half of the period studied to 67% in the second half. This may have been due to an increase at the same time in the proportion of cases reaching direct mediation, which may have enlarged the concentration of difficult cases in the negotiated category. Support for this supposition comes from the fact that the overall rate of referrals reaching agreement did not change over time, as also from the fact that where direct mediation had been offered but refused, success rates of negotiation were lower (71% full agreement, against 81% for cases that had never been offered the opportunity). Victims were also rated as being less willing in those cases that did not reach full agreement: victims seen as 'not keen' were successful only 40% of the time, against 85% for those who were moderately or very interested.

Although mediation was generally successful in producing an agreement, whatever the characteristics of the parties or the details of the process, there was some significant variability in success rates for negotiated cases. Between schemes, this was certainly so, with some (Exeter, Cumbria East, Sandwell) reaching 100% total agreement or nearly so, while Cumbria West reached agreement in only just over half, Cumbria South in 62% and Cumbria North 81%. Full agreement was less likely when offenders were not under threat of official legal action (57% reached full agreement against 80% of all other cases). Those involving either multiple victims or multiple offenders were more successful (all cases involving multiple victims produced agreement, as did 84% of those involving multiple offenders), this probably being due to the fact that schemes would generally have held that such cases were too complex to organise a direct encounter, so that the negotiated sample will have contained many of the more willing parties. Offenders who had previously taken part in the scheme also tended to be more successful (93% reaching full agreement), but this also is no doubt a selection effect, in that the scheme would hardly have taken on again an offender who was uncooperative. More meaningful, perhaps, was the fact that local authority departments who were victims were more likely to come to full agreement (93%), perhaps because it was easier for the scheme to get their understanding and active co-operation in reparation. In terms of the victim's age, the most successful cases were among the young teens (12 to 16) and early twenties (21 to 25), where there were no failures to secure full agreement. The 17-20s and the elderly were average in their agreement rates, and the rest (26-59) less successful (71% full agreement). This may indicate that some age-groups were more likely than others to be sympathetic towards young offenders, either because they were not far removed in age, or because they took a 'grandparental' rather than a parental attitude towards them. Agreement was most likely when the victim had suffered no material loss (93% full agreement), presumably for the simple reason that there was less to negotiate about;

similarly agreement was more likely if any loss had already been fully restored (80% full agreement) and least likely when this was not so (70%). The less there is in contention, the easier it is to secure agreement — a reasonable, if not earth-shattering, conclusion, and one that is in line with Kressel's first hypothesis above. Nevertheless, it is interesting that the type of crime made no difference at all, and that agreement seems to be a matter of the personal attitudes of the parties more than anything else.

With regard to the type of agreement, outcomes were classified into three groups:

(A) those involving only an explanation and an apology

(B) those involving concrete undertakings in addition to an apology

(C) those involving other achievements beyond a simple apology.

Most of the agreements were of type (A), viz. an apology only (57% of all agreements). Just over a quarter involved the offender in some sort of future undertaking. As regards reparation to the victim, this might have taken place in the course of 'mediation' (in which case it would have been recorded as C), or be part of a future undertaking (B). Two-thirds of the undertakings did in fact involve reparation, as did 58% of immediate achievements. Overall, 26% of all agreements involved reparation. In most cases (21%) this was 'direct' reparation to the victim (usually payment of compensation — only one eighth of such agreements involved work for the victim), but in the other 5% it was 'indirect' (usually work carried out for some community cause chosen, or agreed to, by the victim). Amounts paid in compensation ranged fairly evenly from as low as £1 to a maximum of £60. In a few cases relationships were re-established between victim and offender (usually after an assault) through 'mediation' proper, but this was always infrequent (eg. about four cases a year at Exeter).

Schemes varied considerably in the types of agreement they tended to negotiate. Exeter was the least likely to arrange anything beyond an apology — only 20% involved anything further. Two-thirds of the apologies were given in person, one-third by letter only (usually because the victim refused to meet the offender). Achievements were more substantial in other schemes, where simple apologies comprised from

63% (Cumbria South) down to 27% (Cumbria North) and 25% (Sandwell). Specific undertakings (B) were involved in over 60% of the agreements formulated through the Sandwell scheme and 48% of those in Cumbria North, descending to 31% in Cumbria East and West and fewer than 10% at Exeter. Other achievements (C) tended to account for between an eighth and a quarter of all cases in every scheme, slightly fewer at Exeter. Practical reparation did not, however, vary in exactly the same way between schemes. Reparation occurred most often (40-45%) at Sandwell, Cumbria East and Cumbria West. Cumbria South and North both achieved 31%, with Exeter very much lower at 15%. Direct reparation to the victim varied accordingly from around 40% at the first three schemes, to around 20% at the second two, and to 8% at Exeter.

There were considerable differences in the time involved in negotiations between the different outcomes. Overall, undertakings involved the more protracted effort (three and a quarter hours per case on average), other achievements averaged 3 hours, and a simple apology no more than two and a half hours. Reparation was achieved, on average, after 3 hours' negotiation. Contacts with the victim did not vary greatly across the different types of outcome, and the dis-proportions in time taken were largely due to the amount of time that had to be devoted to work with the offender. Direct mediation, where it occurred, also tended to be longer if reparation was to result.

Correlations with other variables showed closely similar patterns, whether one compared (A) with either (B) or (C), or cases involving reparation with those lacking reparation. Here we shall therefore discuss the results in terms of the achievement, or otherwise, of reparation. Victims were most likely to agree to reparation when they were households (40%) or local authority departments (38%), persons aged 17-25 (43%) or over 60 (50%), or persons in work (39%). They were least likely to agree to reparation if they were commercial business firms (17%). Reparation was also more likely when the victim was rated by the mediators as having acted less positively during the negotiation (41%), or when they had not wanted to meet the offender in person (35%), perhaps because it took more to satisfy the less co-operative victims — or because the more demanding were perceived negatively by the mediators. Similarly, reparation was more likely to form part of any agreement if this was negotiated indirectly rather than mediated face-to-face (36% in the former case, 25% in the latter), or in the case of partial rather than total agreement (35% versus 27%).

Offenders were more likely to be involved in making reparation if they already had a court record (39%). They were least likely to do so if they had been cautioned but not convicted before (19%). Where they had known the victim before, they were more likely to make some kind of reparation (34%), especially if a neighbour (47%) or a customer (50%).

The existence or otherwise of any material loss did not, surprisingly, affect the chances of a reparation outcome. Although damage offences more often resulted in reparation (38%), theft offences less often did so (20%). Offences involving violence or sexual assault were unlikely to result in reparation (14%).

Court-based schemes
Full agreement was much less frequent for these schemes than for the police-based, probably because there was likely to be much more in contention in most cases, which involved more serious offences. Over all referrals, exactly a third came to total agreement, and 44% came to at least partial agreement. Over time, moreover, both rates dropped, from 41% full agreement in the first half of the research period to 26% in the second half; and from half reaching some agreement down to 38%. From more recent figures, therefore, total agreement seems likely in little more than a quarter of all referrals.

These overall rates disguise a very large difference between directly mediated cases and those negotiated without a victim/offender meeting. Full agreement was achieved in 83% of mediated cases, and a partial agreement in the rest, whereas only 23% of the negotiated cases ended in complete agreement and over half of them (54%) reached no agreement at all. The agreement rates for negotiated cases did not alter over time, but the success rate for mediation dropped from 88% in the first half of the research study to 77% in the second half, perhaps because more difficult cases tended to be included as schemes gained more confidence. Most schemes were close to the overall rate for success in direct mediation, except perhaps for Wolverhampton where the rate was 73%. The only significant exception with respect to rates of agreement after indirect negotiation was Sandwell, which achieved 71% full agreement and only 29% complete failures. This was possibly due to the lower rate of employment of direct mediation at Sandwell, which may have resulted in more favourable cases on average within the indirectly negotiated group. In its more typical neighbourhood dispute work, Sandwell is much more used to using indirect mediation and the project may well have exercised less persuasion towards a direct meeting than the other schemes.

Whether negotiated or mediated, agreement was affected by a number of other variables. Success was more likely when the victim was a household or a local authority department, and when both the victim and the offender were white. Success was less likely if the parties shared a close relationship or were neighbours, if the victim had suffered emotionally or if the victim was only moderately keen to take part. More than ten pre-mediation meetings between the project and either party or others involved in the case was a sign that the outcome would rarely be productive (fewer than half of these cases got to a complete agreement), as were more than seven shorter contacts (telephone/letter), more than eight contacts with the victim or more than seven with the offender. The fact that negotiations had got so protracted in such cases probably meant that they were proving difficult anyway, but as such obstacles were not usually overcome, one must question whether projects could use their time more efficiently by abandoning these cases after a pre-defined amount of effort. It may be pointless to go on struggling against the fact that one of the parties is clearly reluctant.

Other variables were associated with success in either negotiation or mediation but not both. Negotiated cases were more likely to get to some agreement if the victim was either elderly or just older than most of the offenders (ie 21 to 25) and if he/she was in a manual occupation. Success was less likely in the case of individual victims (rather than corporate ones or households) or where there were several different victims. Male offenders, and those with previous convictions, were also less likely to reach agreement. Theft and damage offences were the easiest to resolve, the most difficult being burglary and offences involving actual injury to the victim. Offenders who themselves had suffered emotionally were more likely to agree to some settlement, as were those who had already fully restored the victim's losses before intervention. Naturally, a refusal to take part in a joint victim/offender meeting or failure to attend such a meeting once arranged were both adverse signs.

Fewer variables were separately correlated with success in direct mediation. The only additional positive indicators were a male offender (thus in the opposite direction to the association with regard to negotiation) and a victim who was not seeking work (eg 'housewife'). Unemployed victims, compared to those in work, were least likely to come to full agreement. Fraud cases were less successful than average. Mediators' ratings of parties' performance in mediation were not necessarily highly predictive of the outcome (despite the fact that one might have expected a 'halo effect' whereby the participants would have been seen to have acted more positively when the outcome was successful). Offender performance was not at all associated with outcome in the case of corporate victims, and only weakly so with personal victims. Victims, however, made much more difference, with 91% of those making what was considered a positive contribution coming to total agreement, and only 63% of those who behaved 'negatively' or in a more ambiguous manner. This may be taken as a sign that offenders are motivated to reach some concrete achievement in most cases, given that it may influence how they are to be punished by the court, so that poor skills or a cynical attitude do not in themselves present an insuperable barrier, whereas the attitude of the victim is much more crucial, given that they do not *have* to agree at all.

Lastly, one should mention that, for all the limitations of getting to agreement on its own as a measure of success, the courts would seem to regard it as a significant outcome. They were far more likely to endorse a complete agreement by sentencing in such a way as to reflect this (often mentioning that if it were not for the agreement, they would have sentenced more harshly). Two-thirds of all total agreements (whether directly or indirectly mediated) were endorsed by the court, and only half of partial agreements. More about court sentencing will be provided, however, in the next section.

Compared to the police-based schemes, the court-based projects were more likely to achieve concrete undertakings rather than a simple apology (45% of all agreements were of type B), but this was largely due to the Leeds project, which placed much greater stress on reparation because of the more serious offences with which it was generally dealing. Leeds achieved such undertakings in 64% of all cases. The Junction Project was also dealing with offenders with more serious criminal histories and employed reparative undertakings in each of the four cases that arrived at some agreement. Although N.E. Essex might not have been expected to place such great emphasis on material achievements, given that its offenders were not generally as serious, it still achieved 62% agreements of type B, perhaps because of the greater stress on victims' interests within this project. The West Midlands projects were much more dominated by simple apologies (over half at Wolverhampton and 70% at Coventry), with type-B agreements applying to only 37% and 24% of their total cases respectively. Anecdotal evidence from the Totten scheme also indicates that the achievements there were also mainly limited to an explanation and an apology, although reparation was also agreed on occasion.

Such undertakings most often involved (44%) some kind of work (almost always for corporate victims or for some local charity), and slightly less often repayments of cash or return of goods stolen (32%). Reparative work varied considerably in the level of commitment. At Coventry and Wolverhampton tasks ranged from helping at a school fete for 2 hours to 20 hours skilled labour at a car repair firm over a period of several weeks. In most cases, however, at both these schemes, reparation was confined to a single work session on one day.

Other undertakings involved promises to try to mend relationships, to stop misbehaving or to keep away from the other party, to seek help for a drink problem, and so on. Only 2% involved repairs to the victim's own property, and a further 5% promises to visit the victim or to help them in some way. Other achievements were relatively rare, at least as recorded by the schemes. In three cases, relations between the two parties were said to have been restored, and in another three the unemployed offender had been offered the chance of a job with the victim's help. In another case the offender had been introduced into a club that might help him stay out of trouble. In one case there had been an agreement to participate in mediation of an underlying dispute after the court had sentenced the offender.

Direct reparation to the victim was relatively infrequent at both the West Midlands schemes (around 10%), most common at Leeds (41%), and was around a quarter to a third at the two smaller schemes. Reparation of some kind (both direct and indirect) could be expected for most cases that were successfully negotiated by the Junction and Leeds projects (all four in the first case, 72% in the second), but was less often employed elsewhere (36% and 39% at Wolverhampton and N.E. Essex, and only 18% at Coventry). Often an offer of material reparation was made by an offender and turned down by the victim. From interviews with victims it would appear that a third of them were offered reparation at Coventry, and 56% at Wolverhampton. The victims tended not to place much emphasis on the material advantages of such reparation. Where it was agreed it was usually as a token to confirm the understanding reached, symbolic of the offender's good faith.

Victims involved in reparation (whether work or financial repayment) were more likely to be households, local authority departments or other agencies, rather than individuals or business firms; aged between 26 and 59; and in a job or seeking work. They were more likely to have agreed to direct mediation and to be moderately or very keen on the idea. Offenders were more often older (26-59), male and in non-manual occupations. Although those who were less keen were more likely to be involved in reparation, the most satisfied at the end, according to the schemes' own ratings, were those who had made reparative agreements.

Reparation was more frequent when the parties were closely related (family, marriage, co-residence or neighbours) or in a business/customer relationship. Unlike the experience of the police-based schemes, the existence of material loss was positively related to the chance of reparation as part of the agreement, with fraud and 'take and drive away' offences being particularly high. Violence offences were the least likely to result in reparation.

Also in direct contradiction to the findings for the police schemes was the fact that reparation was *more* frequently a part of the agreement when this was total rather than partial, and when achieved by direct mediation.

Table 7: Percentage of agreements involving undertakings

	Negotiated	Mediated
Partial agreement	26%	48%
Full agreement	39%	62%

Effect on Criminal Justice Disposals

The evidence in the extant literature with respect to the effects of victim/offender mediation schemes upon the decisions of traditional criminal justice agencies is virtually non-existent. The most substantial statement appears to be that of Smith, Blagg and Derricourt (1986) with respect to the South Yorkshire scheme: "Our tentative conclusion is that in its first year this project had only a marginal effect on the sentencing of offenders". This, however, is not based on any statistical comparison, but merely the opinion of the researchers regarding the sentences meted out to offenders dealt with by the scheme. They felt that the increased knowledge by the court of the victim's reactions and sufferings did not seem to have made sentences harsher, but that only in a few cases did there seem to be any reduction in the likelihood of custody. Their impression is reinforced by the similarly subjective statement of Dittenhoffer and Ericson in relation to the Ontario VORP that it was unlikely to have had much effect as an alternative disposal.

Sentencers may be influenced by a report on the results of victim/offender mediation in one of three ways:

(a) as evidence of the offender's regret and willingness to put things right, which would reflect upon the offender's character and might lessen the severity of punishment needed as an expression of moral disapproval or to effect a change of attitude;

(b) as evidence that the offender has shouldered practical responsibility by making reparation, so that the need for retributive punishment is thereby reduced;

(c) as a reminder of the victim's suffering and needs, which might put them in mind of awarding compensation or another sentence that would help serve the victim's interests. (This might be an alternative to custody which would allow reparation to be made, or it might be a more severe sentence that recognises the particular hurt to the victim in a specific case. Although it would no doubt be improper for a judge to be influenced by the victim's attitudes concerning the appropriate severity of sentence, as these may reflect personal opinion as much as the degree of hurt caused by the offence in question, it would be proper to recognise that some offences are made more serious by the fact that they are committed against more vulnerable citizens, such as the elderly or the infirm, or contained an element of, say, racial harassment.)

The implications of these three are rather different, as they operate on different principles of sentencing. The first may lead to an overall reduction in the level of punitiveness with which an offender is dealt; the second to a substitution of reparation for a part of the punishment that would otherwise have been assigned, so that the sentence is less severe but the onus on the offender remains identical; the third is equivocal, but may lead to an overall increase in the onus on the offender, as the court recognises his/her responsibilities to the victim as being in addition to the proper criminal sentence. (This may be so, even in the event of an apparent reduction of the severity of sentence, if the combined punitiveness of the sentence and the reparation is greater than that of a court sentence alone would have been.)

The degree of influence of reparation upon sentence will, in addition, depend on the degree to which the punitiveness of the court is a reflection of the harm done to the individual victim and to what degree it is a reflection of society's need to condemn the offender's behaviour. Reparation can be seen to provide a more complete replacement for the former than for the latter. Some cases brought to court may seem minor in terms of the threat they appear to pose to the social fabric or general morality, and prosecution largely reflect the need to serve the victim. In the event of reparation, such cases might be deemed unnecessary to bring to court, which is one of the bases for the police-based schemes as a diversionary mechanism. It would also provide a rationale for community mediation schemes that provide an alternative forum for settling interpersonal disputes that have given rise to minor offences.

Such effects are difficult to measure in practice. We have no means of measuring the degree to which victims are helped by reparation; nor can we measure the 'punitiveness' of reparation. In the former case we can only rely on victims' accounts of the experience and how they describe the effect upon themselves, a matter that is the subject of the following section. In the latter case we can examine sentencing decisions and whether they vary according to the degree to which the offender has assumed the burden of material reparation, but these are crude and partial indices. It is impossible, for instance, to measure the extent to which reduction in sentence, if any, reflects the offender's apparent remorse or the fact that the reparation is seen as punitive in itself. Here, and more generally, we can rely only on what sentencers themselves say they do when faced with a victim/offender mediation report. On their own, such comments might not be totally reliable, as one cannot expect magistrates or judges to be entirely dismissive of a local scheme or to admit that it is given no weight at all in their deliberations, but combined with statistical evidence on actual sentencing practice it should be possible to draw some conclusions.

There are few references to sentencers' attitudes in the literature relating to victim/offender mediation. Schneider (1986) found that most rated American juvenile restitution schemes as quite low on a scale of punitiveness. In relation to American VORPs, Coates and Gehm did not question sentencers, but did ask victims and offenders who had participated how punitive they saw reparation to be. Victims generally saw it as at least partially punitive and only 24% saw it as insufficiently onerous. Naturally, no offenders saw it as too light an imposition, while 35% found it excessively punitive. Virtually all, however, saw reparation as a reasonable alternative to prison (95% of victims and 87% of offenders), despite the fact that it was seen as less severe. (That it was seen as a reasonable alternative, therefore, would seem to reflect a general opinion that custody was normally too harsh a penalty.)

Police-based schemes

The only criminal justice decision in question in relation to these schemes is that of the police whether or not to prosecute or pursue some other (lesser) course of action. As this decision is almost always taken before mediation, it is difficult to pinpoint the influence of the schemes on the rate of diversion. This involves a look at cautioning policy generally and changes over time at the police force level. Fortunately, in those police force areas that had juvenile liaison panels (or something equivalent) that used reparation on occasion the practice was usually widespread and could have been expected to have an impact even at county level. This was certainly true of Cumbria, where the arrangements applied to the whole force. Most of the urban areas of Northants are also now covered by juvenile bureaux. The reparation scheme at Exeter, however, was limited, even after recent expansion, to East Devon only, so that its impact on the figures for Devon and Cornwall as a whole might be somewhat attenuated.

Using the most recent available crime figures (Criminal Statistics, 1986), the cautioning rate can be calculated for any police force by expressing the numbers cautioned as a percentage of all those either cautioned or convicted at a magistrates court. (Those convicted at a Crown Court have been omitted as being too serious to be relevant for consideration for a caution.) This was carried out separately for offenders aged 10 to 14 and 14 to 17. All three of those police force areas known to employ reparation schemes — Cumbria, Devon and Cornwall and Northamptonshire — had above average cautioning statistics in 1986. For 10-14 year olds, the average cautioning rate over all forces in England and Wales was 84%. Both Cumbria and Devon/Cornwall achieved 88%, and Northants 90%. Among 14-17 year olds, the overall average was 59%. Devon and Cornwall cautioned 66%, Cumbria 68% and Northants 84%. Few other forces had such high figures among the 14-17s, but a few did have comparable rates, notably (72%) the West Midlands (which does have juvenile liaison panels, and the Sandwell scheme, although the number of cases dealt with by the latter was much too small to have had any overall impact), and Lincolnshire, Northumbria, Nottinghamshire, Warwickshire, Wiltshire, and Dyfed, all with rates between 65% and 68%.

Both Devon and Northants have had their juvenile reparation schemes in operation for several years. Both forces already had cautioning rates well above average in 1983 (58% and 62% respectively for 14-17 year olds, compared to an average across all forces of 46%). In the interim, the number of bureaux in Northants has expanded and the force's cautioning rate has continued to grow, with an especially strong increase between 1983 and 1984 (see the graph below at Fig. 1). Devon and Cornwall, which has only just expanded its practice, too late to affect the figures shown here, had a fairly steady cautioning rate over the same period. Cumbria, on the other hand, in 1983 had a cautioning rate that was well below average (35%), but introduced a pilot reparation scheme in the middle of 1984, followed by a regular arrangement for the following two years with Home Office funding. The graph shows a very steep rise in that force's cautioning rate from 1983 to 1987, especially in the first two annual increases.

It seems clear that in the three forces with reparation schemes studied here there has been a marked change in cautioning rates. The fact that a few other forces, however, were able to achieve similar results without reparation schemes must lead one to question whether the impact is due to reparation or to some other factor. Certainly, the reason why both Devon and Northants have had flourishing juvenile panels for many years is due very much to the support of those particular police forces, especially at the top, and their enthusiasm for reducing the extent to which juvenile offenders were being prosecuted. Evidence for the Cumbria research shows that the productivity of the four regional panels was very variable and dependent by and large upon the enthusiasm of the

Figure 1: Offenders aged 14-17: Percentage cautioned of all cautioned or convicted in a magistrates' court

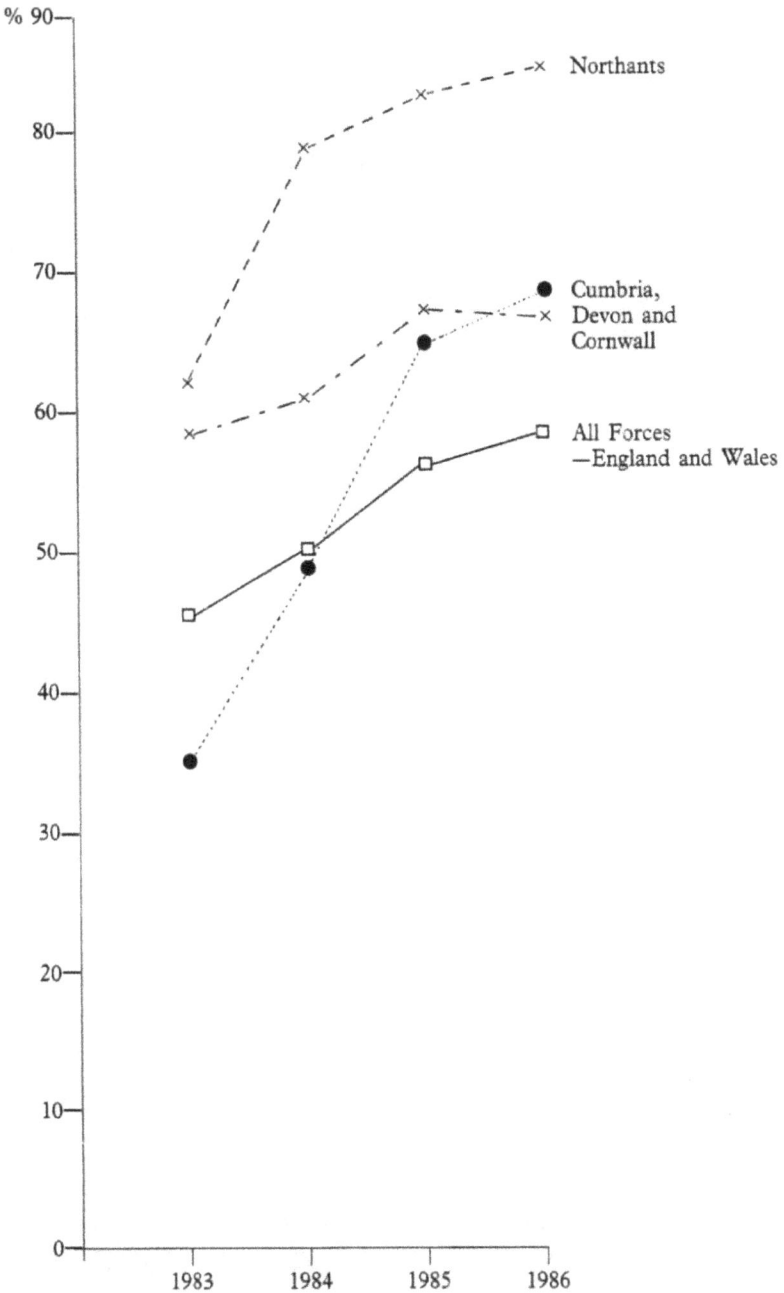

particular police officers sitting upon the panels. There has been increasing pressure over recent years, including from the Home Office, for cautioning rates to be improved, and this has produced a moderate advancement over England and Wales from 46% in 1983 to 59% in 1986, and we have seen above that some forces have exceeded even this trend, with or without reparation arrangements.

The evidence presented so far does not enable one to say that reparation schemes necessarily affect rates of cautioning in themselves, or if they do so it may only be in conjunction with a pre-existent commitment on the part of the police force to prosecute fewer youngsters. Nevertheless, it must be said that there has been a phenomenal rise (almost 100%) in cautioning rate in Cumbria since the introduction of the schemes, and that Northants stands out as exceptional with a cautioning rate for 14-17 year olds well above any other force and as high as the average for 10-14s across all other forces. It would seem likely that police consultative arrangements with social services and probation departments do help to reduce the need to take many juveniles to court, although it is more questionable what role reparation might play within such arrangements.

The research findings show that reparation is employed in only a small number of cases, although it is possible that they are particularly significant cases. The difference, for instance, in Cumbria between what would have been an average cautioning rate (for all forces) and the rate it actually achieved is only about 100 juveniles, while more than this number a year are referred to the reparation scheme. The corresponding difference for Devon and Cornwall is about 125, while the Exeter scheme handles about 65 reparation cases annually. Although it therefore cannot account for the whole of the difference its impact could still be substantial if these same cases would otherwise have been prosecuted. Many of the juveniles referred to the reparation schemes, on the other hand, had not been known previously to the police, and one must seriously doubt whether all these would have been prosecuted for a first offence. Particularly serious offences, which might have warranted prosecution for a first offence, were after all, not referred to most of the schemes. One of the probation ancillary workers on the Cumbria scheme, interviewed by the researchers, complained that many cases not in danger of prosecution were still referred to the scheme for welfare reasons: "...*nearly all are very minor offences, usually where the police have felt it their duty to be seen to be doing something more than just cautioning people — where there is pressure on them, eg petty vandalism, graffiti, cases that would have been thrown out of court any-way...my impression is that the police have been keeping the cautioning rate artificially high by formalising what used to be dealt with informally...*". All in all one must remain sceptical of the claims of reparation schemes per se to have been instrumental in diverting from prosecution more than a small number of juveniles.

Court-based schemes

The schemes examined all operated before sentence. All involved reports by the scheme to the court on what had happened in their attempt to mediate between the offender and the victim. They could all, therefore, have had some influence upon the disposals offenders received when they reappeared in court.

Direct comparisons between offenders who were referred to the schemes and those who were not might not, however, be valid, as the first group would be a specially selected one that might differ in important ways from the general run of offenders. As a control for such differences we have been able to break down all cases according to the sex and age of the offender, the type of offence, and the court by which they were sentenced, before making comparisons of the sentence awarded. Nevertheless, there might be other features that would bias the reparation group compared with the others — they might have had more or fewer preconvictions, for instance, or they might have seemed more amenable individuals, or more likely to be sentenced severely. In the results described above, the offenders dealt with by the projects do not seem to have been very different from the normal range of court defendants, except (especially in Leeds) that they would on the whole have been those more likely to receive the harder sentences. Not only would the projects have been particularly keen to deal with offenders in danger of custody, but the method of selection (apart from a few cases in Coventry) on the basis of referral for a social enquiry report would have meant that the more minor offenders would have been omitted. In most cases, therefore, a custodial sentence, or something more than a fine or a discharge, could have been expected in the normal course of events. On the other hand, with the exception of Leeds, the projects did not attempt to deal with offenders remanded in custody because of the logistical problems involved. This will have had the effect of excluding the most serious offenders for whom custody is the most likely disposal.

Overall, 1% of the cases for which we have the final sentence were dismissed. 1% received an absolute discharge, and 18% a conditional discharge, 1 7% were placed on probation, 16% required to carry out community service, and 2% received attendance centre orders. 21% were sent into custody, while a further 6% received suspended custodial orders. 14% were fined, 5% in conjunction with other orders (largely probation or community service) and 9% as a sole penalty. 32% were also required to pay compensation, mostly in combination with some other sentence, although 3% of all sentences were compensation orders on their own.

The incidence of compensation orders as a sole penalty among these cases is strikingly higher than the overall incidence, in 1986, for magistrates' courts in England and Wales, of slightly less than one in two hundred for offenders charged with indictable offences. The overall incidence of compensation is also higher than the figure of 23% given in Newburn (1988) for indictable offences. It would not be surprising if the existence of a reparation scheme reminded magistrates of the possibility of ordering compensation, a potential which seems at present to be under-utilised (Newburn, 1988), and many of the orders will have been merely enshrining an agreement already formulated between the offender and the victim. (The subsequent Criminal Justice Act 1988 now requires courts to give reasons for not making a compensation order, thus ensuring that the possibility is always considered, although the information before the court about the victim's losses or suffering would not necessarily be improved. Police forces are now encouraged to report victims' losses more systematically.)

The figures do not, however, prove that such an effect did exist, as the sample of cases would naturally have contained only those where there was an identifiable victim. Among court-cases generally there will be a number where no such victim exists and where compensation is not a possibility. Taking into account the offence helps to resolve some of these difficulties in comparison. Only one offence had a particularly high rate of compensation, that of criminal damage, of which 63% resulted in orders at magistrates' courts: a rate exactly the same as that quoted in Newburn (1988) for damage offences across all magistrates' courts in England and Wales. Damage offences are generally those with the highest chance of compensation, however, so that there may be little scope for improvement in the overall rate. Other offences generally had similar rates to the expected ones, however (burglary 34% compared to 36% nationally, assault 26% compared with 23%, fraud 55% compared with 49%), except for theft, where the compensation rate was 32%, as against 18% nationally. Generally, therefore, compensation is ordered at more or less the expected rate at magistrates' courts for cases referred to the reparation schemes (and is certainly not lower), except for a large (78%) increase in awards for theft and a possible rise, too, in awards for fraud (12% increase).

We can compare awards of compensation at Crown Courts only for the Leeds scheme, but here the differences from the national rates (again taken from Newburn, 1988) are more substantial. Compensation for damage was up from an expected 18% to 27%; for theft from 8% to 19%; for burglary, 6% to 16%; and for assault, 14% to 19%. Differences seem to be greater in general when the expected rate is low — ie when there is greater scope for improvement. In sum, then, there does seem to have been an increase in the ordering of compensation in the magistrates' courts and, to an even greater extent, in the Crown Court.

Compensation was more likely to be ordered if the victim was a business firm, or aged over 25. Offenders in non-manual occupations were more likely to be expected to pay compensation, while those without jobs were less likely to be ordered to do so. Not surprisingly compensation was unlikely to be awarded if any material loss had already been made good by the offender (only 8% of such cases resulted in a compensation order).

The likelihood of a compensation order increased directly in proportion to the degree of success schemes had achieved. Direct mediation and indirect negotiation resulting in a full agreement both give rise to higher than average rates of compensation orders, while cases that were not proceeded with for some reason had a low rate. The occurrence of direct reparation also resulted in a high rate of compensation awards (41%). These results appear to confirm that the schemes did influence the courts in the direction of considering compensation more often — sometimes, of course, as a direct consequence of reinforcing a mediated agreement by incorporating it in a court order.

In looking at the other disposals, we compared, for each scheme, the actual sentences received by referred offenders (whether or not there was successful mediation) with the distribution of disposals that would have been expected from their local court for the same distribution of offences, and of ages and sexes of offenders. The local court in the case of the Coventry scheme was the Coventry Magistrates' Court, for the Wolverhampton scheme the Wolverhampton Magistrates' Court and for N.E. Essex the Colchester Magistrates' Court. In each case, virtually all the cases studied were from these particular courts. With respect to Leeds, although the majority of cases came from the Leeds Crown Court, a significant minority were referred by the Leeds Magistrates' Court, so that we had to divide their cases into two groups according to their origin, comparing each with their relevant court.

A special tabulation of disposals for each of the above courts was provided by the Statistical Department of the Home Office for indictable offences in 1986 (the latest available data), broken down simultaneously by sex, age (17-21, 21 and above) and principal offence. From these the distribution of disposals for each court, sex, age and offence combination was calculated, and these 'expected' rates applied to the numbers of referrals to the schemes in each of the same categories. These were then totalled for each court to give expected rates for each sentence for the particular constellation of referrals to the local scheme. The difference between the actual and expected rates could then be tested by chi-square for statistical significance. (The fact that the figures obtained by this method are necessarily 'artificial' means that the parameters of this test may not be satisfied; nevertheless its application does provide some index of the size of difference observed.) For each court the differences were apparently significant at the 0.001 level of probability, except for the Colchester comparison which, because of the low sample size, was significant at 0.5 only (ie not reliably different).

The following table shows the results of this analysis.

Table 8: Sentencing of offenders by court: actual versus expected numbers

| | ESSEX | | COVENTRY | | WOLVERHAMPTON | |
	Expected	Actual	Expected	Actual	Expected	Actual
Discharge	4	5	25	27	20	22
Probation	3	5	12	17	11	22
CSO	1	—	15	24	11	18
Fine	5	4	42	17	36	13
Att. centre	—	—	4	5	1	—
Susp. custody	1	—	5	7	4	6
Imm. custody	1	—	10	10	15	10
Other	1	2	1	7	3	10
Total	16	16	114	114	101	101

| | LEEDS-MAGISTRATES | | LEEDS-CROWN COURT | |
	Expected	Actual	Expected	Actual
Discharge	4	3	6	3
Probation	4	9	13	26
CSO	3	11	23	22
Fine	25	6	10	1
Att. centre	—	—	—	1
Susp. custody	2	7	14	10
Imm. custody	4	6	56	54
Other	1	1	1	6
Total	43	43	123	123

Taking all the schemes that dealt primarily with magistrates courts (Coventry, N.E. Essex and Wolverhampton) one can identify some major shifts in sentencing pattern. 'Other' sentence shows the largest increase, from 5 to 19. This is due almost solely to an increase in the number of sentences which were compensation alone. Just as significant, however, is the huge decrease in the incidence of fines from 83 to 34. (It may be remembered that the original aim of the Coventry scheme, when first mooted, was to provide an alternative for fines.) Part of this shift will have been towards compensation orders (ie a move from the offender paying the state to reimbursement of the victim), but the majority would appear to be due to an increase in the number of probation and community service orders. The former are up from an expected number of 26 to 44, the latter from 27 to 42. There has also been a slight increase in the number of conditional discharges. As far as custodial sentences go there is also some change, a decrease in immediate custody from 26 to 20. This has been mostly absorbed by an increase of 4 in the number of suspended custodial orders. This pattern of changes applies on the whole to each of the three courts, although there was no decrease in custodial orders from the expected level at Coventry.

The cases from Leeds magistrates were omitted from this analysis because the results were different in two important respects:

(a) there was no move towards the use of compensation orders as a sole penalty, and

(b) there was an increase in the number of custodial orders, from an expected two suspended orders and four immediate to seven suspended and six immediate.

In the Crown Court at Leeds, however, findings were similar to those for the other magistrates' courts: an increase in the use of compensation as a sole order, a decrease in fines, and an increase in the number of probation orders. There was little shift in the use of community service and a minimal reduction in the use of custody (from an expected 56 immediate custodial orders to 54, and 14 suspended orders to 11).

These results cannot be accepted too readily, however, as a final summary of effects on sentencing. It has already been mentioned that the controls used in order to create a fair comparison did not allow for the fact that most offenders had been referred for social enquiry reports and were therefore in greater danger of serious disposal than the general run of offenders before the same courts. Although there is no way of controlling precisely for this effect, it is possible to explore the degree to which the results might be affected by this factor. This can be done by assuming that, in the limit, no offenders were likely to receive a simple fine or discharge. In fact, we do not have to go quite so far — we can merely assume that there was no reduction in the level of fines as a result of the schemes (because this apparent effect could be the result of selecting only the subjects of social enquiry reports). We can then take the actual numbers of fines as being, in the limit, the expected number. By reducing the expected number of discharges in the same ratio (a reasonable, if arbitrary, assumption), and re-calculating the expected numbers receiving the other disposals, we can derive another set of expected values which represent the extreme position where all offenders who were not fined are assumed to be in danger of some other disposal than fine or discharge. Comparison with the real figures then shows a substantial decrease in the actual use of custody (for each scheme) and an even larger increase in the use of conditional discharges, probation or CSO (variable across the schemes).

Such extreme assumptions obviously cannot be taken as a picture of reality, but they do provide a limit representing the sample of offenders received by the schemes to be as severe as it possibly could be. The results presented in Table 8 above represent the opposite extreme — i.e. they make no allowance whatsoever for the fact that virtually all these offenders were the subject of social enquiry reports. If both extremes are unreasonable expectations, one can only plump — again arbitrarily but with reasonable hopes of striking near the truth — for a happy medium, the average of the two sets of results, the one underestimating the seriousness of the sample, the other over-estimating it.

The results of these new calculations are presented here with some confidence, despite their relatively imprecise derivation because they are by and large confirmed by independent evidence below that indicates a significant impact on sentencing decisions (as well as anecdotal evidence — see for instance case-study H in chapter 4). Although the figures are estimates they represent a figure between the unlikely extremes produced by assuming that the offenders referred to the schemes were no more serious than those generally before the courts (despite the fact that they had virtually all been referred for reports) or by assuming that no more would ordinarily have been fined than were in fact so sentenced (and that the proportion of discharges would have been similarly low). The range of variation between the schemes, moreover, was not always large, and for some sentences it is possible to say that the direction of effect is more or less certain, even if its quantitative value is not. The range of results is therefore given in Table 9, as well as the "best estimate" according to the above method of analysis.

In summary, these results indicate that 18% of those offenders referred from magistrates courts to the reparation schemes probably had their sentences affected by such action. The results are possibly slightly higher (just over a quarter) for Leeds and Colchester, although the figures for the latter scheme are based on a small sample size and are not reliably different from the average figure. If the relative order of the schemes is reliable, then these results would seem to indicate that sentence change was more likely the higher the emphasis the schemes placed on material reparation (especially Leeds) or advantage to the victim (especially Colchester). Wolverhampton also exceeding Coventry on both these indices. The effect of the Leeds scheme on Crown Court cases seems to have been rather lower at 14% than its effect on magistrates (26%).

In terms of the type of change to sentencing patterns, there were some common tendencies and several differences between the courts. One of the most substantial changes was the increase in "compensation order only" disposals (accounting for virtually all the "other" sentences in the tables). The number of such disposals was always at least double that expected, with the single exception of Leeds magistrates' court which showed no increase in "other" sentences at all. There was also a substantial increase (by 50%) in the number of discharges awarded in most cases — again with one exception, Leeds Crown Court where the seriousness of the cases precluded such a disposal most of the time.

There also appears to have been a substantial (nearly 50%) reduction in the number of fines, and in the number of immediate custodial disposals (40%), both without exception across the schemes.

There was more variability in terms of the other disposals, but probation orders were never fewer, arid usually many more than expected. Community service orders tended to be more frequent, although not at Colchester, nor at Leeds Crown Court.

Table 9: Estimated changes in sentencing decisions by court

	Actual sentence relative to expected (Tab.8)	Actual sentence relative to expected (opposite limit)	Likely change in sentence (estimated)	Change as % of expected
COVENTRY MAGISTRATES				
Discharge	+2	+17	+9.5	54%
Probation	+5	-5	0	—
CSO	+9	-4	-2.5	+12%
Fine	-25	0	+12.5	-42%
Att. centre	+1	-2	-0.5	-9%
Susp. cust.	+2	-2	0	—
Imm. cust.	0	-9	-4.5	-31%
Other	+6	+5	+5.5	+367%
Sample size = 114 *Estimated % sentences altered = 15%				
WOLVERHAMPTON MAGISTRATES				
Discharge	+2	+15	+8.5	+63%
Probation	+11	+2	+6.5	+42%
CSO	+7	-2	+2.5	+16%
Fine	-23	0	-11.5	-47%
Att. Centre	-1	-2	-1.5	-100%
Susp.cust.	+2	-1	-0.5	—
Imm. cust.	-5	-17	-11	-52%
Other	+7	+5	+6	+150%
Sample size = 101 *Estimated % sentences altered = 22%				
COLCHESTER MAGISTRATES				
Discharge	+5	+2	+3.5	+100%
Probation	+2	0	+1	+25%
CSO	-1	-1	-1	-100%
Fine	-1	0	-0.5	-11%
Att. Centre	0	0	0	—
Susp. cust.	-1	-1	-1	100%
Imm. cust.	-1	-1	-1	-100%
Other	+1	+1	+1	+100%
Sample size = 16 *Estimated sentences altered = 27%				
(NB figures unreliable because of small sample)				

[Table continued on next page]

Table 9: Estimated changes in sentencing-continued

	Actual sentence relative to expected (Tab.8)	Actual sentence relative to expected (opposite limit)	Likely change in sentence (estimated)	Change as % of expected
LEEDS MAGISTRATES				
Discharge	-1	+2	+0.5	+20%
Probation	+5	-1	+2	+71%
CSO	+8	+3	+5.5	+100%
Fine	-19	0	-9.5	-61%
Att. Centre	0	0	0	—
Susp. cust.	+5	+2	+3.5	+100%
Imm. cust.	+2	-4	-1	-14%
Other	0	-2	-1	-50%
Sample size = 43 *Estimated sentences altered = 26%				
LEEDS CROWN COURT				
Discharge	-3	+2	-0.5	-14%
Probation	+13	+11	+12	+86%
CSO	-1	-4	-2.5	-10%
Fine	-9	0	-4.5	-82%
Att. Centre	+1	+1	+1	—
Susp. cust.	-4	-6	-5	-33%
Imm. cust.	-2	-9	-5.5	-9%
Other	+5	+5	+5	+500%
Sample size = 123 *Estimated sentences altered = 14%				
ALL MAGISTRATES COURTS				
Discharge	+8	+36	+22	+54%
Probation	+23	-4	+9.5	+22%
CSO	+23	-4	+9.5	+22%
Fine	-68	0	-34	-46%
Att. Centre	0	-4	-2	-29%
Susp. cust.	+8	-2	+3	+18%
Imm. cust.	-4	-31	-17.5	-40%
Other	+14	+9	+11.5	+135%
Sample size = 274 *Estimated % sentences altered = 18%				

*Note: Percentage sentences altered by participation in the reparation schemes was calculated by totalling the total number of changes (ignoring sign), dividing this by two (because one less of a certain disposal necessarily implies one more of some other), and expressing this figure as a percentage of the total sample.

Attendance centres applied only to schemes with a number of younger offenders, but in those cases they were used less often than was expected. Suspended custodial orders were most variable and were probably not subject to any significant change.

In absolute terms the estimated figures indicates a shift from fines and to a lesser extent custody, in the magistrates court, in favour particularly of conditional discharges, but also compensation as a sole order, probation and community service. In Leeds Crown Court there appears to have been a shift more or less equally away from imprisonment (immediate or suspended) and from fines towards probation and compensation only. The number of prison sentences saved over two years may have amounted to 23: 11 (11% of cases) at Wolverhampton, 6 or 7 (4% of cases) at Leeds, 4 or 5 (4% of cases) at Coventry, and one (6% of cases) at Colchester.

These represent the best estimates that can be formed on the basis of the available statistical data. The size of the figures may be questioned — although they are as likely to be on the low side as they are to be too high — but the directions of the schemes' effects on sentencing are usually sufficiently robust to endure whatever the method of analysis employed. The shape of the findings in Table 8 has been affirmed by subsequent calculations, the size only of the differences having been increased.

Fortunately there are other pieces of evidence that can be used to test the viability of the above findings deriving from the associations of other variables with sentence within the sample of clients of the reparation schemes.

Custodial sentences were more likely when the victim was an individual or a household rather than a corporate body. Social agencies as victims were particularly low in terms of the incidence of custody for the offender. Custody was more frequent when there was more than one victim or the victim was aged over sixty (48% of the latter cases resulted in immediate or suspended custody, against 24% of all others). The offender was less likely to receive a custodial sentence if female (6%, compared with 21% for men; women were more likely to receive probation, but were much lower on community service), a first-time offender, or not in a job. Black offenders were more likely to receive a custodial order than whites (37% received immediate or suspended custody or attendance centre, compared to 25% of white offenders). Custody was also more likely if the victim and offender had not been previously acquainted. Fraud and burglary were the offences most likely to be met with imprisonment; criminal damage was the least likely.

None of the above findings are unusual, so that there is no evidence, at least, of any change in the pattern of sentencing in terms of the characteristics of the offence, the offender or the victim. More direct evidence is provided by associations between sentence and variables pertaining to the projects' intervention.

The extent to which the schemes had been successful in mediation was inversely related to the chance of a custodial outcome in court. Thus those referrals that it had not been possible to negotiate for whatever reason had the highest rate of immediate custody (48%). Those negotiated which eventuated in no agreement had a 32% rate of custody. Those cases where the victim had not wanted to take part but where the project continued to work with the offender (usually on the basis of 'offence-analysis' counselling), or where both parties had come to some agreement but had not met directly, had average rates of custody. **The lowest rate of custody was for directly mediated cases, among whom only 13% resulted in such a sentence.**

Reparation *completed by the time of sentence* resulted in very low custodial rates (only 5%), whereas reparation that was only promised appeared to make no difference to the chance of a custodial sentence. Whether reparation was direct or indirect also made no difference. (It seems that deeds rather than words are more persuasive to sentencers.)

There are some signs that a poor outcome to the intervention can have a negative impact on sentence. That a positive performance in mediation by the offender reduces the chance of custody may be reasonable enough, but the finding that an antagonistic victim more than doubles the chance of custody is more disturbing, although it may be that a victim is more likely to be antagonistic if the offence has been a more serious one, and thus more likely to receive a harsh sentence in any case. The chance of the offender receiving a conditional discharge also improved with the degree of enthusiasm of the victim to take part in mediation (not keen, 14% discharge; moderately keen, 20%; very keen, 27%).

Better results were achieved in shorter mediation sessions (ie. under one hour), for which the custody rate was only 9%, and as many as 35% were discharged. This is likely, however, to be a result of schemes putting more effort into cases particularly in danger of custody, rather than an effect of shorter or longer mediation.

Despite the major reduction in fines overall, there are few measures relating to schemes' interventions that are correlated with the rate of fines, so that the reduction seems to have occurred across the board among referrals to the schemes. This tends to confirm the arguments used above that the sample of offenders, referred for social enquiry reports, was particularly unlikely to receive fines compared to offenders generally. Community service orders and probation orders were found to vary inversely with custody rates.

A different approach to examining the effects on sentencing was employed by two of the authors (Judith Unell and Anna Leeming) in relation to the two West Midlands projects. In each of the courts the Clerk to the Justices was provided with a short list of randomly selected cases where direct mediation had occurred. Each Clerk brought the relevant court papers to a meeting with the researchers, without perusing them in detail beforehand. At the meeting each was asked to scan the papers and, in each case, to make a swift intuitive assessment as to whether the offender's participation in the project had been taken into account by the magistrates, while also estimating what the sentences might have been in the absence of such participation. Such an exercise is obviously subjective, and suffers also from the disadvantage of retrospection, but it makes a useful adjunct to the above statistical analyses (which, in any case, contained their own uncertainties).

The Clerks said that they made their assessments on the basis of the following factors:

(a) the nature of the charge and the appropriate range of sentencing options;

(b) mitigating factors apparent in Social Enquiry or Medical Reports;

(c) the quality of the mediation, especially the amount of contrition and genuine concern shown by the offender, and evidence of willingness to forgive on the part of the victim, such assessments depending essentially on information given in the projects' reports;

(d) the level of compensation that the offender appeared likely to be able to afford;

(e) the offender's previous convictions.

The results of this exercise, although admittedly based on only a small number of cases (18 in all), appeared to indicate that, in general, offenders who had taken part in mediation and reparation were treated more leniently by the magistrates when passing sentence. In 14 of the cases, Clerks considered that sentences were more lenient than they would otherwise have expected. In one case the sentence was more lenient than usual but was considered to have been because of other powerful mitigating factors rather than participation in mediation. In the other three cases the sentence was considered unusually harsh, although the Clerks had not felt this was because of the reparation report. Even in those cases where the reparation report was felt to have been influential, the social enquiry report was sometimes felt to have contributed as well, so that it is not possible entirely to separate the effects of the two.

In terms of the actual sentences this exploratory study showed a trend away from fines towards conditional discharge (noted in about a third of the cases); a reduction in the level of compensation awards; and a movement away from custody (again in about a third of the cases), usually in favour of community service, a suspended sentence, or a probation order. (These proportional changes in different types of disposal compare very well with those estimated statistically.)

When asked their general impressions, the Clerks suggested that in most cases reports of completed mediation and reparation were likely to help the offender or at least do no harm. Where cases were specifically referred for reparation by magistrates, it was assumed that the sentencing magistrates (usually, of course, a different bench) would take note of what had been achieved. The expression of forgiveness by the victim, in particular, it was felt, weakened the case for the prosecution, making it difficult to impose a harsh sentence unless necessitated by the offender's previous record.

In addition to this study, the Coventry scheme itself tried to monitor its own effects by asking defence solicitors immediately after the hearing whether they thought the sentence had in any way been affected by the offender's involvement in the scheme. This was done for 66 of the 81 cases dealt with in the first year. In the solicitors' opinions, 57% of the total who had at least some involvement received reduced sentences. Whereas 72% of offenders who had taken part in a joint meeting with the victim were seen to have received a reduced sentence, 63% of those involved in indirect negotiation showed no such benefit. In no case was the sentence considered harsher than expected.

In some cases, magistrates made an unsolicited statement in open court about the influence of the reported mediation upon their sentencing decision. In the 18 instances where statements were made and noted in Coventry, 15 concerned offenders who had taken part in joint meetings, and 3 offenders who had participated in indirect mediation. In all these cases the magistrates said they were giving a reduced sentence. Moreover, the Honorary Recorder of the Crown Court has written of the first twelve cases dealt with there *"in all cases...the offenders were confronted with the consequences of their crimes in a far more concrete way than ever before. The principal function of the Scheme's officers was to act as go-betweens and channels of direct communication between victims and offenders. Because they gained the confidence of the victims and the respect of the offenders, the endeavours of the Scheme's officers brought comfort to the former and a real sense of guilt to the latter...the experience for the offenders of being confronted with the effects of their crime in personal terms is uncomfortable. As far as the Crown Court Judges are concerned, the depth of the reports by the reparation officers has provided an insight into the particular offence which neither the Social Enquiry Reports nor the prosecution papers can provide, either severally or jointly. In all cases the reparation reports had a direct relevance to sentencing"*. (Information from Rose Ruddick.)

In relation to the Leeds project, the researchers studied sentencing comments where available and other sentencing data to arrive at the conclusion that about ten to fifteen cases might have been diverted from custody over two years because of mediation. This estimate is twice that made on the basis of the controlled comparison, and at least indicates that the latter has not over-estimated the schemes' effects.

A survey of magistrates' opinions was also carried out by the researchers at both Coventry and Wolverhampton. Just over half of all magistrates in both areas agreed with the statement "The courts should usually deal more leniently with someone who has tried to make amends to the victim". In both areas combined they were split more or less evenly as to whether they agreed or disagreed with the statement that "It is more important for the offender to do a practical job for the victim than to offer an explanation and an apology", with slightly more of the Coventry bench disagreeing and more of the Wolverhampton bench agreeing. This at least shows that a significant number of magistrates are prepared to mitigate sentence even where practical reparation has not taken place. In both areas magistrates generally disagreed that referral to mediation was inadvisable because it created delays, while around three-quarters agreed (many of them strongly) with the statement "Reports from a reparation scheme can help the courts make better sentencing decisions by providing new information".

This survey showed that magistrates generally valued intervention by the schemes, and are prepared to take offenders' attempts at making amends into account. Taken together with all the other evidence, there does seem to be a presumption in favour of the schemes having had a favourable effect on sentencing, especially in those cases which were more successful and had reached a joint victim/offender meeting.

In the case of the Crown Court judges who presided over most of the Leeds cases, only a few were openly supportive, most being sceptical or positively opposed, perhaps due to the fact that they were not involved in the initial planning. Nevertheless, a number made favourable comments in court in relation to the intervention in specific cases. It may be that faced with evidence in an individual case a judge will react more positively to the idea of mediation than when discussing it at a more abstract level. As will be shown in the next section, actual empirical evidence of the scheme tended to lead to more favourable attitudes across all agencies.

Attitudes of Participants

Any experimental scheme of the type studied here depends for its survival on the support of members of the public and of specific agencies who must be willing to participate voluntarily if the work is to be actuated. The results must not only be positive but people must also perceive the idea positively and wish to support it. It is therefore important to obtain not just indices of performance from a detached viewpoint, or from the point of view of the social system as a whole, but to obtain an idea of how clients themselves experienced and rated the schemes (cf. Merry, 1982).

The most important participants in the case of these projects are the victims and the offenders. The fieldwork we carried out placed a substantial emphasis on interviews with both parties after mediation. These interviews were carried out usually some months after the experience. This has the advantage of allowing the parties time for mature reflection — and also time to experience how well any long-term agreements have worked out. Given the emphasis we have found in practice, however, on the immediate emotional experience of a mediation session, it is possible that memories soon begin to fade, or that people will quickly become embarrassed at admitting such feelings, experienced some while ago and now less relevant when the whole business has been put behind them, especially to a researcher arriving out of the blue. Certainly, some people who were quite obviously full of enthusiasm immediately after the mediation gave much cooler, critical, even cynical, accounts later on. It may be in the nature of the experience that with the perspective of time one begins to have doubts about its validity that were not countenanced at the time of involvement.

Despite this problem, surveys of participants' reactions reported by other studies have shown predominantly positive results. Almost all say they would go through it again. With respect to American VORPs, Coates and Gehm (1985) report that 83% of offenders and 59% of victims were very satisfied, a further 30% of victims being 'somewhat' satisfied. It was assessed that parties' perspectives on one another had been improved in a third of cases and their attitudes to the criminal justice system had become more favourable in nearly a half. Victims were more likely to have been happy with the ultimate 'contract' (94% versus 85% of offenders) and were more likely to have felt that they had a substantial input (63% versus 22%). These facts might well reflect a certain 'bias' towards the victim's needs in the American schemes (reflecting the strongly political nature of the victims' 'movement' in that country and in Canada, cf. Rock, 1986). Certainly the incidence of monetary agreements is very high there compared to the outcomes of British experiments in victim/offender negotiation. Such payments can often be quite large, too: nearly half of all offenders, according to Coates and Gehm, had difficulty meeting payback schedules, although in the end 82% of financial contracts were completed as well as 90% of reparative work agreements. Generally it would seem, too, that monetary restitution is preferred to work for the victim (Hudson, Galaway and Novack, 1980).

Completion rates are generally reported to be high. Galaway (1983) quotes 81% completion for the early Elkhart, Indiana, VORP. American juvenile restitution programmes show similar rates: 82% (Schneider and Schneider, 1980; Schneider, 1986) completed in full, with a small number of others completed after the payments were scaled down to a more feasible level; only 1 out of 409 offenders did not complete in Kigin and Novack's (1980) research. The Finnish Vantaa Mediation Project also claims 82% completion (Iivari, 1987). Mediation generally is thought to lead to higher rates of compliance, because the involvement of the parties in formulating the agreement increases their commitment and leaves them with more positive attitudes towards one another, as well as having been more satisfied by this kind of process than by a court appearance (Pearson, 1982). This has been an especially important argument in favour of divorce mediation, given the high rate of breakdown in court-imposed settlements. Generally rates of 60% or higher are quoted for client satisfaction with divorce mediation (60-76% in Irving and Benjamin, 1987, 70-90% in Kressel, 1987, the latter making the point that such a rate of satisfaction is better than that achieved by most professional services). An experiment using randomised allocation of potential clients in Canada (Bahr, 1981) revealed that 25% of them felt 'much better' after taking part in divorce mediation, compared to 9% after going through the normal court process. Pearson and Thoennes (1985) found, in a study of the Denver juvenile restitution project, that 92% of clients were satisfied after achieving an agreement, 61% were even satisfied after failing to do so, while only 46% were satisfied after a court decision without mediation.

British results, to date, are very limited. With respect to completion, Mackay's (1986) report on the early stages of a Scottish pilot scheme showed five agreements completed, two not kept and five more still outstanding, out of 12 agreements monitored. He also interviewed seven victims who had taken part, of whom six said they had found the project helpful, and ten offenders, of whom nine were of the same opinion. In the study of the first years of the South Yorkshire project, Smith, Blagg and Derricourt carried out victim and offender interviews that showed that 10 out of 13 offenders gave a positive account of the experience, but only 9 out of 15 victims. When the victims gave a positive response, it was usually to the effect that it had helped to reduce their fear or anxiety, had revealed the offender as an ordinary human being who was not threatening, had given them a chance to vent their feelings before the person at fault, or, in the case of two cases involving already acquainted parties, had eased the strains in their relationship. Offenders who were positive about it, said that the schemes had helped change their behaviour, that the meeting was a good experience in itself apart from any effect on court sentence, and that it was harder to face up to than appearing in court. Most victims, however, did not only give as their reason for participating the benefits to themselves (usually described as 'curiosity' or a desire to 'tell him what we thought of him'), but also a concern to help the offender or contribute to his/her reform.

A major conclusion of most studies is the need, not only for researchers to explore participants' experiences, but for projects themselves to monitor the agreements they promote and the later satisfaction of the parties, especially the victim (eg Umbreit, 1985). Given the possibility that the experience 'fades' over time, it may be important to give it a boost by showing the victim that they are not forgotten entirely after making the effort to take part. This could overcome the effect, that one or two interviews reported below found, of a victim coming to suspect that he/she had been 'used' by the scheme in order to help the offender rather than out of concern for his/her own feelings and needs. This becomes all the more important when, as in the British schemes, the meeting is the central event and its 'psychological' achievements are often not backed up by any concrete reparation.

Coates and Gehm (1985) found that one major source of victim dissatisfaction with VORPs was "inadequate follow-up", and in describing the Minnesota VORP Galaway (1985) lays great stress on the fact that all agreements are monitored either by the scheme or by the probation service, and that all victims are contacted again later by the project to check that they still feel satisfied. Regular follow-up is also mentioned in connection with the Finnish Vantaa Project (Iivari, 1987). Mackay (1986) reinforces the importance of projects themselves monitoring outcomes from his Scottish experience.

As far as the attitudes of the general public or social agencies go, there is little reported in the literature. Schneider (1986), however, did show that members of the judiciary were overwhelmingly supportive from their experience of juvenile restitution projects.

Police-based Projects
There was hardly any follow-up of cases in any of these projects carried out by the mediators themselves. While monitoring of the longer-term outcomes may consume valuable time and resources, its importance makes such a cost well worth bearing. Without such regular information, it will be impossible for schemes to develop in the most productive way, for the ultimate effects of what they do will remain unknown. The primacy of avoiding juvenile prosecutions which runs across all these projects no doubt contributes to this oversight.

The only evidence we have, therefore, comes from research interviews carried out in relation to the Cumbria panels. Given the complexity of contacting victims, and especially offenders, and arranging mutually suitable times to visit, and also the widely scattered communities dealt with in such a rural area, the number of interviews achieved was not as substantial as one might have liked, but was as large as possible in the time available. (Quite often a researcher would drive a hundred miles for an appointment, only to find the person had 'forgotten' about it and was out.)

Thirty-three full interviews were completed with victims and forty-five with offenders in the East and West regions, about half the number originally contacted. Those refusing interviews gave as their main reasons (victims) that there was nothing to discuss or they preferred to forget the incident, or (offenders' parents) that their children might be upset by having the matter resurrected. A few did not respond to letters or telephone messages at all. It is likely, therefore, that the sample was biased towards those who felt more positively about the scheme — or at any rate felt something strongly enough to want to communicate it. The sample also concentrates on those who met the other party, all of the offenders and all but one of the victims interviewed having taken part in direct mediation. The fact that those who did not have this experience were more likely to refuse to give an interview may in itself tell us something about the relative worth of indirect and direct mediation as far as the parties are concerned. Accounts from offenders were broadly positive in their evaluation of reparation, but those of victims were more critical.

A striking feature of victims' accounts was the social concern that motivated most of those who gave positive accounts. In several cases this was enhanced by an imaginative sympathy with the offender's experience and by a feeling that "*it could have been my own son (or daughter)*". For instance, a couple who suffered a break-in to their caravan which entailed considerable damage said that they had agreed to a meeting because they had been involved in the Scout movement and felt a general sense of social responsibility towards young people. They were "*used to young boys*" and felt no anxiety about the prospect of a meeting, although they were sufficiently affected by the offence to feel they could not use the caravan again. They were in sympathy with the idea of diversion and even felt frustrated that there was nothing more concrete they could do. They considered a suggestion of practical reparation (digging their garden) but rejected this on the grounds that a face-to-face discussion might have a more telling effect.

A similar concern appeared in an account given by a priest, from whose church collection box money had been stolen. He said he had spent 15 years in youth work and *"had done this sort of thing off my own bat"*. The encounter itself had been brief: *"There was not a lot more he could say after he'd said his piece...he'd obviously been briefed on what to say, and it was brief...It wasn't in any sense a confrontation, he didn't have an awful lot to apologise about...It was low-key, but the point was made — low-key because I wasn't the irate victim...It was difficult to feel very aggrieved."* He thought the scheme *"better than a caution because it takes it one stage further...it brings home that there's someone on the other end of this. Especially in a close-knit community like this, it could have a fair amount of deterrent value...yet it doesn't have the notoriety of a court case. There's nothing glamorous about being taken round to apologise to your neighbour."* He illustrated the point about the close-knit community and the feasibility of dealing with offences informally with an anecdote. A fence had been erected round a clinic on the estate by a YTS group. It looked as if it would not stay up and one night two girls decided to prove it would not. The police were informed, but one of the girls' mothers went to the clinic and offered compensation, which was accepted. *"So while the police couldn't do anything it was sorted out behind their backs. Nobody wants to get their neighbours into trouble."*

A similar sense of wanting to help was conveyed by a licensee of a public house which was a frequent target for burglary. His wife was very much opposed to the idea of meeting the offenders in the latest incident, but he had gone ahead on his own. He received some compensation at the meeting and felt he had *"got through"* to one of the two boys. He felt that the fact they had come to face him showed they were not all bad, and then he found them *"quite ordinary-looking"*. One of them later came in for a drink, but was ordered out, significantly by his wife — he himself said he would not have recognised them. This case seems to show that possibilities for reconciliation existed but that the refusal of one party to take part prevented full realisation of them.

176

More personal factors could inform victims' responses. A mother of three teenagers, one of whom had had a bicycle stolen, thought that *"the boot could be on the other foot"* when the reparation worker proposed a meeting; she had been *"mad at first, but when you sit down and think about it, these things happen"*. If it happened to her own children she hoped someone would be prepared to give them a chance. *"With teenagers you can't condemn anybody's because you never know about your own."* The two offenders she met both lived nearby, one a school contemporary of her eldest daughter. Both paid quite substantial sums in compensation when they came, and the reparation worker had visited only a week before the interview with their final instalment — a surprise to the victim, since she had forgotten about the money, which was unimportant because the cycle had been insured. The reparation worker had, however, suggested that to pay their share of the value of the cycle would nevertheless *"teach them a lesson"*.

Some accounts from victims were predominantly negative. In one of these, the parties had not met and the issue for the victims was simply the payment of compensation. The case illustrates the problems that may arise when the scheme becomes nothing more than a debt-enforcement agency. *"If I hadn't gone and sat in the probation office they wouldn't have pressed the boys for payment...It's no deterrent whatsoever...nobody seemed to think they should do anything to pay for the loss and damage...They're too soft with them life's not like that They pat them on the head and say, Good boy It's too airy-fairy we were rather disgusted with the whole thing."* In some of these cases victims had been misled into higher expectations of compensation than the scheme could actually guarantee. Victims who expressed the most satisfaction with the scheme tended to be those where there has been a direct meeting and where financial reparation was of less importance to them.

In another case two boys who had assaulted a third came to an isolated farm to make their apologies. At the time the meeting had gone well enough, but on reflection the victim's parents wished that the meeting had taken place elsewhere. In an isolated rural situation they felt vulnerable to burglary and possible revenge, although nothing of this sort had in fact occurred.

Other victims were suspicious that the apology they had received had been insincere — a problem that might have been less prominent if the mediation had been more substantial and revealing, although this uncertainty permeated some of the court-based cases as well, where mediation tended to be more intensive. A special problem arose in multi-offender cases, where the offender taking part in reparation was usually the least implicated, while the leading offender did not take part because he or she was being prosecuted. To the victim it would then often seem that the lesser offender was being unfairly put upon and the other 'getting away with it'.

Generally, and not surprisingly considering their age (the youngest interviewed was only twelve), the offenders gave less fluent and elaborate accounts than the victims. Some seemed to have been very unclear about what was happening. One boy, who had previously been cautioned, got the impression from the reparation worker that he would be prosecuted if did not agree to the meeting. He said he was "*not really bothered*" about going for a predictable telling-off, it was better than going to court. Neither he nor his mother were sure it had done him any good, although he had not been in trouble since.

Other offenders, too, had gained the impression that they would at least improve their chances of being cautioned if they agreed to meet the victim. This was true of one of the boys who broke into the caravan mentioned above. He had a relatively serious criminal record (and a very disrupted home life) and he thought he might go to court if he did not agree when his probation officer suggested a meeting, though she did not actually say so. He was nervous before the meeting but become less so during it, since it did not entail the expected 'telling off'. Like other offenders he seemed to have said little: it was the victims who did the talking. He said he was glad he agreed to go because it helped him to get a caution; but after some thought, added that he had felt he ought to apologise, and would probably have gone even if he had already been cautioned; he was glad to have the chance to say sorry.

A drunk who had broken a fence had also been unclear whether he was going to be prosecuted or cautioned. He admitted to being "*a bit scared at first*" at meeting the victim, "*but it was worth it in the long run. She was a nice woman...but I wouldn't go through it again...I thought it was my bit to do it, I thought I had to really, because it was pretty nasty, breaking her fence...It should be done more often, it's better than going to court. It scares you a bit, checks you a bit, but gives you another chance.*" Despite this relatively positive experience he had been in trouble twice since — what he called "*daft things*".

One girl met the owner of a shop from which she had stolen clothing. Initially expecting to be prosecuted, the reparation worker came and said that she would not be, and it was clear to her and her father — though not her mother — that this was not conditional upon her agreement to a meeting. She agreed because "*It just seemed the right thing to do, really.*" She and her friend had been thinking they might go back to the shop anyway, and the reparation worker's suggestion gave them the opportunity. The meeting, however, was not a success. After she had apologised, the owner of the shop began by saying "*Oh, I thought it would be you*" and began to shout abuse, saying "*You'll never be a mother, you'll never get a nice fellow. Look at your hair, it's all wet.*" She threatened to call the police if she ever entered the shop again. The reparation worker had had to withdraw the girl from the meeting. "The latter said she had "*tried to forget*" the experience and felt that if she was a victim she would be prepared to meet the offender, but not to shout at them. She considered that the shopkeeper was preoccupied with shoplifting, and "*would not have minded if she'd just shouted about the stealing*" without the personal abuse. Nevertheless, she approved of the idea in principal: "*It's harder to go up to someone and say, I'm sorry, say you did wrong and all that.*"

Perhaps the most noteworthy point about this case is that it is apparently so exceptional. It seems likely that most victims who might have reacted in the style of this shop owner refused the offer of a meeting. It raises the dilemma for practice, in that even if the worker had realised the shop owner was so angry she could not easily have refused to arrange a meeting when the victim had expressed willingness.

Overall the interviews suggested that the majority of victims (at least those who had met their offenders) expressed some satisfaction with the experience, though a significant minority did not. Their views overall were less positive than those of offenders. Victims who expressed dissatisfaction spoke variously of having had high expectations of compensation, sometimes encouraged by the police, which are unrealistic given the nature of the project; of feeling they were being asked to do something for the offender rather than vice versa and resenting this; of feeling that they were not kept informed of the progress of events; and of fearing that the attitude of offenders had been exploitative or cynical. Victims who expressed satisfaction did so largely in terms of feeling that they had an opportunity to do something useful — helping to keep young people out of the criminal justice system. They tended to be people with a sense of social responsibility, sometimes sharpened by a feeling that if their own children were in trouble they hoped that they would similarly be given a chance. Victims who took this view did not mind being 'used' — they welcomed it as an opportunity to contribute. They were not interested in compensation, or were satisfied with a token amount. Victims who were primarily concerned with compensation were less likely to be satisfied, because it took so long to be paid or it was never paid in full. There were few cases in which victims felt that meeting the offender resolved a sense of hurt or anxiety associated with the offence; this was mainly because the project dealt on the whole with minor offences which had not aroused much sense of personal victimisation. Some victims did, however, report relief on knowing that the offence had been committed by juveniles rather than hardened criminals; and for some, among them a teacher who was going to have to continue teaching the offender, the meeting was a useful way of clearing the air; they could put the matter behind them after an apology had been offered and accepted.

For offenders the experience of reparation, whether or not it entailed meeting the victim, was intimately tied up with their feelings of relief at avoiding prosecution; they sometimes had unrealistic ideas about the severity of sentence they might have received. By no means all were clear that they would not be prosecuted anyway; some had picked up a message, whether conveyed intentionally or not, that they would only be cautioned if they agreed some sort of reparation. Their feelings about meeting their victims were usually anxiety beforehand and relief afterwards — that they had not been shouted at or bullied as they had feared (with the one exception described above). Some offenders, despite knowing they were going to be cautioned, wanted to apologise to the victim in any case, because it seemed the right thing to do; the idea has a wide intuitive appeal, and the project provided a structure which made it possible to put the idea into practice. In the meetings themselves, which were very brief, the offenders were usually passive participants, but some — generally the older ones — did report feeling better because they had apologised for something they considered wrong. Negative feelings expressed by offenders were sometimes based on unrealistic expectations that the project would somehow keep them out of trouble in future, or arose from resentment at the demand for compensation. The parents of offenders, however, were overwhelmingly in favour of the idea of reparation, and it may be that the project brought benefits to them of an unanticipated kind, by reinforcing the moral message they had wanted to convey.

Court-based schemes

The Leeds scheme helped to arrange several episodes of reparative work or compensation by instalments, and was therefore often involved in post-mediation contact with victims and offenders in order to supervise the arrangements, but apart from this the schemes rarely carried out any follow-up visits (or telephone calls) with either party. As most of the reparative agreements involved small amounts of money or time (see above), they were usually carried out immediately, so that the question of supervision rarely arose. Nevertheless, it would have been useful to have had some systematic feedback on clients' later attitudes and feelings. As it is we have to rely on samples of parties interviewed by the researchers, as we did in relation to the police-based schemes.

Coventry and Wolverhampton

The fieldwork in relation to the two West Midlands schemes included interviews with a sample of cases referred during the first 9 months (September 1985 to June 1986) and during the first 3 months of 1987.

Only those cases that had reached direct mediation were included, because it was felt that these clients had participated most fully and were likely both to be better informed and to have more considered views than others. No victims refused interview, but two could not be contacted and one was excluded because she had been previously interviewed for a television programme. In total 33 victims were interviewed in Coventry and 27 in Wolverhampton. Three offenders refused interviews, and 35 could not be contacted. Thus fewer offenders were interviewed, 19 at Coventry and 23 at Wolverhampton. Of those eligible, the victims interviewed represented 92% at Coventry and 100% at Wolverhampton; the offenders represented 43% at Coventry and 64% at Wolverhampton.

(a) Offender interviews

Offenders were asked who had first suggested they take part. In both areas defence solicitors had been active in introducing offenders — almost half in Coventry and just over a quarter at Wolverhampton. Almost all the remaining offenders said they had been approached directly by project workers, usually at court. One Wolverhampton offender made the approach himself, having heard of the scheme through a friend who had participated. He was the only one who had any prior knowledge of the scheme.

Recollecting their initial briefings by the project workers, three-quarters said that they had understood that the schemes aimed to bring victims and offenders together in a face-to-face meeting. Only a few remembered being told they would be given a chance to make practical reparation. 16% at Coventry and 22% at Wolverhampton said they were told that participation might help them in court, and about a third saw the schemes as being mainly to help the offender. They were outnumbered, however, by those who thought that both parties were intended to benefit equally (58% in Coventry and 43% in Wolverhampton). Very few (about 10%) thought the victim might be the principal beneficiary.

Asked their reasons for taking part, the majority of Wolverhampton offenders (57% of the total) said this was in order to get their sentence reduced. Predominantly these offenders felt that their choice in the matter was limited by the vulnerability of their position before the court. Experience had taught that it was usually wise to go along with 'official' suggestions. To quote the mother of one juvenile offender in Wolverhampton:

"I don't think he had much choice, did he? No, because if we hadn't have took part it would have gone bad things against him at court so we went along with anything that was offered to us. [Their solicitor] said best to do what they want you to do and it all makes it look, you know, better for him, so we went along with everything...If they [the court] thought he'd been co-operating they'd be more lenient with him but then if they thought he had a no care attitude or that we weren't bothered, well then it might not go off so easy."

Mitigation was given as a reason for only 16% of those at Coventry. About a third in both areas gave 'communication with an unknown victim' as the reason, while a number at Coventry also mentioned 'reconciliation with a known victim' and 'easing their conscience'. Practical reparation hardly featured as a reason (one offender only).

Even if it might seem prudent to take part for one's own good, it did seem that many offenders had already felt some regrets about their offences. A majority reported feeling uncomfortable about it soon after the offence. Most described it as 'spur of the moment' with no obvious motive and many claimed drink as a factor. Once the effects of drink and excitement began to wear off, many had begun to think about what they had done and to feel foolish. Occasionally there was a reaction of profound depression. Those who had had a close personal relationship with the victim before the offence had more complex feelings, the incident in question belonging to an accumulated history of grievances and disagreements. In such cases feelings of guilt were often tinged with a sense of satisfaction.

Less often had they apparently made the imaginative leap from thinking about their offence to considering the plight of their victim, especially at Wolverhampton where only 26% claimed to have thought about this before the scheme intervened. At Coventry 58% claimed to have done so, however. In preparing for the meeting, the victim became the focus of feelings of nervousness and embarrassment for nearly all of them, heightened by uncertainty about how the victim would react — whether or not they were previously acquainted. More of the Coventry offenders said that they had discussed such feelings with the project workers before the meeting than did those at Wolverhampton. Pre-meeting discussions were usually organised, at both projects, around the background to the incident (more often explored at Coventry than at the other scheme), a plan for the meeting itself, and consideration of practical reparation (more often at Wolverhampton). The plan for the meeting was the most frequent topic addressed in both schemes, not only practical details but contents as well: "*I was given quite a bit of guidance...but she always said that she wasn't telling me what to say — that would always be my decision and I had to work it out for myself*" (Coventry offender).

Most offenders looked forward to the joint meeting as an opportunity to achieve an understanding with their victim. They perceived is as a self-contained event rather than as a means to an extraneous goal. In other words they tended to be more concerned with the process of the meeting than with any practical outcome. A sizeable minority hoped the meeting would enable both parties to air their views and feelings, but it was rather more common for the offenders to see the meeting as a setting for their own explanation and apology, the emphasis more on a one-sided contribution by offender to victim. Few anticipated that the meeting would give primary emphasis to the victim's view of the offence.

The opportunity to make practical reparation hardly featured at all in offenders' hopes of the meeting, and comparatively few said that the meeting was designed to attract a reduced sentence. This might be a prime reason for taking part in the scheme in the first place, but it was not seen as the purpose of the meeting. At least temporarily, the prospect of facing their victim concentrated offenders' attention upon problems of communication — "*What shall I say to the victim?*" — rather than "*What do I get out of taking part?*".

Despite the range of expectations, descriptions by offenders of the actual meeting were remarkably consistent. They were usually structured around three key events, in varying order: the apology, the victim's account of the distress and inconvenience caused, and the offender's explanation of how it occurred. For offenders who had given little attention at the time of the offence to the consequences for the victim, the meeting therefore introduced important new information. The change in perception this could bring about is illustrated by one of the Coventry offenders who had, he claimed, taken part merely out of curiosity:—

"We all just sat down and started talking about why it happened. It was a spur of the moment job...we explained all this to her. We said we had no intention to do the robbery because we had no tools on us and she agreed to that part...She said you should think of your family and all that as well as committing crime...she said it weren't just her. It was the family being called at that time of night plus the work with trying to find call-outs to fix the place up...We both felt very guilty over that. She accepted everything what we was telling her and said 'I don't think you'll be doing it again' and from then I haven't done anything yet, touch wood...Since that meeting I've took different views about it. I think 'What should I go out and commit crime for?' because I've seen what it done, the damage. It's not just doing the crime, you have a part in it afterwards."

Most offenders described their offences as opportunistic and many appeared to believe this somehow diminished their culpability. What offenders like the one above were learning through the encounter was that an offence like burglary causes damage, distress and inconvenience to the victim whatever the motivation.

Offenders against public institutions and businesses were also confronted with the human consequences of an act committed against an apparently impersonal victim: *"I was getting really bad, nervous, because he was saying all what I'd caused damage and it was really getting to me then and I realised how extensive the damage was. It wasn't just the windows. It had upset the whole work and upset it for a few weeks...It was all hitting me like a sudden shock, realising the extent of everything"* (Wolverhampton offender).

The evidence from these interviews suggests that there are ritualistic elements to the encounter — the 'expected' apology and explanation — but that, once confronted with their victims, offenders are required to consider the consequences of what they have done. Not all offenders benefit from this, or will change their behaviour as a result, but it does seem that the mediation session opens a window through which offenders can view their behaviour from a new perspective, which may have a radical impact upon some.

A surprising aspect for most offenders was the sympathy and understanding offered by their victims. Almost all considered that their victims had been either reasonable or demonstrably sympathetic and had accepted their explanation and apology. The very 'niceness' of the victim could add to the embarrassment (*"That made me feel a little bit worse actually, you know, the fact that he wasn't angry"*). It seems that an atmosphere of acceptance is essential, in fact, if an offender is to be enabled to reflect constructively upon the information given by the victim. If the victim openly challenges the offender's credibility and sincerity, the latter is likely to be forced on the defensive, trying to excuse rather than take responsibility for the action. Very few meetings, however, seemed to have been hostile, just as was found in relation to the Cumbria scheme. One meeting at Wolverhampton had escalated into a row which had to be stopped by the mediators and the offender physically restrained, but this was a rare exception, where the victim had himself been threatening. Only three offenders interviewed had met any hostility of this kind.

It may be argued that victims have every right to be sceptical and hostile, and this points to one of the critical dilemmas for a mediation service trying to benefit both parties at once. A distressed victim may have a real need to vent hostile feelings — how is this to be balanced against the offender's need to learn something useful from the encounter? When such cases are encountered, much more time is needed, and perhaps greater mediation skill, to be able to work through the passionate phase of the meeting to a more constructive one, a process which, after all, is very familiar to family mediators dealing with divorcing parties, and one which can be controlled.

In no case did the question of negotiating practical reparation appear to be a central concern during the meeting. An offer did not usually come until near the end, and if at all, was most likely to be used as a token to confirm the understanding. Usually, however, an offer of practical help was turned down by the victim.

Almost all the offenders said they had been glad they met their victims. They identified two main kinds of benefit: achievement of an understanding with the victim and changes in their inner feelings and outlook. By the end of the meeting concern with mitigation had almost disappeared. At Wolverhampton only 17% gave this as one of the benefits of meeting (compared to 57% who gave it as the reason for first taking part), and at Coventry only 11% identified this as a benefit. This suggests that offenders' original motives may be challenged and changed through mediation. For the offenders who had known their victims, the offence had become a barrier to resuming a normal relationship. In several cases they had been in regular touch but unable to discuss the impact of the offence on their relationship until the meeting provided a safe setting for dealing with its consequences.

The easing of a sense of guilt was an important theme. A sense of being understood and forgiven by the person who had suffered the offence was seen by several interviewees as an important step back to self-respect. Occasionally mediation was even followed by more concrete offers from the victim (eg of permanent employment) that might bring the offender even further back into the community, as in one of the Wolverhampton cases: "*I have benefited from it. He has talked to me not just about my offence but he has talked to me about my future as well, what I'm going to do with my life, what I want to do. And it's really put me at rest.*" Many reported new perspectives on themselves and that meeting the victim 'made them think'. The impact of such a personal encounter seems to stand in sharp contrast to the formality and artificiality of the criminal justice process.

(b) Victim interviews

'Corporate' victims made up 45% of the Coventry and 63% of the Wolverhampton samples, interviews being held with representatives of those bodies. None in either city had been in contact with victims support schemes. Most (over 80%) had been informed already by the police that an offender had been apprehended.

They were generally appreciative of the open and tactful way they had been approached by the project workers, and explanations of what the scheme was about were usually full and clear: "*I was in no doubt as to what it constituted by the time I had agreed to take part in it*" (Coventry victim). Almost half had even heard about their local scheme before being contacted, usually from the mass media (not that all the schemes received the same amount of local attention — most of those interviewed at Leeds had never heard of the scheme before being approached by the mediator, despite reasonably wide coverage in the local media). Around 60% of them had formed a positive view about it while others were originally more cynical. The aims as they saw them were varied, although the predominant response referred to the idea of bringing victims and offenders together in a face-to-face meeting. Apology, reparation or reconciliation were mentioned only by 14 or 15%.

Quite a few victims felt their scheme was run mainly to help the offender, especially at Coventry (42%, as against 30% at Wolverhampton). Similar proportions (36% at Coventry, 41% at Wolverhampton) thought that both parties benefited equally. Only around 10% saw the victim as principal beneficiary. Many, indeed, did not see themselves particularly as 'victims' anyway, especially among the corporate representatives. These people were more likely to see themselves as acting for the general public good by helping to reform or deter the offender.

Most victims had made a considered decision to take part. The predominant reason given in both areas was a sense of social responsibility: "*...being hopefully a good citizen, I said I would agree to assist the scheme*" (Coventry victim). Some of these identified with the offenders' parents; "*If I'd got children their age [18-20], I'd think it was only fair that someone should sit and listen to what they'd got to say*" (Coventry victim). Another frequent reason was based on sympathy with the schemes' aims and philosophy.

Together the two categories above accounted for 39% and 49% respectively of the Coventry and Wolverhampton victims. The higher figure at Wolverhampton is probably due to the predominance of corporate victims there. Other victims gave less altruistic responses, 'curiosity' being a particularly prevalent reason — especially what the offenders might be like or why they had committed the offence. To some a joint meeting offered an opportunity for reconciliation. Expectation of reparation or an apology accounted for only small numbers. Some were sceptical of the idea but went along with it because it did not seem that it could do any harm. Only two mentioned feeling under any pressure to agree to participate, and these were both corporate victims.

Feelings before the meeting were more or less evenly spread between eagerness or curiosity, some anxiety, and ambivalence or unconcern. Altogether, 30% were apprehensive, although most of these acknowledged that their reservations had been addressed in discussions with project staff. About two-thirds of all the victims remembered some kind of preparatory talk with the scheme before meeting the offender. In about half the Coventry cases, but only a third of the Wolverhampton ones, the conversation turned on the feelings of the victim in anticipation of the encounter; in the remainder the main topic was either practical or factual. Two victims in Coventry claimed they had never even met a representative of the scheme until the meeting with the offender. There may, therefore, be some victims who might benefit from more preparation but are not at present getting the opportunity. At least there should be one prior interview to assess whether a victim is suitable or a meeting appropriate.

Whereas offenders were found to be more concerned with the process of the meeting, victims were more concerned with its outcome — its potential for deterrence, reconciliation, or reparation. The deterrent effect was the most frequently quoted purpose of the meeting by victims, although almost as many saw it chiefly as a chance to hear the offender's explanation and to receive an apology. Mitigation of sentence for the offender was identified as the purpose in only two cases (both at Wolverhampton).

Describing their experience of the meeting, most victims concentrated on the offender's contribution, but many had over-estimated offenders' verbal skills and had had to make more of a contribution themselves than they had anticipated. Most felt the meeting had gone roughly as they had anticipated, and in all those cases where this was not so the results had surpassed their expectations, not disappointed them. The reception of an apology could be surprisingly affecting; "*I was very happy that he did apologise because some people...when you say to a child 'Now apologise', they refuse to do it, but he didn't refuse and he did say it and he was quite genuine about it...It was a surprise to see a person apologise because it's very hard*" (Coventry victim).

The mediator's handling of the meeting was usually seen as impartial and described in complimentary terms. Generally the mediator was regarded as a neutral figure who introduced the meeting and then withdrew to the sidelines, only intervening when necessary. As one Coventry victim described it: "*He just remained silent. He just let [the offender] and I talk it out amongst ourselves...I think that by remaining out of it he just established quite clearly that he was neutral and that he was not influencing me against [the offender] or [the offender] against me...But I think although he remained neutral he was in control of the situation, yes.*"

Offers of reparation were usually remembered, although only a third were accepted at Coventry, slightly more than half at Wolverhampton (a difference which again may be accounted for by the different proportion of corporate victims in each case). Reparation was remembered far more than just an apology, so that not everyone was as impressed by the latter as the victim quoted above. The main reason for turning down offers of reparation was difficulty in deciding on a suitable task. Others were averse to the idea of someone working for no financial reward. A concern common to both corporate and private victims, moreover, was the question of security if the offender were to be given access to their premises. If one weighs up the potential benefit to victims of what is perceived as a token act against the further investment of time and the security risk reparation may involve, it is not surprising that a substantial proportion will decline the offer.

Most felt that the idea of apologising or making reparation was a matter of the offender's own initiative, although in fact such an idea had normally been suggested to the offender by the scheme. If victims had realised this, they may have had a different picture of the meeting, as did one Coventry victim: "*The impression I got was that it was he who wanted to come round and apologise, not that it was the scheme. I didn't know that till afterwards, I mean it was actually suggested to him that he goes round and apologise. I didn't know that.*" To this victim, the sincerity of the apology was obviously compromised by the fact that it was not originally the offender's idea. Most of those interviewed did, however, feel the apologies were sincere, especially at the time, although some were more cynical in retrospect: "*I was glad to receive an apology. Whether it was meant or not, of course I couldn't tell*" (Wolverhampton victim).

The majority of victims who had some definite feelings towards the offence or the offender said that they were able to express these in the joint meeting. At the time of the offence itself, almost half had felt angry, others shocked or depressed or left feeling foolish. By the time of the interview virtually all of them felt less strongly or were not concerned at all any more. Such feelings are likely to diminish over time, but about half said that the scheme had been helpful in this respect. Asked what it was about the scheme that had proven most valuable; 37% focused on the meeting: "*...Just meeting the fellow and realising that he was another human being the same as I was with his own problems, and really that his problems were indirectly the cause of what happened...that was the most valuable thing as far as I was concerned — just physically meeting the guy*" (Coventry victim). This reinforces the growing conviction among staff at both schemes that mediation has intrinsic value per se. Other victims concentrated on the benefits derived: 17% referred to reconciliation, 13% to the insight gained into the problems and motivations of offenders, 10% to the apology or other reparation. Asked if they would have been happy to have the meeting only, without the apology or reparation, however, two-thirds felt this would not have been sufficient. Similarly, the idea of apology or reparation without meeting was rejected by 65% as inadequate. The combination of the two aspects is therefore what seems to make the experience valuable, and sufficiently so for over 80% of all victims interviewed to recommend that the facility of mediation and reparation should be made available to other victims of offences like theirs, as long as the final decision to proceed should rest with the victim.

Whether the victims were corporate or not made little difference to these judgements, about half of both the corporate and the private ones had found the experience helpful, although corporate victims were more likely to stress the meeting in its own right, private victims the reconciliation that ensued. In general corporate victims experience more frequent criminal damage and petty theft, and it may be therefore that the meeting serves as an outlet for a build-up of emotions stemming from a series of crimes committed in the past. The meeting is likely to be more constructive and more memorable as a result. Reparation also appeared to be more relevant to corporate victims than to others.

Many victims felt that there had been some impact upon the offender's attitudes, often attributing this to their own efforts. Some felt that their offenders had benefited from a mitigated sentence as a result, but several nevertheless felt sympathetic towards them because of their circumstances or youth. Some were pleased that they were receiving support and guidance through their involvement in the schemes, and that they would benefit from receiving the message that 'society cares'.

Victims generally did not feel competent to comment on court decisions, and were not anxious to have a say in sentencing. Just over 40% did, however, consider the sentence their offender had been given as fair, while a smaller number (21% in Coventry, 26% in Wolverhampton) considered it unfair. The latter were equally divided between those who saw it as excessively harsh and those who thought it too lenient. Such assessments by the victim were based on the nature and severity of the offence, with little consideration given to the offender's participation in mediation. Therefore the victims did not appear to feel that such participation should influence sentence. While some were prepared to accept mitigation as a result of their involvement, a few felt they had been misled about the scheme's intentions and, to an extent, exploited.

When doubts are formed either about the offender's motivation (and implicitly the sincerity of any apology) or about subsequent incidents, including any apparent mitigation of sentence, these doubts are difficult to dispel. It is likely that follow-up discussion or counselling by the schemes would help victims cope with any such uncertainty. In addition, some victims would have appreciated more information about what happened to the offender after sentence. Many had clearly invested a great deal of time and interest in the scheme — at times to the extent of offering long-term friendship and help to the offender — and several were anxious about the offender's well-being, or wanted to know whether they had kept out of trouble since the meeting.

Any policy to follow-up cases on a regular basis would run into problems — how to monitor offenders' subsequent careers, the issue of confidentiality in sharing information with the victim, the implications of passing on negative news, and how long the scheme should keep in touch with former clients, for instance. But certainly it seems that victims are likely to benefit from at least one 'debriefing' session, whether immediately after the meeting or delayed until the court has passed sentence. 22% of victims in Coventry and 15% in Wolverhampton identified issues which they considered unresolved at the time of their research interviews,

(c) Attitudes of Criminal Justice Agencies
Given the current reliance of the mediation schemes on criminal justice agencies for referrals, the attitudes of sentencers, police, probation officers and defence solicitors are obviously crucial to success. Questionnaires were therefore sent to all magistrates, justices' clerks, main grade and senior probation officers, all defence solicitors on the courts' duty rosters, and a sample of police inspectors. Of 566 sent out, 373 (66%) were returned. No one group in either city fell below 50% response rate. Everyone who replied had heard of the scheme, except for a very small number of the police officers. Over half had even had some dealings with the schemes.

38% expressed a favourable attitude to the schemes, while only 9% said they were unfavourable, 8% not having enough information to form a view. This leaves a large middle ground of 'court users' (44%) who had mixed views. Direct personal contact with the schemes increased the chances of forming a favourable opinion — 47% of those with such contact indicating positive attitudes, against 25% of those without. Even among this more favourable group, however, there were still 40% who expressed some ambivalence, so that the schemes would still seem to have some way to go in persuading local professional opinion.

Whether favourable or not, most respondents saw the primary purpose of mediation and reparation to be the provision of help to the victim, and a large majority (78%) of both groups thought that the schemes should continue. The difference between the two groups lay in whether they thought the schemes were achieving what they should. 82% of the favourable saw the schemes as promoting the victim's recovery, as against 48% of the doubters. 79% of the first group saw their work as an effective deterrent, compared with 47% of the others.

Support for the schemes was strongest amongst defence solicitors and probation staff in both areas, and among justices' clerks at Wolverhampton only. Support was weakest among the police in both areas and justices' clerks at Coventry. There were, in fact, more unfavourable than favourable responses from both these agencies in Coventry. Magistrates' views ranged in between in both cities.

On more specific attitude items, it was found that:

- court users broadly share the schemes' view that mediation and reparation should be widely available as an option for dealing with offenders;

- court users broadly share the schemes' view that meeting the victim is not an easy way out for an offender, although the justices' clerks are less convinced than others;

- court users are divided in their views about the relative importance of communication between victim and offender and practical reparation — the police and magistrates were the most likely to emphasise the importance of reparation, while the schemes themselves would strongly emphasise the mediation itself;

- defence solicitors, justices' clerks and probation officers are broadly in line with the schemes in their acceptance of mediation for crimes of violence, but magistrates and, to a lesser extent, the police were opposed to this;

- most court users are inclined to share the schemes' view that they may have a deterrent effect, but are more cautious or uncertain;

- most court users strongly endorse the schemes' view that the needs of the victim are paramount, but probation respondents were ambivalent on this question.

Leeds

Interviews were carried out with 43 victims and 39 offenders (reparation sample) who had participated in direct mediation, and with 149 others who had not done so (71 victims and 78 offenders), matched as far as possible for area of residence, offence and sentence (control sample). As always, such matching is inevitably far from perfect, but it does enable one to compare the response of participants with a roughly similar group that have not had the same experience.

(a) Injury and harm suffered by victims

Offenders generally rated the level of injury or harm done to their victims as less serious than did the victims themselves. However, those offenders who had been through the reparation project, and in most cases met their victim, rated the level of injury or harm as more serious than did the control group offenders. 32% of offenders in the reparation sample viewed their victims' suffering as moderate or severe compared to 17% of the control group offenders. This difference may be an artefact of the selection process of cases for the reparation project — offenders who recognised the harm done to their victims may have been seen as suitable cases for referral. However, given what we know about the referral process this seems unlikely to account for the difference. It seems much more likely, therefore, that the experience of going through mediation, and especially meeting their victims, did make the offenders more conscious of the harm they had done. The majority (56%) of victims who met their offender in a mediation session reported that they did not feel any different about the offence as a result of the meeting. Indeed only 39% said the meeting had made any difference to such feeling. 15% of victims who had experienced mediation and reparation felt that the meeting had achieved nothing, 22% said that it had helped relieve their worries about the offence, while 60% gave other reasons why they felt the meeting had been valuable — including the possibility of reforming the offender. It does seem, therefore, that the great majority of victims did believe that some good came out of their meeting with the offenders. Similarly, a majority of the offenders who had met their victims also felt that the mediation session had achieved something useful.

(b) The sentence as viewed by victims

Reparation project victims who met their offender in mediation were more satisfied with the sentence passed on the offender than the control group victims. Control group victims who were not satisfied with the sentence generally felt that the sentence was too lenient, whereas the reparation sample victims who were dissatisfied were so for a wider variety of reasons including the absence of a compensation order.

Although the numbers of respondents to the relevant question were small it does seem that where compensation was ordered by the court, reparation sample victims were more likely to be satisfied with the amount. Where compensation was not ordered by the court, 60% of control group victims thought it should have been, compared with 38% of the reparation sample.

40% of reparation sample victims stated that the compensation would be a sufficient sentence for their offenders, in contrast to 13% of control group victims. The converse of this is that 48% of control group victims definitely felt their offender should go to prison, whilst 10% of the reparation sample felt this. Mediation clearly affects victims' punitiveness towards their offenders, and leads them to be more satisfied with less severe sentencing. However, 53% of reparation sample victims and 27% of control sample victims thought sentencing was inconsistent. All this seems to suggest that the experience of mediation significantly affects victims' punitiveness towards their offender, but less so towards offenders in general, although reparation sample victims were more likely to end up believing that sentencing was inconsistent.

The sentence as viewed by offenders

Reparation project offenders, who attended a mediation session, were slightly more able to predict their sentence and were more satisfied by their treatment by the court than were the control group offenders. Furthermore, if the sentence passed was not what the offender expected, then reparation group offenders generally felt it was less harsh than expected, whereas control group offenders were equally divided between those who felt the sentence was too harsh and those who felt it was less severe than expected. 65% of the reparation offenders who did not receive the sentence expected thought it was less harsh than expected, while 45% of the control group thought their sentence less harsh and 43% thought it harsher than expected.

86% of the reparation group said that they were satisfied that they received fair treatment from the court, as compared to 59% of the control group. Although the difference in the degree of satisfaction may be due to the differential ability to predict sentence, it cannot entirely account for it, since the majority of both groups did not receive the sentence expected (70% of reparation group, 80% of control group).

(d) Ascription of responsibility

The reparation sample offenders and control group offenders differed markedly in their ascription of any blame to the victims. 55% of control group offenders felt that their victims were to blame in some way for the crime. In contrast, 23% of the reparation group offenders who had met their victims in mediation, thought that their victim was to blame in some way. This difference may be a consequence of the effect of mediation, and meeting the victim, on the offender's perception of the offence. However, it may just as well reflect the selection process of suitable reparation referrals. Only those offenders showing remorse should have been referred by probation officers to the scheme and furthermore, if the offender's plea was uncertain then referral was unlikely (90% of the reparation group pleaded guilty compared with 80% of the control group).

(e) Mediation meetings

24% of the reparation sample victims said that the mediation meeting was a difficult experience for them. 75% of the reparation sample offenders made the same comment. A further 22% of the victims said that their meeting was difficult at first, as did a further 7% of the offenders. In all, therefore, 46% of victims and 82% of offenders found the mediation meetings difficult in some way. The mediation meetings were not an easy option for any of those involved, especially the offenders.

The difficulties of mediation meetings were also recognised by the other parties. 72% of the victims realised that the meetings were difficult for their offender, 11% stated that they could not judge whether it had been difficult for the offender or not.

Offenders who found the mediation meeting difficult did so because they felt awkward and embarrassed about being face to face with their victim. Some mentioned that they expected them to be more angry than they were. One offender's remarks are typical: *"He wasn't in a mood, I expected he might be. I expected him to be angry but he was 0.K."*

Victims who found the mediation meetings difficult did so for a number of reasons, because the meeting was stressful due to embarrassment, there was pressure to reach an agreement or the victim felt they wanted to hit the offender. One said *"I would have loved to hit him because of what the break-in did to my young one (3year old child) — it gave him nightmares. It was difficult meeting him because I felt like hitting him but I knew that I couldn't."*

Another victim, who knew her burglar, agreed to a meeting because *"It was a way to get some money back and to avoid a prison sentence for him — prison would not solve the problem...but I had doubts and felt pressurised to meet."* She described the meeting thus — *"I didn't like it. The main reparation man behaved in an embarrassing way towards the offender. I didn't want to do it in the first place, it was such a strain. I didn't say much at all. I felt nervous and embarrassed. The whole thing was farcical."*

Another victim felt uncomfortable in the mediation meeting because she knew that the offender was a friend of her son. Because he was still a friend of her son she said that she felt *"...an additional strain of divided loyalty to her son"*; she agreed to the meeting *"for my son's sake...and to make the offender realise what he had done."* About the meeting she said, *"when I first walked in I felt strange about it. The two ladies handling the meeting — I give them ten out of ten. The lad did come out with an apology and an offer to do reparation for my son. It cleared the air to a certain extent but he didn't talk freely — we were both behind a wall. If he had been a total stranger it would have been easier. The four of us sat around a table — that was slightly off-putting, it could have been less formalised.*"

The primary reason which victims give for agreeing to meet their offender was to help reform them and help stop them re-offending. A victim of attempted burglary said that the crime "*didn't affect my life much but I told him it did. I told him that I was angry; that I couldn't sleep. I was asked by the mediator to say this. I could see the reason for this: to shock him. By helping him I was helping other people — saving others from being burgled*".

This belief that meeting their offender might help reform them was common among victims. It is interesting that although belief in reformation has somewhat faltered in official policy debate, it seems still to have support among victims of crime. Not only do victims still believe in the possibility of reformation, but they are prepared to go to personal inconvenience and difficulty to help try and achieve it.

The belief in reformation meant that for many victims the test of whether the mediation meeting had been worthwhile depended on whether the offender re-offended. For others, however, there was the added test of whether or not the offender kept his reparation promise. Where offenders failed to keep such promises this led to inevitable disillusionment with mediation and with the reparation project.

A doctor, whose surgery was burgled, explained: "*He seemed very reasonable but he had his tongue in his cheek and was laughing all along...he was very apologetic and promised to pay back £5. I wrote it off as a huge joke and he probably wrote it off as a joke as well*".

This offender, who reneged on his promise to pay £5, later re-offended and then failed to keep another reparation agreement made with a different victim. The doctor said that he felt 'conned'.

Another victim helped to arrange a community service placement for the offender he met. He felt let down by both the reparation project and the offender: by the former because they did not keep him informed of what happened to the CSO placement agreement, and by the latter because he found that he had evaded the court and was on the run.

At the mediation meeting this particular victim (of a household burglary) had: "*...said what I wanted to say. I tried to get him to think* *about what if I had been in the house at the time of the break-in. Was he prepared to use violence? If he felt bad why didn't he bring the cassette player back? I wanted to confront him with some of the points...judging by the results I don't think that it did anything for him. There appeared to be some remorse...I was mindful of him using it as a vehicle to get off, so I put pressure on him at the meeting.*

"I suggested working at a local Boys' Home where deprived children live. He told me he had actually been there (as a resident) and so work should be arranged elsewhere. So I suggested work at a Hospice instead.

"I feel quite angry that I put in all this time and he let me down. Also I feel let down by the Project because they haven't informed me what's happening. I drove back specially to Leeds for the reparation meeting."

The pressure was to form a contract and pressure might sometimes result in an unsatisfactory contract.

We have quoted this particular victim's experience at length, not because it is typical, but because it illustrated some of the dangers in reparation and mediation. Victims may generally believe that they can personally influence reformation by a mediation meeting, but that belief is often naive and failure can quickly produce disillusion. Reparation projects are in a dilemma: they need to respond positively to victims' belief in reformation if they are to achieve a mediation meeting, yet by doing so they can create the conditions for ultimate dissatisfaction on the part of the victim. The positive side is that victims are not necessarily simply punitive towards their particular offender.

There was sometimes a problem when an agreement to carry out work for the victim was incorporated by the court in a Community Service Order, one victim complaining that the intervention of a formal supervisor made the offender feel resentful and spoilt the personal relationship previously established.

One of the potential advantages of reparation and mediation schemes is that they bring the victim more positively back into the process of dealing with offenders. Our evidence suggests that at least some victims appreciate this more positive role. However, this appreciation may be turned into disillusionment if the victim is then re-marginalised by formalising agreements through court orders. This is a complex issue: not all victims will want to play a more positive role and some of those who do will welcome more formal support. It is an issue which further, more detailed research could explore. In the meantime, it is a problem which reparation schemes need to be sensitive to in dealing with reparation agreements.

Having raised a series of issues around victims' dissatisfaction with their experience of the project, and having drawn on some of the negative comments made by victims who were interviewed, we would not want to suggest that there was overwhelming dissatisfaction with the project. On the contrary many victims expressed positive support for the idea of mediation and their experience of the project. The negative comments have been used, however, to illustrate some of the pitfalls and dangers of reparation work with victims.

There was a positive side to victims' experience as well. Three victims, two women and a man, who each had sons mentioned that one of the reasons why they agreed to meet was because they could identify their offender with their son, or in one case, grandson.

One said "*I felt it was right to help him (by meeting) as it was his first offence and he stood outside (whilst his co-defendant broke in). I felt sorry for him. They don't realise until afterwards what harm they have done. He was a thin, pale-faced boy. I imagined it could have been my stepson sitting there*".

Another, whose vehicle had been stolen: "*I think the young man was silly, foolish. For the younger set to be a bit lenient is a good thing but not a soft touch. I'd like to think that making this mistake, and realising his mistake, he can gain something by it*".

One reason for meeting him was because "*…there was the possibility about learning how to deal with my grandson who's also been in trouble. I thought: if it was one of mine how would I approach it?*"

A shop worker who, with his employer, agreed to meet in mediation said: "*I wanted him (the offender) to see how upsetting it was; to see we're only ordinary folk. We didn't want to be anonymous. He was a genuine lad. He was crying at the meeting…we've both got sons. My lad is 18. Makes you think it could have been him*".

When asked whether the offender was the sort of person that he expected to meet he replied: "*He was different. You expect the criminal to be young, drinking every night, stoned. But we could probably have given him a job. He could have been my son*".

Some encounters between victim and offender challenged the stereotypical images about offenders. One victim said of her mediation meeting: "*I expected him to be wearing a striped jumper. I didn't expect him to be like the guy in the street you walk past. He was an ordinary kid. Given the right opportunities he could be a decent lad*".

Mediation may also increase a victim's understanding of crime. A headmaster said: "*It gave me a little more understanding about crime. What he said relates to him; but others possibly think in the same way. So I've more understanding of offenders in general*".

However, the meeting had not lessened his concern about crime: "*I'm more concerned about crime because of hearing the offenders' side*".

The irony is that whilst mediation meetings might make victims realise the ordinariness of offenders this realisation may not lessen their worry about crime; indeed it may increase the worry. Such an increased worry about crime in general could of course, be channelled positively — for example, by involving people in a community crime reduction programme. However, if this is not done there is a danger that mediation can, in certain circumstances, simply increase the fear of crime. Mediation schemes need to be aware of this danger. Work with some victims may need to continue after the mediation sessions to ensure that the results are positive and beneficial for victims. Ninety per cent of the reparation sample victims we interviewed said that they did not feel any less concerned about crime in general after meeting in a mediation session.

Attempts to generalise or summarise victims' views are fraught with problems due to the heterogeneous nature of crime and victims. Victims varied in their attitudes and opinions about mediation and a wide range of views were expressed by the victims whom we interviewed. If one common thread emerges from the interviews with victims it is that they see the mediation process as one of confronting the offender with the harm done and helping the offender to reform: that is mediation is seen as a sort of moral encounter. This theme is so prevalent that it obviously relates to a deeply felt need by victims and a need which the traditional criminal justice system does not respond to. The implicit assumption of the existing system — that such encounters are generally to be avoided — is questionable at least in this specific regard. Of course, there are other reasons for insulating victims from offenders but we can only report that some victims see positive reasons for engaging in mediation.

We have already pointed out above some of the pitfalls of mediation work with victims but the other common theme which emerged from interviewing the Leeds mediation victims was that they saw the reparation project as primarily offender focused with the primary aim of reducing re-offending. The latter was something which fitted in with their own views of what mediation might achieve. However, the former was more of a problem. In part this was a (perhaps inevitable) product of the referral route into the project via the offenders, with probation officers seeing the possibility of helping their clients. Since the probation service has traditionally worked almost exclusively with offenders this is bound to occur and victims perceived the Service as offender orientated. The Leeds project was well aware of this problem and did try and overcome it but was not entirely successful from the victims' point of view. One conclusion to draw from this difficulty might be that the probation service is not the best location for a reparation and mediation project.

CHAPTER 6

Ultimate Objectives and Quality

The previous chapter has dealt with all the shorter term measures of schemes' achievements. None of them alone, however, provides a sufficient criterion on which to judge, overall, whether schemes have been successful or not. For one thing, many of the expectations were of effects more remote in time or more subjective in their nature, and, however difficult such factors might be for the social researcher to study, they are no less important to the evaluation of the developing process of victim/offender mediation. For another thing, it is important to be able to assess the balance of achievements over a range of objectives and from a number of viewpoints — the offender's, the victim's and that of the criminal justice system. This also involves passing beyond the mere exposition of empirical data and entails subjective judgements informed by such data. Those who have observed the schemes closely over the last years, from as dispassionate standpoint as they could maintain, have inevitably formed overall impressions of the relatively 'good' and 'bad' aspects of their work and these impressions are as much the data of social science as the more statistical indices that were the greater part of the substance of Chapter Five.

The sections of this chapter are focused on different long-term objectives that the schemes under study have commonly espoused, the categories largely corresponding to those listed in Marshall (1988b). We deal first with the victim's interests, then the offender's, followed by the reconciliation of the two. We then proceed to consider the more traditional aims of the criminal justice system and how these may or may not have been served by these schemes, followed by a section on the alternative aims for criminal justice that the ideology behind victim/offender mediation supports. Lastly there is consideration of the quality of the action observed — attributes such as justice, fairness, commitment to the original aims, costs and efficiency.

Serving the Victim

All the British projects espouse the aim of increasing victim satisfaction or of meeting victims' needs. If pressed, some would probably give such objectives priority, although most would probably prefer to say they exist to serve the offender and the victim equally. Serving the victim was certainly one of the major aims behind the Home Office decision to fund four experimental schemes (Brittan, 1984).

In some ways, emphasis upon the victim has been greater in the American schemes which, as we have seen, can be quite onerous upon the offender in terms of reparation. This is partly, no doubt, a response to the politicisation of the 'victim movement' in North America, partly a response to the greater punitiveness of the existing criminal justice system, but certainly also a reflection of the fact that services for victims are much less developed there than in Britain. Compensation is a much greater issue in a country that has no 'free' National Health Service, so that the medical costs of injuries (and these can be massive) come out of victims' pockets, nor universal arrangements for compensation ordered through the criminal courts, nor federally-funded criminal injury compensation. Many of the schemes that have blossomed in the United States have been in large part a response to these gaps in provision, whereas in Britain such schemes have had the luxury of taking many of these things for granted and being able to work towards the introduction of newer, non-material ways in which victims may be helped.

Describing American VORPs, Coates and Gehm (1985) suggest four types of satisfaction that victims might derive from such schemes:

(i) understanding of the offender and the offence;

(ii) reparation;

(iii) experience of the offender's remorse;

(iv) concern shown by the mediator.

These may be more simply grouped into two types — material satisfactions (reparations) and psychological or emotional satisfactions.

The American VORPs aim to serve both objectives equally. They may, however, conflict with one another in practice. There have been examples earlier of victims, in a joint meeting with their offender, waiving offers of reparation (cf Case study F, Chapter 3), or accepting a token contribution in preference to an extended commitment. A stress on material negotiations about the appropriate quantum for reparation may be seen as sullying the enlightening exchange of views that the more successful mediation meetings can provoke. As Marshall and Walpole (1985) observed, *"the possibility of the offender merely 'paying' to put things right may even be slightly repulsive and unwelcome"* (p.46). Wright (1986) argues that British schemes have over-emphasised the role of compensation in serving victims' needs (an emphasis that is reflected in the common usage of 'reparation' in the title of such schemes), preferring a stress on 'conciliation', on what the schemes have to offer that is new, rather than that which our present court system already has potentially on offer.

Over time, American schemes have tended to place greater and greater emphasis on compensation over the quality of the meeting between victim and offender itself:

"Although there seems to be consensus that offender-victim meetings are desirable when both parties agree to them, the results have been mixed, and offender confrontations are now reported to be declining in some restitution programs. Individuals involved in either side of the restitution process seem more and more inclined toward the position that it is the payments that really count rather than meeting between victim and offender and a possible resulting relationship. Among possible reasons for this development is the problem of victims' lashing out at the offender during their meeting and as a result alienating him from the restitution process. Jurisdiction is also a problem; offenders can be compelled to attend such meetings but victims cannot. Many victims have no desire to confront offenders, preferring to remain strangers to them and desiring only to receive restitution for damages. As caseloads for restitution program staff grow, this aspect of the program comes to be de-emphasised, ultimately affecting the initiation and maintenance of offender-victim relationships.

"The decline of offender-victim meetings and interchange results in an essential part of the program being lost, for a major aim of the restitution program is to counteract the prevailing impersonality and anonymity of much criminal behaviour by making offenders aware of the personal harm that they have caused." (Alper and Nichols, 1981).

In different social circumstances, British projects have moved in the opposite direction. Most, as Davis et al. (1987) observe, soon began to emphasise the psychological benefits over material reparation, a trend that previous chapters of the present book confirm.

Are they right to do so? Public attitude surveys, such as that of Sessar (1984), usually find that the public favours *"material redress"* over *"reconciliation, apology or personal service to the victim"*. Such results may merely reflect the fact that such respondents have not experienced a joint meeting with the offender, and the nature of the psychological benefits that may ensue. While it may be true, however, that material or financial concerns fit uneasily into the personalised context of direct mediation, it may also be true that outside of this context the same victims may still feel a right to material compensation — by means, for instance, of a court order. Some of those interviewed seemed, indeed, to be expressing just such a point of view: *"[The reparation] was quite over and above the thought that we would have of being compensated for our loss...at that time we thought we would be compensated-for our loss...no award was made for compensation, so that reflects £100 loss to my business partner and myself..."* (a victim at Coventry whose offender had cleared the garden of an empty property as reparation).

One must remember, too, that there are inherent limits to the use of victim/offender mediation as a means of serving victims' needs. As Davis et al (1987) point out, such schemes can only be relevant to a small minority of victims (just as court-ordered compensation is), because the majority of offenders are not apprehended and prosecuted. At the same time, considerations of offenders' needs and those of criminal justice generally, will restrict even further the number of cases where victims may actually get the chance to take part in the scheme.

The present research indicates, indeed, that among the police-based schemes there is a low emphasis on victims' needs (because of the focus on diversion) and most of their victims were corporate (60%) rather than personal, and that even the court-based schemes tend to exhibit a bias towards the offender merely because of their position in terms of referrals, even though they certainly wish to be able to serve victims just as much. At least most of these schemes (with the prominent exception of Wolverhampton) tended to select personal victims (70%), apparently representative of the general range of such victims. All the schemes, of whatever type, have tended to use material reparation to only a slight extent (the highest rate of personal reparation was 41% at Leeds, but it was 10% at Coventry and Wolverhampton), and indeed there has been a tendency for those victims who stress recompense to be uninterested in meeting the offender.

There is no straightforward resolution to these issues. It is apparent that different victims will have different needs and will be amenable to different kinds of service. Rather than trying to impose a single ideology of what victim/offender interaction should be like, schemes should strive for flexibility in response to victims' wishes. This would mean spending more time than is often done at present in discussion with the victim, to establish how they might be assisted and to prepare them properly for whatever process, if any, they choose. They should be placed under no illusion that the schemes are there solely to serve their interests, and they should be clear that fruitful participation in a joint meeting will involve some effort in trying to understand the offender's point of view and a willingness to be reconciled to him/her.

The next two sections will look at the two main types of victims' needs in more detail.

(a) Material assistance

Reparation is an explicit and central aim to most American restitution programmes and many VORPs, such as that at Ontario (see Dittenhoffer and Ericson's, 1983, discussion of its aims). Even in Britain, where other compensation arrangements exist, there may be advantages to determining payment by means of personal negotiation between victim and offender, rather than by fiat of the court. Newburn (1988) has studied the problems of compensation orders in England and Wales, finding that this provision is under-used by the courts, largely because of a lack of sufficient information on which to base a decision as to the quantum. This would not be such a difficulty for the parties themselves, although disagreements over the extent of damage of what was stolen and its value might be far from easy for the mediator to manage, apart from any effect such wrangling might have on the newly-formed, and fragile, relationship between the two. The impression one gets from the research is that victims would find it inappropriate to enter into personal negotiations in this way, and would rather leave it to the court. Where, however, the victim has no interest in demanding full compensation and perceives it as a token of remorse rather than an end in itself, it may be easy to come to some agreement about payment that bears only slight relationship to the actual loss. Magistrates and judges, in any case, can only award compensation that is within the offender's means to pay. Offenders in this research were representative of those generally before the court in being predominantly unemployed and often in debt already (cf Case-study A in Chapter 3), so that many victims, even through the court, will only receive what is, in effect, a token payment. The fact that the sum is reduced from what the victim might otherwise think is owed him or her may be much more acceptable if voluntarily agreed in a meeting with the offender, whose circumstances are evident, than when ordered by a court with no explanation of why the sum is smaller than expected and without any conception of what the offender may be like.

Another problem bedevilling court compensation orders is that they are limited to being financial. In a meeting with the victim, the impecunious offender will have the opportunity to suggest other ways in which he/she may be able to make amends, especially by carrying out some form of work for (in the main) the corporate victim. Or the victim may be satisfied with other achievements, such as the offender's attendance at a youth club, that might keep him out of trouble, or work for some local voluntary agency. There is much more flexibility and creativity that can occur in the mediation of reparation than is available to a formal court when considering compensation.

Although Newburn (1988) found that victims were generally happy to have been awarded compensation, they were very often dissatisfied with the way it was actually received — usually in fortnightly instalments (or less frequently if the award is shared among several victims) of small sums stretching over a year or two. This process only serves to remind victims periodically of an experience they would rather put behind them. In practice, therefore, they may have been happier with smaller sums within the offender's current means that could be paid forthwith. They have no chance of telling a court so at present, or even of knowing anything about the offender's circumstances. Participation in one of the mediation schemes would therefore be one way of finding a solution which was practicable for the offender and acceptable to the victim. Once faced with an offender who obviously is not rolling in the rich profits of ill-gotten gains, but is suffering from difficulties in making ends meet and in establishing an acceptable position in society, resentment over the material loss may well diminish in favour of more constructive ideas. Any financial payment arranged voluntarily with the offender probably has a higher chance of being paid in any case (cf Case-study E, Chapter 4). There have been few cases in the schemes studied where an agreement of this kind was not kept, whereas, despite the sanctions available to a court, compensation ordered by sentencers is quite often not paid (or time-consuming to collect).

As cautioning rates increase, at least for juveniles, another problem emerges in relation to court-ordered compensation: more and more victims will now be losing their chance of such an award because the offender never comes to court. There is a strong *a priori* case, therefore, for considering the use of victim/offender mediation in conjunction with cautioning as a means of satisfying victims' needs in such instances. As most such cases only involve juveniles, there will usually be little chance of large financial sums changing hands, but at least the victim will have a chance of finding out why full compensation is not possible and of exploring other ways of allowing the offender to make amends, at least in a token way. Unfortunately, the schemes we have studied here that intervene at the cautioning stage have been much more concerned with diversion than with victims' interests and they have not been operated in such a way as to test out the use of mediation except in a few cases where the offender has been in danger of prosecution. Where this has been done, especially in the Cumbria scheme, those victims who have been solely motivated by economic concerns have usually been dissatisfied with the outcome if they have taken part indirect mediation, although most will have seen that what was on offer was of little use to them and not taken up the offer of a meeting at all. Many of them, in any case, will have been insured, even if there was a significant loss, so that there are few cases in practice where money is really a central issue.

It has often been supposed that material reparation would be more relevant to corporate than private victims, especially when work for the victim is being considered. Although this may be so to a degree, the evidence from the schemes' experience so far is that such reparative work is still relatively rare even in the case of corporate victims. This is so because it is not true that the only interest corporate victims might have in mediation is material. Most corporate victims suffer from repeat offending, and one of the most valuable lessons they may gain from participation in mediation is in learning more about the causes of this (especially in the case of persistent 'mindless' vandalism) and possibly being able to take preventive steps.

If a victim's only interest is in compensation, however, it is unlikely either that a meeting will be very productive (for either party), or that it will be worth the bother involved for the victim. One of the reasons victims gave for not wishing to participate, in the study by Coates and Gehm (1985) of American VORPs, was that it would be too much trouble in relation to the loss they had sustained. If the loss were greater, however, the chances of the offender being able to afford to compensate them would usually be scant. It is difficult, then, to justify the time and effort of setting up mediation if the purpose of the meeting is to be restricted solely to negotiating compensation, although this could be justified as an element within the context of a more wide-ranging meeting. Experience of reparation schemes in this country indicates, however, that most victims offered the chance of some resolution of the aftermath of their victimisation will give less priority to compensation than they would if that was all that was on offer.

Other practical problems also arose. There was, for instance, a lack of clarity about situations in which compensation was agreed in a mediation contract but then the court passed sentence without a compensation order before the offender has paid off all, or indeed any, agreed compensation. In some circumstances the offenders were sentenced to custody and the victim recognised that they would not get compensation. In other cases, where the sentence was non-custodial and no compensation order was made, the offender was under no legal obligation to honour the agreement, and the victim may have felt cheated or let down by non-payment. Mediators did warn victims that court sentences may not necessarily acknowledge their mediation agreements, but not all victims clearly understood this, not realising that it might mean no compensation or reparation work even though a contract had been signed by the offender.

There was further confusion about the time to commence payment, whether this should be before sentence was passed or whether it should wait until the court had passed sentence. The matter of whether any money paid under a reparation agreement was to be deducted from money ordered to be paid under a compensation order was also uncertain. In general, payment of such money did not commence, if at all, until after sentence.

If compensation was agreed at mediation and then 'endorsed' by the court, then the victim received payments through the court. This could create confusion with some victims and offenders who expected the payments to be made direct, or through the probation officer or mediator.

Offenders who agreed to do service for the victims usually commenced this service before sentence, in contrast to the situation with compensation agreements. Often the service was completed by the time the offender came to court for sentence. In such cases the supervisor of the work would usually provide the project with a letter reporting on the offender's performance which the project would usually present at court.

Offenders might gamble and perform the service after a mediation session and before sentence in order to prove their 'worth' to the court in the hope that this would affect their sentence. Some were to find, or to feel, that it made no difference. Although they may not feel bitter, some did feel a sense that they had received a 'double sentence', and that they had lost the 'gamble'. Alternatively an offender might wait for the court sentence, but the mediation agreement might then weigh less heavily as a mitigating factor in sentencing. In practice, however, the offenders had little choice as to when to commence service agreed. The choice of date usually rested with the victim, or the agency where the offender was to work. In cases where it was not possible for the work to commence before the sentence was passed the leader of the Leeds scheme usually requested an adjournment or deferment period to enable reparation to take place.

There were, thus, problems in deciding when compensation or service should commence. Some judges and recorders suggested that monetary reparation might be construed as a bribe so they preferred compensation ordered in a sentence. Others, however, said that if the offender was genuine in their remorse then they would have repaid some of their debt by the time sentence was passed.

One victim said, when interviewed by a researcher, "*I want a lump sum of £42. I thought he'd pay it before court. I still expect to get the money. If the court don't order it, I'll get a solicitor to get it.*" In fact the mediation agreement between this victim of theft and the offender stated that the amount of compensation would be £25, a sum which the court ordered to be paid in a compensation order. The problem of unfulfilled agreements remains unresolved, and can be the source of dissatisfaction amongst victims.

When the contracts were 'endorsed' by the court then the compensation or service was systematically followed through. In other cases the agreement was voluntary with no court sanctions, and not systematically followed through. In cases where the offender was sentenced to custody most voluntary agreements broke down, as did many other post-sentence voluntary contracts.

The use of the word contract is perhaps an unfortunate choice, as the mediation agreements were never intended to have legal force. The onus was on the mediators to make this clear, but some victims do not appear to have fully appreciated that there was no legal mechanism to enforce voluntary agreements.

Projects which encourage reparation payments to victims which are not 'endorsed' by court compensation orders could lead victims into difficulties with insurance. With compensation order from the court the amount awarded should be deducted from any insurance payment. Payments agreed under mediation agreements and not made part of a compensation order by the court may not be paid in full, or even at all, which could result in problems with insurance payment. In an early case at the Leeds project, the victim and offender were unable to agree on the amount of damage done, the discrepancy amounting to £400. This left the magistrate in difficulty deciding the appropriate level of compensation. The magistrate insisted that the insurance company be notified of what had happened, and decided that due to the uncertainties he was unable to make a compensation order. The offender was fined £100.

The Leeds project also identified two victims who were inflating their insurance claims. This raises the interesting possibility that mediation might help check inflated insurance claims by victims. More generally, any future reparation schemes ought to explore the relationship to insurance claims more fully. Interviews with victims at Leeds found that 43% were insured and claiming for the loss or damage incurred. Thus a resolution of these problems is certainly necessary.

(b) Psychological benefits

Meeting the offender and being able to express one's feelings to the culpable party, to witness them as human beings rather than vague impersonal threats, to receive their apologies and exercise the privilege of forgiveness may help victims restore their social and personal equilibrium in a more direct and immediate way than would otherwise be possible. Strange as the idea may seem *in the context of our formal justice system*, it is in fact the most natural way of resolving transgressions between individual persons, one that has existed as far back as history can record. The upset cause by crime is as much symbolic as actual, and often it is only through a corresponding act of contrition and making amends that the full impact of the crime can be exorcised. Compensation may be welcome, but if that is all it may still leave a bad taste in the mouth. There are examples in the great variety of cases dealt with by the schemes studied here of mediation successfully resolving problems of fear, anger, anxiety, and self-esteem resulting from the original offence. The importance of these feelings to victims of crime has been recently well documented (Shapland, Willmore and Duff, 1985; Maguire and Corbett, 1987) and can also be testified to by victims support volunteers who have visited thousands of victims around the country annually. Victims in this research, too, were often concerned more with the inconvenience or the invasion of privacy than any material loss (cf Case-studies A, E and G in Chapters 3 & 4), and were sometimes desirous of confronting the offender even before this was offered by the scheme (Case G). More often the initial impulse was more curiosity than anything stronger, but even these participants were likely to be surprised by the feelings evoked once engaged in the meeting with the offender, feelings otherwise suppressed and perhaps never positively resolved. One of the most prevalent needs of all is that of putting 'closure' on the offence, a point in time after which one can say 'it is all over and done with now', and that psychological moment is often defined by the experience of the offender's remorse and the act of forgiving (see Zehr, 1985).

Dealing with such problems has always been an explicit aim of American VORPs, although not of restitution programmes that placed emphasis solely on reparation. In the description of the aims of VORPs by Coates and Gehm (1985) they include victims' needs to share their feelings, to gain understanding of their victimisation, and to be able to experience the resolution of the offence in a personalised context. The courts have no place for them except as witnesses under hostile cross-examination that may only increase their self-doubts and upset.

Victim fear and anger are often given as reasons for not going ahead with mediation. Obviously one does not want to precipitate a violent episode, but such feelings, if not too extreme, can be dealt with in the context of mediation by a properly skilled mediator. They are coped with all the time in divorce mediation. Strong feelings may have a greater capacity for impressing the offender if channelled in a constructive way. They may mean there is more to resolve and hence more to achieve. It is sensible that schemes in this country in their early days, while mediators themselves are still learning their jobs, should enter with caution into such troubled waters, but the aim should be to develop the capacity for dealing with such powerful emotions. Most of the meetings we have documented have not been pitched at a high emotional level, and the victims involved, at least by the time the meeting took place, were not feeling overwhelming despair or anger. They were more inconvenienced than traumatised. This may be partly a matter of case-selection, partly a matter of timing. As a result we have yet to see the full power of mediation between victims and offenders, or to see this tested out, except in a few atypical cases (eg the initially vindictive victim in Case-study B, Chapter 3).

Certainly, even within the limits of the kinds of cases dealt with, schemes have generally found, and interviews with participants afterwards have confirmed, that the meeting as a psychological event, as an emotional process, has been much more remarkable than as a mere forum for arranging reparation. Participants of American VORPs also tended to see the greatest strength of such meetings residing in the humanisation of the justice process and the service provided to the victim thereby (Coates and Gehm, 1985). In police-based schemes, the level of hurt and anxiety evidenced by victims was usually very low, given that these were in any case minor juvenile transgressions. The court-based schemes saw more serious cases, just as Mackay (1986) found that the victims involved in the experimental Scottish scheme still showed noticeable emotional effects from their victimisation, but often by the time of intervention the intensity of the problems has subsided considerably. It is evident that timing is a difficult problem. At the moment this is geared to the exigencies of the formal criminal justice process, which is irrelevant to the choice of the optimum time as far as the victim is concerned. One can suggest a meeting with the offender at too early a stage as well as too late. Defining the exactly right moment could be extremely difficult, and arranging mediation for precisely this time almost impossible.

For this last reason, just as one could not see reparation schemes or compensation orders as a solution to the material problems of most victims, so one cannot see victim/offender mediation as a means of coping, on its own, with the psychological pains of victims. Such mediation could be a significant part of the support given to victims in the resolution of their problems, if it happens to be offered at a time when feelings are neither extravagantly high nor diminished altogether, but it should be seen only in the context of a more general plan of support for emotionally affected victims. The most appropriate source for this is victims support, a rapidly growing movement of voluntary schemes that now covers two-thirds of the country and has recently received a moderately large contribution in the way of governmental funding. Despite this success such schemes still lack universal coverage even in the areas where they have been set up. Ninety per cent or so of all their cases are burglary offences, which means that many deserving victims are still not getting any help or support (cf Maguire and Corbett, 1987). It was a remarkable finding that in the experience of virtually every reparation scheme we examined (with the special exception of N.E. Essex) hardly any of the victims contacted had received a visit from a victims support volunteer.

Workers in most projects, found as a result that they were inevitably involved in giving support and advice of a general kind to victims they visited, quite aside from their principal mediation work. The mediator's visit was usually welcomed even if the victims did not agree to meeting the offender. From the mediator the victim may at least gain some reassurance that the offence had not been directed personally at them, or that the offender had been caught. The visits also enabled the victim to share some of their anxieties and fears about what had happened with the mediator. Without more of a background of support for victims, it is difficult for more of them to be able to take advantage of the opportunities that meeting the offender could offer, or to be able to make full use of them.

There was one unexpected finding of this research pertaining to victim/offender mediation as a service to victims. It would seem that many — both academics and practitioners — have done victims the discredit of regarding them as motivated solely by personal gain. It seems that many have imagined that victims might go away with great glee with a wad of banknotes in their hands, or the promise of someone to slave in their garden. It is reassuring to find that the great majority of victims involved in these schemes were not so grasping, and indeed that they even seemed to feel rather guilty about taking something from the offender that by the usual norms of justice might have been seen as owing to them by right. The most frequent motive evidenced by those taking part in the schemes was, by contrast, a desire to help, a feeling of social concern.

Perplexing as it may seem as a reaction to victimisation, it does have a definable logic. It is the replacement of a negative anti-social experience by a positive socially responsible one, the replacement of feelings of vulnerability by the experience of doing good, the denial of a threatening environment by working towards social reintegration. The sense that some good has thereby been achieved may constitute a hitherto unregarded source of satisfaction to victims. It was the general experience of the research interviews with victims that more were motivated by such a sense of social responsibility, tinged perhaps with curiosity, than by a desire to heal personal hurt. It is deceptively easy to dismiss this as evidence that schemes were exploiting victims' social consciences in order to help the offenders, but the interviews, coupled with many of the case-studies, show that many victims really did value such involvement and were thankful for the opportunity. On the whole they tended to be the more satisfied victims when interviewed later. Sometimes it can lead them, entirely voluntarily, and often at the expense of the mediator's embarrassment, to try to help out an offender who is no longer seen as an attacker but as an unfortunate individual who needs to be helped back into the community, for that person's good as much as everyone else's. The lengths to which this can go is evidenced by Leslie Jerman's account (Guardian, 16 January 1988, p.9) of his own involvement in the fluctuating fortunes of his 'own' offender over a period of years, something which arose from his own initiative, and with the assistance of the offender's probation officer, rather than being the suggestion of any organised scheme. While such altruism will not be within everyone's resources, nor should it be expected of anyone, the fact is that in very minor ways many of the victims involved in mediation in the schemes studied here were making just such a contribution to reducing the gap between 'us' and 'them', the law-abiding and the outcasts, and gaining a modest amount of satisfaction from the effort. Indeed 80% of victims, in interviews later on, gave a positive account of the experience and emphasised the meeting itself rather than any reparation as the essential contribution. Mere involvement can be beneficial in itself. One of the Cumbrian participants summed it up:

"I think the victim should be involved in some way. I have been a victim before and it all went to court and I knew nothing about it at all, I didn't get anything...this way I got to see them and I got compensation. I think you should be able to voice your opinion and I think it was good for the boys to come and apologise."

Benefits to the Offender

One can question whether there need be any benefits as far as the offender is concerned. Does such a person not have a duty to make amends to the one who is harmed?

Even if one admits this is so, nonetheless the process of victim/offender mediation is the more productive the greater the genuine commitment of both parties. Given some sign of leniency or willingness to abet social reconciliation, the offender's commitment may be enhanced. The chance of mitigation, or even of diversion from prosecution altogether, may not therefore simply be seen as a bribe to help out the victim, but as a real contribution to the avoidance of the alienating experience of formal justice and the substitution of at least an element of trying to restore relations between society and the offender.

The movement, in some quarters, away from so many prosecutions or prison sentences, is a recognition of the need to give offenders the chance of finding an acceptable niche within society, which is only made all the more difficult by branding them as criminals and reinforcing their careers as outsiders (cf Bianchi & Swaaningen, 1986). All the schemes we have studied have accepted, at least initially, that one of their aims was to effect such social reconciliation by alleviating the punitive impact of the criminal justice system on offenders. Those schemes associated with diversion tried to do this most comprehensively, by trying to avoid the labelling of offenders as such altogether. Whether this is avoided simply by not prosecuting is another matter. If the alternative is a formal process of cautioning and an addition of the offence to one's criminal record, which may be quoted in court if one is prosecuted in future for some other offences, one may question how far the labelling of the offender has been avoided. This problem has led many devotees of diversion to resist any alternative that gives such formal recognition to the crime, a movement that seems to have been taken furthest, in this country, in Northamptonshire, where several stages of 'no further action' and 'informal caution' have been introduced to avoid any formal record of criminal involvement.

Logical as this stance is, given the premises on which it is based, it does mean that although the negative impact of social sanctioning is avoided nothing positive is put into its place. The door to social reconciliation is open, but it leads nowhere. In their resistance to any form of recognition of persons as offenders, not only is punishment avoided but also any form of help or counselling that might actively contribute to social reintegration. Thus we have seen that reparation has been used very sparingly in association with cautioning in order to avoid the possibility of labelling offenders by social intervention predicated on the fact of an offence. While the offender may thereby avoid learning the unfortunate lesson that society is determined to reject him/her, the more beneficial lesson that transgressions against other people are incompatible with a fruitful social career may also be evaded. The lesson that seems to be getting across in such circumstances seems to be that one can do what one likes and need have no responsibility for the effects on others. While one does not want to encourage people, especially young ones, to see themselves as 'criminals', one equally should not want to encourage them to see themselves as lacking any moral obligations.

Diversion will be discussed further in a later section. As far as the present section is concerned, one may accept that diversion may be a benefit to the offender, and will certainly be perceived by the latter as such, but that on its own its impact may be more one of avoiding negative implications rather than positive in its own right. The experience of meeting the victim, on the other hand, and having to regularise that relationship — often a distinctly difficult challenge — can provide a learning process that should be far more influential than that occurring in the courtroom (cf further discussion in Marshall, 1988b), because it demands active involvement, personal contact that is starkly meaningful, and self-confrontation, precisely because the context is not retributive but co-operative (see, especially Case G in Chapter 4 and Case II in the appendix). Such a meeting cannot be dismissed in the way a court appearance can be — it is difficult to distance oneself from what is going on when that is in your own hands rather than those of criminal justice officials and lawyers. Most importantly, criminal justice administers *punishment*, often accepted by offenders as just, but viewed as a means of *paying* for their past transgressions. Personal reparation, however, does not reduce crime to a commercial transaction but introduces the notion of *atonement* that involves future as well as present obligations. It may (as interviews with participating offenders sometimes showed) teach the crucial lesson that crime hurts even if it was 'unintentional' — that excuses (neutralisation) are not relevant to the issue of responsibility. The emotions that permeate a personal encounter make it an instrument of tremendous power for reform when handled well (see, especially, Case II in the appendix).

The evidence of this research is that the existence of reparation schemes does allow some offenders to avoid prosecution, although they may just as often involve an added burden to what would otherwise have been a straightforward caution. If this burden, however, constitutes a constructive learning experience, and is not seen as punitive, it can be conceived as a benefit to the offender. It may even be perceived to be so by the offenders themselves if the meeting affords them emotional relief through the expiation of guilt and the experience of social re-acceptance by being forgiven (and in many cases by being the subject of active concern). In Case A (Chapter 3), for instance, the offender received a rare opportunity to experience acceptance by others after being thrown out of home and suspended from school.

As far as the court-based schemes were concerned there was evidence of altered sentence patterns, although their implication in terms of mitigation was unclear. There was probably some chance of a custodial sentence being avoided, but the most likely effect was away from a fine to probation or community service, less often to conditional discharge. While a fine may be generally seen as less onerous than the longer-term commitments involved in the first two alternatives, with respect to impecunious offenders it may be a personal matter as to which would be the preferable disposal. On top of this was the increased likelihood of having to pay compensation. Mitigation, then, could occur, but it was uncertain. VORPs in America have similarly found only marginal effects on court decisions — Coates and Gehm (1985) found no evidence for reduced probability of imprisonment, but did find a substantial reduction in the length of sentence for participants in the schemes. As in the British schemes, the researchers found that offenders generally took the process seriously — an attitude of cynicism seems to be much easier in front of the judicial bench than in front of the victim — and that they appreciated the fact that the victim is willing to listen to them and give them a chance to 'make things right'.

Whatever the chances of being treated less punitively, some offenders will in any case have been so disturbed by their arrest, and realisation of what they have done, to want to make amends. For such individuals — and they were not, apparently, rare (cf. Case-studies B and C in Chapter 3; many offenders indicated when interviewed that the commission of their offences was soon followed by regret) — the reparation schemes offered a chance to atone, as an approach to the victim without their assistance might have been difficult to make, or even liable to misinterpretation. If taking responsibility and apology are natural processes — and from some of the evidence in the last section of the preceding chapter, it seems they did have great intuitive appeal — then means should be provided to allow them to occur: even if criminal justice agencies do not wish to adjust their own decisions, formal processes should at least not obstruct the achievement of these ends. It is one of the major goals of American VORPs to provide a niche for the acting out of atonement and accountability, and this, it seems, can be achieved as long as victim/offender encounters are not dominated by artificial or material issues. As far as the offender is concerned, just as much as for the victim, it is a way of putting a boundary on the past offence. Not all offenders, however, will feel this way without prompting, or realise the benefits to be gained, so that one must question how many would be willing to face up to the victim with the incentive, which most seem to have assumed, of possibly receiving easier treatment at the hands of criminal justice. Although many offenders feel it right to apologise, it is not something any of us finds easy to do, and their accounts to researchers in the interviews often relate how difficult it was and the sense of relief that followed the achievement.

Dispute Resolution

The rise of VORPs in North America has been connected, as described in Chapter 1, to a religious ideology that stressed the achievement of harmony and reconciliation. One of the founders of the early schemes, Howard Zehr (1983) stresses the priority of reconciliation among their goals, just as it has been accorded the prominence of a place in the title VORP itself. He views this process as not simply applying to those who were previously acquainted, but, on the basis of crime as a disruption to social relationships generally (cf. the discussion in Marshall, 1988a, of crime as a 'dispute'), sees it as the development of mutual awareness between victim and offender as individual persons, mutual understanding, the exchange of remorse and forgiveness, reaching agreement, and shared satisfaction with the process. In this sense, all victim/offender mediation is concerned with reconciliation. (Not that all American schemes accept this view — the Minnesota VORP, according to Galaway, 1985, does not conceive reconciliation to be its aim. It seeks merely to provide the opportunity for reconciliation, that parties may use or not use as they wish.)

There are three ways, however, in which victim/offender mediation may be more specifically concerned with resolving conflict between individuals. In the first place, they may have been already acquainted — quite often the offence has arisen from a relationship problem. Half the cases referred to the court-based schemes involved victims and offenders who already knew one another, as did nearly 40% of those referred to the police-based schemes where personal rather than corporate victims were concerned. Offences of violence involved related parties between two-thirds and three-quarters of the time. In a tenth of all cases the offender was known to have a definite grievance against the victim. In the second place, the offence may have arisen from a relationship problem the offender had with some third party (such as his/her parents) — see Case-study B in Chapter 3, where the mediation was concerned with the offender's relationship with his mother as well as his victim. In the third place, although not previously acquainted, they may live close enough to be likely to encounter one another in future, a fact that may be mutually embarrassing and may even be fraught with danger if one or other feels vengeful (cf Case-studies A and G, Chapters 3 & 4).

This last situation is a common occurrence. Victims and offenders tend not to live far apart, and over half of all victims lived in high crime areas (almost as high as the proportion of offenders who did so). Many cases dealt with by the reparation scheme enabled the two parties to be able to meet again later without fear or feeling discomforted.

There is also the opposite danger that, by putting the offender in touch with a victim whose address was previously unknown, the offender is in a position to take revenge later. A small number of victims interviewed were anxious, looking back, that they may have put themselves into this position. Any subsequent offence, if unsolved, is likely to be interpreted as further depredation by the same individual. Continued communication with the victim after mediation by the mediators may help to allay such fears, which are probably groundless in nearly every case. At present, some schemes are likely to carry out mediation at the victim's home or place of work for the victim's own convenience, but they probably should have more regard to the security issues if this involves revealing a previously unknown address. Even if retaliation is unlikely, all precautions should be taken to prevent any possibility of it happening. At the same time, probably the best preventive measure is a satisfactory meeting that disperses ill feelings on either side. (There is also the possibility of victims taking revenge when they get to know who the offender is, and there were several cases where this, too, was a potential problem successfully diffused by means of mediation — most notably a case at Leeds of threatened revenge by the brother of a girl killed in a traffic accident against the family of the person convicted of her manslaughter, who was himself serving time in prison for the offence.)

Previously acquainted parties, however, pose special problems to victim/offender mediation. In some ways, they seem to be the most suitable types of case for such a process, there being that much more to resolve, and many schemes have indicated as much to referring agencies. A large group of schemes, in Australia and America, normally called Neighbourhood Justice Centres or something similar, take only referrals of 'related' parties from criminal justice agencies, often diverting cases from the courts. By distinguishing such cases from the usual run of crimes, however, these schemes are moving the issues from an offence/sanction context to a dispute/resolution one. The mediation is more or less identical to that of community mediation schemes that try to resolve interpersonal conflicts (usually neighbour problems) that have not been given a criminal label, except that one or other party who may be under threat of legal action may be more committed to achieving a resolution than would otherwise have been the case (cf Harrington, 1985).

In the case of the schemes we are studying, however, the cases are not diverted from the legal process, and mediation take place in a context where one party is clearly identified as the victim and the other as the offender. The research data show that a large proportion of cases do involve such previously acquainted parties, unlike, apparently, the American VORPs (Coates and Gehm, 1985). At the same time, there seems to be little difference in how these cases are treated compared with cases involving strangers. Little effort seems to have been put into resolving the underlying dispute, although the case-studies in Chapter 3 show that this cannot be entirely avoided as an issue. There are several possible reasons for this apparent failure to act as dispute-resolvers as well as reparation-negotiators. In the first place, the victim/offender definition of their work may blind mediators to other possibilities for resolution when they occur, or the time available may prevent more extended mediation. In the second place, the circumstances may be inappropriate. Lastly, one or other party may tend to resist opening up the meeting to wider considerations.

In the case of some schemes, notably the police-based, the stress on reparation as a more or less superficial expedient to enhance the likelihood of the offender being cautioned probably does lead to a neglect of underlying relationship issues, just as the victim's needs take a back seat. A very small number of cases at Exeter, and no doubt elsewhere, have involved mediation proper and an attempt to resolve an interpersonal dispute, but this is both rare and peripheral to their main activity. We have already seen above one example (Case-study C, Chapter 3) where mediation might have had much to offer in Northampton, and the police had suggested as much, but the reparation scheme was unwilling to get involved. The researchers found that the Northampton Bureau took the same stance with respect to all assaults between acquaintances, arguing that mediation would only exacerbate ill-feeling or 'raise the temperature'. In the case of the court-based schemes, however, there is not the same offender-dominance and the mediators and scheme co-ordinators do appear to show awareness of the potential for dispute-resolution. Even so, there was still some apparent reluctance, perhaps partly based on confidence, to become involved in morally ambiguous issues where the criminality was not clear-cut, or where strong feelings were involved. It may have simply seemed more comfortable to work with black-and-white conceptions of victim and offender, but, if so, the schemes were adopting just those traditional conceptions of justice and offence-processing that many thought they were meant to be challenging.

It is possible that once a dispute has turned to criminal action by one or both parties, it has gone too far for resolution of the underlying problems until this escalation has in itself been resolved. It is most apparent that this might be so in cases of domestic violence, which most mediation schemes will be very wary of tackling because of the danger of negotiating the violence of one party along with other relationship problems — the 'I promise not to hit her if she gets my meals ready on time' syndrome. Mediators have generally agreed that such behaviour is non-negotiable, that violence must be negatively sanctioned and the offender made aware that no progress can be attempted until this kind of behaviour is abandoned unilaterally. Given these conditions, it is possible to accept a dispute between husband and wife for mediation, the violence problem having been dealt with in the normal way, and a case at N.E. Essex was of this kind (see Appendix). Whether or not a dispute can be mediated in the aftermath of criminal action will, in fact, depend on the nature of that action (which may be minor) and the attitudes of the parties. In some instances the offence may have precipitated a change in the attitude of the other party, who has thereby been brought to realisation of the effect their own behaviour was having on the other. Nevertheless, resolution of longstanding interpersonal problems can be a difficult, uncertain and time-consuming process. As Merry (1982) observes, disputes over material issues (such as reparation) are far easier to conciliate than those involving behavioural change. The success of mediation for fundamental relationship problems, in fact, has probably been oversold generally, at least insofar as small local schemes with relatively limited resources are concerned: "Like most brief interventions, mediation cannot address deep-rooted emotional and social problems and is clearly not a substitute for more sustained counselling and support services" (Pearson, 1982). Mediation, as offered by the type of scheme studied here, is probably, limited to the achievement of specific agreements and the modification of mutual perceptions between the parties, rather than anything more fundamental, although it may make a contribution at the appropriate time to the resolution of deeper issues in the context of longer term counselling (which would not be within the schemes' own resources unless caseloads were to be severely restricted).

Another stumbling-block to dispute resolution in the context of victim/offender mediation is likely to be resistance to the idea by the parties themselves. The research data indicated a tendency for *victims* with a prior relationship to be less keen on direct mediation, while *offenders* in this position were usually more keen. Where the emphasis of the meeting was placed on reparation or an apology, rather than on more general issues, however, such an offender was often less keen — there was one case which the researchers came across in Totton in which the offender blamed the victim in part for what had happened and was therefore not prepared to apologise, although he would apparently have been prepared to meet the victim otherwise. Surveys of victims' attitudes to reparation have uncovered the same reluctance among those who already knew their offender personally (eg O'Brien, 1986). It seems likely that the reason for this in the context of an ongoing dispute is that the commission of an offence represents a temporary advantage for the offender over the victim, which the victim will want to see redressed before being willing to negotiate other matters. A criminal prosecution is, from the victim's point of view, a way of restoring the balance, because the fault is placed wholly on one side, even though the victim may have precipitated the offence. Agreement to mediation of the underlying dispute (rather than the superficial matter of reparation for the offence) would mean agreeing to take part as a more or less equal party, rather than as the advantaged 'victim' in relation to the disadvantaged 'offender'. As Blagg (1985) observed, the offender wants mediation to correct the balance of blame, but the victim has a vested interest in preserving the imbalance.

Compatibility with Traditional Criminal Justice Aims

(a) Prevention of Recidivism
This was one of the original aims in the minds of those at the Home Office who agreed to fund a few experimental victim/offender mediation schemes on an experimental basis (cf. Brittan, 1984). Virtually all schemes, here and abroad, had adopted some such aim as at least a long-term hope, even if they did not see it as likely to be a short-term reality. Any short-term intervention like that offered by these schemes was unlikely to alter patterns of behaviour formed over a long period of time and influenced by strong community, family and peer-group forces. A more likely effect of the reparation schemes is an indirect one, through a gradual influence on community attitudes to offenders and a reduction in general readiness to reject them (Marshall, 1988b). One of the Cumbrian cases outlined above provided an example of what appeared to be a positive experience for the offender followed by a continuation of trivial offending. Any effect may, in any case, be mediated by other factors. One might expect that it would be greater, for instance, the more obvious and affecting was the degree of victim suffering, but in most of the cases

referred to the schemes, especially the police-based, this was not considerable. Young (1987) observed of the Sandwell scheme, for instance, that "Few of the victims who took part...had such a sense of personal injury and this is reflected in the offenders' accounts of meetings." The effect may also depend on an offender's ability to absorb it. Van Voorhis (1985) suggests that offenders with a higher level of maturity or moral development will be more affected — he found some empirical evidence for this proposition in that those measured by psychological tests to be more mature were more likely to pay court-ordered compensation and were better able to appreciate the reparative aspects of compensation (rather than equating it with a fine as mere punishment). On the other hand, younger offenders may be more malleable and less committed to crime, and thus more easily affected. The court-based schemes tended to concentrate on the lower age-range, probably for this reason, although the research provides no evidence for greater success with younger offenders. The fairly long sessions of 'offence-analysis' conducted with some offenders at Coventry may also have contributed to an effect on recidivism quite aside from any meeting with the victim. The skill of the mediator may also be important in separating the conciliation experience from one of punishment, as Blagg (1985) has argued: "...reparation can be a highly complex process requiring skill and sensitive handling and...its value as a lesson for juveniles may well be lost if it merely replicates the punishment paradigm, albeit by a more insidious route."

Data on recidivism for American schemes is sparse. Schneider and Schneider (1980) reported that only 8% of the offenders who had passed through the juvenile restitution project they studied had come back to court for a subsequent offence after the scheme had been in existence one year. (A further 4% had come to court for not complying with the restitution order.) But such figures make no allowance for the type of offender referred to the scheme, and in any case the time elapsed for most cases was very short. In a later paper, Schneider (1986) it was claimed that participants had lower recidivism rates than non-participants, but there had still been no attempt to control for other differences. With respect to adult restitution schemes, Hudson and

Chesney (1978) employed an experimental/control group design in relation to Minnesota Restitution Center and found that the experimental group were more likely to be committed to prison for new offences than the controls, although they were less likely to be committed for violations of the parole to which they had been allocated in order to take part in the scheme. Guedalia (1979), in his study of restitutionary probation found that victim contact reduced the offender's chances of re-offending, but other variables might well have affected the comparison. In their major study of VORPs, Coates and Gehm (1985) failed to produce any evidence on recidivism, although they noted that offenders tended to fear meeting the victim and seemed to be affected by the encounter, in much the same way as research described above on the British schemes has shown.

In the research into the Leeds scheme, it was shown that participating offenders rated the injury to their victims more highly (and more closely to the victim's own rating) than did other offenders, so that the scheme did seem to have some effect on an offender's response to the harm caused. Interviews with offenders in other schemes also seemed to demonstrate some impact on their attitudes and understanding.

The only evidence we have on re-offending comes from an analysis of the criminal records of all adult offenders referred in the first twelve months to the Coventry and Wolverhampton schemes. A few records could not be traced, leaving a total of 163 offenders followed up (88 from Wolverhampton, 75 from Coventry). Only local records were searched, so that only offences committed in the West Midlands area were included. They were classified according to the extent of involvement with the reparation scheme into four categories:

(i)   those referred who did not participate at all;
(ii)   those whose victims were unwilling to take part, but where discussions took place between the offenders and the project workers;
(iii)   those who were involved in indirect mediation;
(iv)   those who met their victims face-to-face.

Most offenders had several previous convictions. Consequently their records were analysed to show comparisons between their criminal behaviour before referral and during a comparable period afterwards, taking account of both the number and nature of offences committed during a maximum period of 18 months. For each offender an offence score was calculated for the period before referral and the period afterwards by multiplying the number of offences by their severity ratings, the latter based on victims' mean seriousness ratings of offences (Kapardis and Farrington, 1981). The post-referral score was subtracted from the pre-referral score to give a 'behaviour improvement index'. First offenders could not be analysed in this way and were treated separately. With respect to offenders with previous convictions, the results for Coventry were as follows:

Table 10a: Behaviour Improvement Index for Coventry

	No work	Individual work	Indirect mediation	Direct mediation
Number in sample	8	13	16	21
Ave. improvement	-1.17	+0.44	-1.23	+0.88
Standard deviation	7.17	3.96	11.75	5.50
Ave. days monitored in each period	310	346	394	402

There is no significant difference between the 'no work' group and the others, but the sample size is rather small to expect statistically significant results. All one can say is that there does appear to be a trend towards better results for the direct mediation cases and those where the project had worked with the offender alone. Around 55% of offenders in these groups had improved their criminal behaviour scores over the period of participation in the scheme, as against about 45% of the others, ie, they commit either fewer or less serious offences.

For Wolverhampton the results are shown below. Again the samples are too small to achieve statistical significance. The trend is clear, however, towards participation leading to better chances of improvement in later offending. Unlike Coventry, however, the indirect mediation group are the most successful, and those where the scheme worked only with the offender, the least so. 74% of the indirect mediation group and 55% of the direct group had improved their scores, against 46% of the individual work group and 36% of those not involved at all.

Table 10b: Behaviour Improvement Index for Wolverhampton

	No work	Individual work	Indirect mediation	Direct mediation
Number in sample	2	29	8	19
Ave. improvement	-0.93	-1.06	+5.38	+0.94
Standard deviation	2.53	9.82	8.17	7.04
Ave. days monitored in each period	333	327	309	342

As far as the first offenders were concerned, only 2 out of the 46 had re-appeared in court for another offence between their referral to the scheme and the end of the monitoring period (between 300 and 400 days for most of the cases), 1 in each of the cities. One of these, moreover, was one of the two who had not actually participated in the scheme.

These findings are highly tentative. Generally they indicate that involvement in the scheme leads to a better prognosis in terms of recidivism. The difference in the results for the two schemes, however, is somewhat perplexing. The Coventry scheme puts a good deal of effort into individual work with the offender, which might explain the good results with this group, but why the indirect mediation group in Wolverhampton should turn out so much better than the same group in Coventry and even than the direct mediation group in the scheme is problematic. If these results are reliable — and one must have reservations about this — they may indicate significant differences in the way the two schemes go about mediation. The greater emphasis on reparation at Wolverhampton may be better suited to the indirectly mediated cases, for instance.

(b) Diversion and Mitigation

Diversion has commonly been associated with the aims of reparation schemes. It was so in the reasons given by the Home Office for supporting experimentation in this area: *"What might be involved could be at one level a community resource enabling a case to be resolved without need for recourse to the courts"* (Brittan, 1984); *"Direct and immediate reparation could in some instances satisfy the victim, so that the police might feel that prosecution was no longer in the public interest. Obviously this could apply only to minor offences...Or once the case is before the court, it might be considered in place of a sentence"* (ibid.).

This is considerable pressure contemporaneously for the diversion of more offenders, for theoretical reasons (see below) as well as pragmatic ones (cost of prosecution). It is easy, in these circumstances, for diversion to dominate other aims and to side-track reparation schemes from their principal objectives (see Davis, Boucherat and Watson, 1987; Marshall, 1988b). In particular, the diversion aim can lead action away from the concept of restorative justice to one simply of another *"alterative punishment"* (Coates and Gehm, 1985). This tendency is already present in the Home Office statement quoted above, and is made even more obvious in a further passage from the same speech: *"And there will be many cases which are simply too serious for any conceivable form of reparation to be a sufficient penalty...Above all reparation must not come to be seen as a soft option; it should take its place as part of the criminal justice system's total response."*

Davis, Boucherat and Watson (1987) point out the aims of diversion itself are multiple. It may be seen as a way of reducing the negative impact of the justice system on offenders' self-attitudes and careers; it may be seen as a way of providing alternative services to offenders (increasing the positive impact); or it may be encouraged by purely cost considerations. The present day is one where formal measures against crime tend to be used in preference to private settlements. Ramsay (1981) instances the widespread use of 'making-up' (restitution plus apology) in the 18th century as an alternative to prosecution, and Mackay (1986) makes a similar point; *"...reparation in the forms of monetary compensation and of kind formed an important diversionary function in the Scottish criminal justice system until the 19th century."*

However, the cost-benefits of such private settlements were predicated on the victims being able to take such steps of their own accord. Nowadays, with fewer crimes being committed by persons known to the victim, or discoverable by him or her (Marshall, 1985, p.47), such reparation can only occur by the provision of special more or less formal arrangements, such as the reparation schemes studied here. This involves a cost which will mean that any potential savings will be limited. Indeed, studies in the United States lead to the conclusion that the hopes of producing cost savings are usually unfulfilled (Pearson, 1982), although better offence resolution at no greater cost may be feasible (see section on 'quality' below).

We have seen in previous chapters how the intention of reducing the negative impact of the system on offenders has led many social workers to advocate a policy of minimal intervention and that this has led many of the reparation schemes associated with diversion to intervene on as few occasions as possible, which has, ironically, minimised their potential impact on diversion. If this is one's sole aim, diversion can be achieved more swiftly and without cost merely by a change in prosecution policy, which several police forces have shown to be quite possible, at least as far as juveniles are concerned. If reparation is to serve the victim as much as the offender, it is not compatible with the idea of minimal intervention. As a factor in diversion, therefore, it can only be justified as an additional (or alternative) service that is likely to have a more rehabilitative effect upon offenders. Given the dominance of the minimalist position among those social workers and probation officers associated with the operation of the schemes, however, this model of reparation at the pre-court stage cannot honestly be said to have been tried in this country. The research would tend to indicate that the police force representatives on these schemes would usually be happier with the more interventionist model. It would, however, have the consequence that costs would be increased as a result of intervening in many more cases.

A particular problem associated with the police-based schemes is the matter of whether reparation precedes or not the decision whether to caution or prosecute. As far as offenders go, this position was often, it seems, left deliberately unclear in order to ensure their participation. Such deception is not a good basis for any sort of intervention. One or other model should be clearly followed and all participants should be in no doubt where they stand. The crux of the matter is whether a caution be conditional on the performance of adequate reparation by the offender. If, as will often happen, the victim is not willing to participate, the offender would have to be provided with an alternative task — either writing a letter of apology to the victim and sending compensation, or performing some work of a community service nature. This would, however, smack of sanctioning (including judgements as to the appropriate level of sanctions) without the protection of the judicial apparatus constructed to make precisely those decisions. This could only be countenanced in very minor offences with predefined maximum limits to the type and severity of task that could be assigned.

If, however, one removed reparation entirely from the decision to caution, there would be no incentive for most offenders to participate, except for those who genuinely felt remorse already. This is what has led to the well-meaning deception of offenders as to whether or not they were to be cautioned. If reparation is to have any substance at all it must be seen as a *duty* owed by the offender to the victim. If it is a duty, one can expect it to be performed, and if it is not performed, then alternative sanctions can be justified by this dereliction. The application of such sanctions would, however, necessarily involve the courts (except for minor breaches as indicated above) and hence prosecution. There is no reason, it would seem, in principle why private reparation should not be facilitated pre-court, but in cases where the victim does not waive his or her right to compensation, and where the offender is not able to make recompense without assuming more than a minimum burden, the necessity of prosecution would have to be faced. Such a process could decrease the rate of cautioning, although it would not necessarily have this effect.

There are still possible justice problems with such a process. The level of compensation voluntarily agreed by the offender and the victim might be based on a falsely high assessment of the damages by the victim. There would be no judicial oversight of such agreements. Although theoretically a problem, it seem unlikely that an offender would agree to a settlement that was absurdly high, and mediators could refuse to accept an agreement that did seem to be based on pressure rather than empirical reality. Where compensation claims were very high, it is unlikely that the offence would be diverted from court anyway, and even if it did come to court there would be little scrutiny of the claim, other than that already exercised by the police in documenting it.

A more serious problem, perhaps, is that offenders who could afford to pay compensation might be able to avoid prosecution when the impecunious could not do so. In court, however, those who can afford to pay a fine or compensation order may feel their sanction to be a much lighter burden than those who are poorer, so that legal justice is incapable of compensating more than marginally for wider social inequalities. Moreover, reparation schemes offer alternative means to financial compensation with a capacity for creativity that the court does not possess. It would be a more important matter if a caution did not become part of an offender's record, as the decision to prosecute or not would then become equivalent to a decision whether to assign a criminal record or not.

A third problem is that defendants who are innocent may plead guilty in order to participate in private reparation and avoid a public prosecution. This seems unlikely, although it is certainly possible. It would seem to be less likely that this would happen than that someone would plead guilty in order to be simply cautioned, a possibility that already exists.

An argument often levelled against diversion schemes is that they may lead, in practice, to the opposite effect — either to the involvement of offenders who would previously have been dealt with informally, or to the expenditure of more effort and time on each case than heretofore (in relation to reparation schemes, see Marshall and Walpole, 1985, p.45; Marshall, 1988a). The latter was certainly a concern in the police-based schemes studied here, hence the reason for a minimalist approach. It has led some to criticise those intermediate treatment (IT) schemes who become involved in such work, as, according to one IT officer, *"There is a great danger that an effect of increased involvement in this type of diversionary scheme by IT workers will be to expend scarce worker time and agency resources on work which will ultimately focus on soft-end juvenile offending and not on consolidating the use of IT as an alternative to care and custody for the serious persistent (heavy end) offender"* (Woodward, 1985). The same arguments could be put forward in relation to ordinary social workers or probation officers.

The above problems all stem from the interdependence of personal reparation and criminal justice decisions, yet these have no necessary connection. It would seem preferable to disentangle the two completely. The decision whether to caution or prosecute could be taken purely on the basis of society's needs — whether the person's behaviour is sufficiently threatening or chronic to deserve the additional sanction that prosecution brings about. The marginal distinction between a caution and a prosecution could be subject to change over time, but a decision would be based on the behaviour of the offender up to or at the time of the offence and not on any subsequent reparation. Reparation could be seen as a duty of the offender, whether or not prosecuted (assuming that guilt has been admitted), an approach which avoids the ethical dilemmas about offender compulsion, double punishment, and demonstrating 'sincerity' that Davis, Boucherat and Watson (1987) discuss. Reparation would be facilitated by a mediation scheme, whether the case was going to court or not, and quite independently of that fact. In the event of a victim's failing to be satisfied with the reparation received, procedures would have to be instituted for a legal claim for compensation, which could be a civil rather than a criminal matter.

As far as mitigation goes, the main advantages would be cost or the avoidance of a deleterious effect on the offender from a custodial sentence. Courts often declared themselves impressed by the reparation carried out via the schemes, and there was evidence for some reduction in the use of custody. North American VORPs have often adopted such an aim (although Galaway, 1985, notes that such an aim was resisted by the judiciary in the case of the Minnesota VORP and was hence dropped). Coates and Gehm (1985), however, found no differences in terms of imprisonment rate, only a major reduction in the average term served from 212 days to 38 days (which would have cost advantages, but would not avoid the negative effects of imprisonment on the offender; but presumably the judges did not see these effects as likely to be all negative). They also found that criminal justice officials *claimed* that reparation was being used as an alternative to prison (in as many as one-fifth of all cases they estimated) — a difference which may be evidence of inadequate statistical controls (the same problem that the present research encountered). One problem may have been that cases were selected where imprisonment was not really under consideration —

Dittenhoffer and Ericson (1983) found that courts working with the Ontario VORP saw the uncommitted offender with the means to pay as an ideal subject — someone, in other words, unlikely to have been sent to prison.

In our own research, there was a large reduction in the application of fines. As this was partly in favour of increased use of probation and community service, the effect on process costs was possibly to increase them rather than reduce them, at least in the short term. In the longer term, the avoidance of fines may reduce the extent of the problem of fine-defaulting (and hence the use of imprisonment for this reason), a problem serious enough to have been the original reason for proposing the Coventry reparation scheme. The shift from fines to the other disposals possibly occurred because the courts were anxious for some post-sentence supervisory contribution to ensure that reparation agreements were carried out. The change may therefore be seen as introducing a more 'restorative' element into sentencing, although it cannot be justified on the basis of economy alone.

There is a chance that an offender's sentence may be more severe because the full circumstances of the victim's suffering are brought to the notice of the court through the scheme's intervention. It certainly seems that compensation is more likely to be awarded in some cases, although usually just reinforcing the agreement already voluntarily made by the offender. In a case observed at Coventry a young man who had committed several minor acts of vandalism, had received a cuff round the ear when caught by one of the victims, had to meet with the mediator on several occasions, and met one victim (this occasioning a great deal of anxiety), was ordered to pay £260 compensation, despite being employed only on a YTS scheme and the fact that his victims were all insured.

Once again one cannot ignore the effect upon the victim if mitigation is achieved on behalf of the offender. Research into victims' attitudes after sentence at the two West Midlands schemes showed mixed feelings about courts taking into account reparation when considering sentence. To a large extent, however, the dissatisfactions that did occur may have owed as much to misperceptions of what was a likely sentence as to fundamental objections to court cognisance of the mediation. The research findings demonstrate only a moderate mitigative effect, so that victims concerns about offenders 'getting off' too lightly are probably not justified. The problem of victims' attitudes could, however, be alleviated further by divorcing the aims of the mediation more clearly from the sentencing process, so that the decision whether or not to take into account what has already been done in the way of atonement by the offender is seen purely as an option of the court, no different from the discretion it may already exercise with respect to offenders who have made reparation or shown their remorse of their own volition without the prompting of an organised scheme. The report from the scheme would then be seen as a more neutral statement, rather than one which just makes out a case on behalf of the offender.

Broader Social and Legal Implications

(a) Promoting the involvement of the parties
As explained in the introductory chapter, one of the intellectual sources for the movement towards victim/offender mediation was Christie's (1977) paper on 'conflicts as property'. The idea that taking crime and disputes out of people's hands was depriving them of involvement that could be personally and socially therapeutic or educative proved fairly persuasive, especially given empirical findings concerning the lack of criminal justice agencies' liaison with, or attention to, victims of crime, and their often negative, alienative impact on the offenders with whom they dealt. Mediation was intended to give both parties an active role in resolving crime and its aftermath (and the criminal justice system was rarely interested in the aftermath).

Hofrichter (1980), for instance, examined American restitution schemes from the victim's perspective and reached the following conclusions:

"Our study of restitution...has only reinforced our belief that it is good for the victim, good for the system, and good for justice, if victims are restored to a participatory role in the adjudication of criminal offences.

"More specifically, our preliminary findings indicate that where victims are involved as central participants in the restitution process, the likelihood that they will receive monetary and psychic benefits is

enhanced. To the extent that victims are seen as important actors who must be kept informed and available for participation rather than perceived as instruments of other officials, they may experience greater satisfaction and reciprocate by co-operating more fully...

"Where disagreements exist between victims and offenders, and where emotional conflicts arise that might be partly resolved if the consequences of the incident were explained by the victim to the offender, well-planned, face-to-face negotiations appear to offer the most promising form of direct participation. While negotiation poses potential problems of exacerbating victim trauma and creating inconvenience or delay, it affords an opportunity to resolve conflicts and ensure benefit payments that less direct forms of participation cannot achieve."

Such meetings can help restore the 'psychic' balance between victim and offender, and give each party the chance to have their say. As Albert and Howard (1985) put it: *"The need to be heard is often as important as the need to resolve the problem."* Moreover, it can help reform the stereotypes that each party has of the other, such as happened with the Cumbria offender who had expected to meet *"a gigantic fellow with a whip in his hand"* and — fortunately — was pleasantly surprised.

To all true mediation schemes, the aim of involvement is central — a 'basic aim' for the American VORPs (Coates and Gehm, 1985). The fact that the police-based schemes seldom seem to place much emphasis on an extended meeting with a free exchange was primarily due to the fact that these were really diversion, not mediation, schemes. The court-based schemes were motivated to arrange a direct encounter whenever possible. The Ontario VORP, according to Dittenhoffer and Ericson (1983), looked with disfavour on reparation without such a meeting. Even participation in a meeting, however, does not guarantee that victims will feel they have been 'involved' in the criminal justice process. Interviews with participants showed no real evidence that victims saw the schemes in this way. Involvement is seen rather as involvement with the offender or in a community initiative rather than with the justice system. This might, however, be what they would prefer, as did the victim involved in Case D, Chapter 4. As far as information about the progress of their 'case' within the criminal justice system is concerned, 80% had either witnessed the offence or heard about it subsequently from the police. On the other hand, participation in the schemes did make them much better informed about the nature of the offender and the circumstances of the crime.

Nevertheless, schemes could not always achieve such a meeting, without which the involvement of the parties was necessarily more perfunctory and less of a learning experience. The Coventry scheme tried to compensate for this in the case of offenders by fairly long offence-analysis sessions, but rarely was there any compensating attention to victims once they had rejected the idea of meeting. The signs from the research are that a direct meeting is much more productive than indirect mediation, and it would appear justified to make a joint meeting a central aim.

There are, however, certain dilemmas for the mediator, who is in charge of the meeting, but wishes to give participants every chance to use it to their own ends. A certain degree of control is essential if the exchange is to be really fruitful — the avoidance of any threat to either party, the rectification of any imbalance in social skills or personal power. Blagg (1985), writing on the Corby Juvenile Bureau, observed that institutional victims tended to be authoritarian and punitive, and that this obstructed the freely flowing learning process by putting offenders on the defensive. This, in the light of the current research, is something of an over-generalisation, in that the corporate victim was often the most accepting, and certainly all victims, of whatever type, need careful preparation in order to gain maximum advantage from the meeting, as well as to ensure that the demands made of the offender are restorative rather than retributive. The schemes tended to spend more time in preparation with the offender than with the victim. To some extent this may have been justified, in that the offender will more usually lack the necessary social skills, but more attention to victims' needs also seemed to be called for.

While mediators obviously need to steer the meeting, to which neither party is likely to be accustomed, there is the danger that they have their own goals — eg as many reparation agreements as possible, or *avoiding* material reparation, or maximising the impact on the offender — and that they will be tempted to steer the meeting in their own direction rather than the parties'. Davis, Baueherat and Watson (1987) observed that *"mediators exercise considerable influence over victims' choice of remedy"*. The greater the stress on extrinsic goals, such as diversion or mitigation, the greater the temptation to manipulate the negotiation process. As an example one can cite the obvious 'coaching' of victims in preparation for a meeting observed at Exeter. Davis (1985) has spoken of the "theft of conciliation" in the same way, when professionals usurp the opportunities that divorce mediation provides by substituting their own ideological predilections instead of yielding control to the parties. Similarly it was noted by research observers of the present schemes that, rather than exploring victims individual needs and aims, mediators would tend to present the prospective meeting as a chance to put offenders 'through the hoop' and reform them. In doing this they may have obtained the cooperation of some victims, but have alienated others, and they certainly missed out on the chance to offer a valuable service to victims. Once in the mediation session, some victims were able to turn it into a fruitful exchange, but at other times the meeting could be stilted and dominated by the scenario established by the mediator.

While such issues have not featured prominently in schemes' development so far — they have tended to be dominated by more material concerns such as obtaining referrals — they will demand increasing attention in the future. Questions about the autonomy of participants and the degree of control exercised by mediators will have to be seriously addressed during the training of mediators. The preparatory discussions with parties *before* mediation may be particularly important in setting the 'tone' in this respect, and the way mediation is presented needs to carefully considered. In particular, potential conflicts of interest between victims and offenders should be more openly recognised and dealt with in training and practice.

(b) Community involvement
That local communities should come to be involved in, or even have control over, the processing of at least minor crimes committed in their midst has been a strong aim in some quarters, especially as expressed by Ray Shonholtz, initiator of the San Francisco Community Boards (see

Chapter 1). As Nelken (1986) points out, however, community involvement usually means much less than community control in practice. It has been argued elsewhere (Marshall 1988a,b) that complete community autonomy is neither possible within the type of social structure found in modern large-scale nations nor even desirable, and that the aim should rather be to achieve a balance of community and professional interests which recognises that what occurs in the local community has implications for, and is properly the concern of, other communities too (eg the prevention of the scapegoating of minority groups). This even seems to be recognised by some of the advocates of community control, such as Bianchi (1986), who concedes that many communities in modern society are not ready and able to take over the control of crime on their own.

Projects in this country come nowhere near the community control ideal. The closest approximation is provided by the Newham Conflict and Change Project (see Marshall & Walpole, 1985), which stands out as a purely local initiative that puts the interests of the local community first, although even then it must be admitted that the small group of activists that comprise the project are not typical of local residents in their aspirations and social sensitivity. This project takes only neighbourhood disputes and does not divert offences from the criminal justice process, although some of the disputes dealt with could otherwise had been construed as criminal events if the parties had chosen to have resort to the police. Although some of the initiators of the American VORPs were strongly in favour of the devolution of criminal processes to the local level, the projects' aims have typically been rather lower key — such as 'enhancing community under-standing' (see Coates and Gehm, 1985). They seek to achieve this partly by means of involving victims and partly by means of using mediators who are local volunteers specially trained for the role. The training itself, which is often quite intensive (20 hours or more), is educative, in that it helps to break down stereotypes of 'offenders' and 'victims' prevalent in the local community. The mediation is carried out entirely by such volunteers (averaging 15 per scheme at any one time). As more and more people have been involved in some way or another, as victims, offenders or mediators, the aims and views of the project become diffused throughout the neighbouring area, although there is still no evaluation of whether this has resulted in any significant changes in attitudes to crime and community responsibility. Just as with the Newham project above, those running the projects, and probably also the mediators, are not a typical cross-section of the community; they tend to be members of the caring professions or others with a strong sense of social responsibility, despite attempts to obtain volunteers from different backgrounds.

Most of the projects studied in this research made little use of volunteers, although the practical difficulties of doing so anticipated by some schemes have not really proven to be serious after the initial expenditure of time on training and selection, provided there has been a sufficient flow of referrals for the supply of trained mediators. Unfortunately, allowance was rarely made for a lengthy pre-project stage that would have made it possible to recruit a body of volunteers, while pressures to begin mediation work immediately were high. One problem that does occur with the use of volunteer mediators when time is short (only three, or at the most, four weeks in general), is finding people willing and able to take a case at a moment's notice. The Leeds scheme got around this by paying their volunteers sessional rates (not just travelling expenses), thereby being able to expect both a prompt and a more committed service.

An exception, initially at least, to the lack of concern with community involvement was provided by the Leeds project, whose original proposal emphasised that the community should be enabled to deal with its own problems: *"It will aim to engage the community to a substantial extent in dealing with problems of crime in order that it can be perceived in perspective and as capable of being managed."* No mechanisms for instituting this aim were constructed, however, and the project's location in the Crown Court House actually set it apart from the community. Nevertheless, it was the only scheme to employ volunteers on a widespread basis, and it was always intended to move from sessionally-paid workers to purely voluntary work. The project leader saw the future in terms of a community-based mediation project taking referrals from outside the criminal justice system as well, and there are currently plans for starting such a scheme.

There has not, as far as we can tell, however, been any significant difference in the impact of those schemes that use and do not use volunteer mediators. Any differences may only emerge in the long term — it probably takes a longer time to reach optimum efficiency when using volunteers, but there should eventually be gains in terms of running costs if nothing else. Certainly, if community involvement is an aim, then the use of volunteer mediators is one of the main ways in which this can be pursued. At the end of the two experimental years, community involvement in all the areas studied could be said to be very limited indeed, although substantial publicity for the West Midlands schemes has meant that at least most victims had already heard of them before being contacted. Even awareness in those professional agencies that one might have expected to have some recognition of 'kinship' with such schemes is not high if one excepts those personnel that had had direct dealings with the project. This was found also in relation to the South Yorkshire scheme (Smith, Blagg and Derricourt, 1986).

It is early days, however. Such innovations take time to percolate through to the mass of residents, and one cannot expect to move from what is generally a condition of mass apathy (not necessarily an indictment, as a passive attitude is encouraged by the current legal process whereby everything is taken out of the parties' hands) to one of active concern and personal engagement in a couple of years, especially given the uncertainties of direction and management that experimental schemes necessarily exhibit. As the projects grow in confidence, so may the confidence of others also expand, although it will also involve the managers of such projects in being able to give up some of the professional control they currently exercise in favour of the democratic injection of local ideas and norms.

There are signs, however, that in the right conditions, relationships can be forged, through mediation, at an individual level between victims and offenders (cases E, F and G in Chapter 4, for instance) and this holds out hope for the expansion of community responsibility to match the acceptance by some offenders of more personal responsibility for their behaviour. It should be noted, too, that those victims who had a stronger sense of community attachment, or who felt some sympathy with the social circumstances of their offenders, were more likely to be prepared to go ahead with it. Offenders were generally surprised at the positive reception they got and were often visibly affected by the victim's generosity in accepting them as individuals in spite of what they had done. There is nothing in traditional criminal justice procedure that offers to match a successful personal meeting of this kind in destroying delinquent self-images or the assumption that everyone is "against them" and will be rejecting (the experience offenders had almost always anticipated).

(c) A more constructive response to crime?

Most of those who have initiated victim/offender mediation schemes have had at least in the back of their minds that this was a modest first step on the way to the introduction of 'revolutionary' new ideas on how to deal with the problem of crime. They have sought to promulgate a positive response to the offender instead of what is seen to be a wholly negative stance of traditional criminal justice, predicated on punishment and retribution. Although, traditionally, the criminal justice system has always sought, in addition to such retributive aims — or even by means of them, to reform offenders, the results over a century of changing approaches have not been encouraging in this respect. It is argued by the advocates of a 'constructive' response that such reform is impossible in the conditions of a purely legal system. While they do not reject the need to hold offenders *accountable*, they would reject the idea that any additional burden of punishment, over and above the duties involved in making reparation, has a beneficial effect. The fact that a person has been led to break the law means that he/she already stands to some extent outside the regular community, they argue, and reform can only occur — and most importantly the personal motivation to reform oneself — if the community takes definite steps to involve such persons and to find a place for them in a society that is able to approve them for their virtues rather than condemn them for their transgressions. The failure that is crime is seen as a failure of the community, or the society generally, as much as an individual's failure. Only by a mutual co-operative effort can such a failure be righted.

To some extent, success in such aims is beyond the schemes themselves (Marshall, 1988b). They can, however, help to spread knowledge about such new approaches and to gain the confidence of the uncommitted by demonstrating their worth in practice. The principles of 'offence-resolution' or 'offence-analysis' (see Raynor, 1985, for a description of these) have already been adopted by a minority of social workers and probation officers, moving the focus in dealing with offenders from general social casework and a concern with 'contributory background factors' per se to a more integrated, active counselling that tries to involve both the offender and his/her community (eg by meeting the victim). The Coventry Reparation Scheme has been very prominent in the development of such offence-analysis techniques and is seeking to incorporate the experience in training for local probation officers. Those probation officers who were involved in the South Yorkshire scheme have also been active in similar training and the promotion of what, perhaps, should be seen as offender/community mediation rather than simply offender/victim mediation. As they become known as 'experts' in mediation, the staff of such projects inevitably get asked to help train others in such techniques, even beyond the sphere of victim/offender mediation. In their work with corporate victims who often suffer repeated crime, for instance, schemes could promote discussion of how to cope with the problem more constructively, and, through meetings with offenders, help to formulate ways of preventing it. Case-study G in Chapter 4 also provides an example of how 'constructive problem-solving' could emerge quite naturally in the context of mediation with a personal victim — the problem in this instance being the offender's unemployment which was identified as a principal cause of the trouble he was in.

All the schemes seem to be making some headway in these respects, so that their benefits pass beyond whatever they may immediately achieve with respect to the victims and offenders they deal with directly. It may, indeed, be suggested that victim/offender mediation is a false distinction — that the sort of inchoate approach involved in such conciliation sits rather badly with rigid 'stereotypes' like offender and victim, and that mediation should be offered on a more general basis, as a resource for many agencies and individuals, whether these are concerned with legal actions or not. In this way schemes could avoid that subjugation to traditional justice concepts that seems to interfere with their proper development (see next section). While those who mediate between victims and offenders may need some specialist training, the bulk of what they learn they hold in common with mediators in any other context — labour relations, divorce conciliation, neighbourhood disputes, or whatever. The experience of the experimental victim/offender mediation schemes has made this clearer rather than otherwise.

(d) Reparative Justice

If the schemes have had some limited influence outside criminal justice, the evidence for their effect to date on criminal justice itself is equivocal. It was a major contention of Davis, Boucherat and Watson (1987), indeed, that the influence was more the other way around! They concluded that schemes should either operate non-selectively, across the board, within a criminal justice setting, or wholly independently of the justice system. Many have resisted the siting of victim/offender mediation completely outside the justice system, because that seems to amount to abdication from any intention of influencing that system, but given the power of an already established system to bend any innovation to traditional ends, it would appear to be necessary for schemes to establish themselves as independent in order to create a base for promulgating a different approach to crime. If, at the same time as trying to introduce reparation principles, these schemes must also be orientated towards diversion of offenders or mitigation of sentence, they will fail in a fundamental way: because, as Davis et al. note, they are then forced to operate in terms of *desert* instead of *need*, and the latter is an essential element in any attempt to erect an alternative system of justice. The present mixed situation unduly limits the schemes to taking cases only *when the offender stands to gain* and they are especially limited by the fear that the formal justice system will take a stricter view of offenders who do not take part in reparation. If the schemes only existed to promote reparation, the ultimate disposal of the offender would be irrelevant, but most espouse the additional aim of reducing the retributive effect of formal justice. This would be unobstructive if it were a long-term aim, achieved as a result of influencing courts to a reparative view in a general way, but it is destructive of the confidence of victims — and might also in the long-term be less influential with sentencers — when pursued as an immediate aim in every case, and not only as an aim but as a principle of selection too. What we see at the moment is too often reparation with justice rather than reparation as justice.

In the Home Office's plans for the experimental schemes, it did not really envisage them as an alternative system so much as supplying an additional penalty (see Brittan, 1984). Their actual influence has, however, not been as simple as this. As a punitive burden the reparation agreements that have resulted have been slight, when they have occurred at all. Nevertheless, courts have represented themselves as being swayed by the report on mediation from time to time, and the analysis above has shown that some change in sentencing as well as in general attitudes towards victim/offender mediation seems to have occurred. It is not a change that can be represented as more or less punitive, it is more a change in the style of disposal. In some ways, sentencing may indeed have become more reparative — a probable increase in the number of compensation orders (especially used as a sentence in their own right), and an increase in community service orders. The shift from a straight fine to probation orders, as well as the other sentences above, could also represent a new attitude to the offender generated by the different kind of information laid before the court.

One might have expected courts to have been most influenced by substantial material reparation, but this was not necessarily so. They do appear to have recognised the value of symbolic reparation, and the importance of a personal apology. The latter is an element which has no formal standing in Western law, although it is not neglected in other legal philosophies, most notably in Japan, where it is one of the cornerstones of the system (Wagatsuma and Rosett, 1986). These authors comment that *"The underdevelopment of American legal doctrine based on apology suggests the degree to which other, individualistic values —*

most notably compensation, declaration of right, punishment, professional self-interest, and administrative convenience — have been elevated at the expense of the restorative capacity of law and social ceremony. The American lawsuit is designed to deal with claims of economic loss; indeed, its lawyer-dominated, adversarial structure is not suited to resolve other kinds of issues. The legal system tends to reduce disputes to the types it is comfortable handling. Claims for personal injury are treated as if the issue is how to put a dollar price on pain and suffering, while claims essentially based on insult and psychic hurt are not dealt with well, if they are recognized at all."

Even the concept of what is involved in an apology may be different between the American and the Japanese systems: "*The behavior we have described as typically American is a transactional apology, that is, the person explains and justifies behavior and may admit responsibility and perhaps liability for this one act. The Japanese behavior we have described is characterized by much stronger relational elements, with less emphasis on the specifics of the hurtful transaction for which the apology is being offered and much greater emphasis on the expression of commitment to a positively harmonious relationship in the future in which the mutual obligations of the social hierarchy will be observed.*"

Haley (1986) agrees with Wagatsuma and Rosett, and adds that "*There is little question that the use of apology relates closely to the frequency and type of litigation in Japan. Perhaps most importantly, the use of apology reduces the likelihood that a dispute will be taken to court. Japanese judges uniformly acknowledge that the failure of an injuring party to apologize and offer at least 'a nominal sum to express sympathy' (mimaikin) is more likely to produce a lawsuit even in cases in which there is no dispute that the injuring party lacks any legal liability. Following the 1982 Japan Air Lines crash in Tokyo Bay, for example, its president met with victims or their families to offer apologies and full compensation. No lawsuits were filed. The combination of apology and adequate compensation eliminated any incentive to sue.*"

Critics of alternatives to courts have feared that the role of law as part of a crusade towards social reform would be lost in favour of conservative social control by local communities, and the stress that

Wagatsuma and Rosett recognise in Japan on restoring harmonious relationships and upholding the status quo might be seen as confirmation of such a tendency. While such a stress may have a conservation function, Haley argues that the role of the apology and the restoration of relationships need not be restricted to a static function, and that in conditions of social change they have been used in quite a different way — "*as a recognition of redefined social norms and as an act of submission to a shifting hierarchical order*": (A similar distinction between positive and negative social control is made in Marshall, 1988a.)

As a part of 'natural justice' it seems that reparative concepts have a rationale that is readily recognised and accepted by social actors in all cultures. Legal institutions in the Western world, however, pay scant, if any, allegiance to these ideas, and this is the basis of much dissatisfaction with their product, not least among the victims of crime. The victim/offender mediation schemes examined here have begun to open the debate on the role that non-material factors should play within criminal justice. It is a debate that will continue. The experience of the reparation schemes, however tentative, should continue to inform that debate and increase its level of sophistication. Already they have helped to move forward notions about the nature of apology and reparation from the materialistic ones typical of Western (especially legal) culture to a view not unlike that which constitutes the Japanese ideal.

The Quality of Mediation

Knowing what the experimental schemes achieved does not tell us how good they were. Most evaluations, unfortunately, are limited to quantitative measures of attainment. Merry (1982), amongst others concerned with mediation schemes, complains of their lack of evaluation in terms of the quality of justice displayed and of the process of mediation itself. Davis (1983) observes that since most disputes will be settled one way or another, the crucial issues are how quickly and how well the process works (to which one might add how cheaply). The next section will deal with the cost and timing issues. This section will deal with aspects of quality. The questions asked are:

(a) how far was justice served?

(b) how well did the mediators achieve a balance between the need to regulate the interaction and to instil a sense of ownership of the meeting in the parties?

(c) how far did the mediators manage to maintain a position of neutrality or fairness between the parties?

(d) how well did schemes monitor the quality of their work?

(e) how well did schemes manage to maintain their original aims?

Legal justice is a very special kind of justice and its criteria are not necessarily the same as those that apply in other contexts (see Marshall, 1988a, on the nature of justice in relation to mediation, and also Heister, 1987). Marshall and Walpole (1985) state that a 'just' outcome may be different in law and in mediation: "*In law, the decision is an allocation of degree of blame upon one party, on the basis of consideration of limited constellation of events surrounding a single past act...from the point of view of a 'reasonable', experienced, emotionally detached fellow citizen. In mediation, the decision is not made by the third party but is a compact between the two main parties. It is not in itself a judgement upon the past and it does not relate to any previous compacts that have arisen from other similar cases. Strict legal rights may be foregone in the interests of future peace or forgiveness. It is a private co-operative enterprise, not a public statement of condemnation or of principle. The justification for this form of resolution — that which makes it, in a sense, 'just' — is that it is freely entered into by the parties primarily affected, on the assumption that they are fully aware of the alternatives, and that the parties themselves know the details of past altercations, the subtleties of possible future developments, and the limitations imposed by their common environment or community, which makes their decisions more intimately knowledgeable than that of any third party could possibly be.*"

The elements of justice that apply to a mediated settlement, then, are

(i) that the parties think it is fair;

(ii) that the parties had the freedom to involve themselves in the settlement as much as they desired;

(iii) that the parties were as fully informed as possible of their legal rights and of the probable outcome of proceeding in other ways.

Interviews with parties showed that they normally conceived the process and its outcome as 'fair'. This finding is not unusual — 80% of both victims and offenders questioned in Coates and Gehm's (1985) study of American VORPs saw justice as having been served. There seems to be little doubt that personal reparation is consistent with public conceptions of natural justice.

Given that the experimental schemes were embedded within the criminal justice process, however, potentially affecting decisions of these other agencies; questions of legal justice also arise. Here there seemed to be more room for criticism. Some victims in the West Midlands schemes saw the ultimate sentence as too lenient, although they had been satisfied with the mediation in its own right. They just did not accept that it should have any impact on their legal 'rights'. On the other hand, many victims had gained a degree of sympathy for 'their' offender which led them to hope that the court would be merciful. It is interesting to compare the greater uniformity of satisfaction with decisions to which victims had been a party (in mediation) with the spread of views and proneness to criticise decisions taken without their involvement (in court): a point that appears to support the contention that personal involvement is valuable in producing greater satisfaction, one of the justifications for mediation.

Another problem arises when there are multiple offenders or victims. If only one offender is given the chance to participate, or only one agrees to do so, he/she may end up paying the full losses (a feature noted by Dittenhoffer and Ericson, 1983). This is, in fact, only a special case of that general unfairness that only some selected offenders are involved in the mediation schemes. In so far as this inequality of involvement is taken into account by the courts, as mitigation in proportion to the voluntary burden assumed, there is no ultimate unfairness, but it cannot be assumed that mitigation will occur. Those offenders who make reparation may also feel better, but one wonders how many would assume such a burden if this was their only compensation. As long as the criminal justice process and victim/offender mediation are interlinked such justice problems will occur. One of the reasons for the lack of emphasis by the schemes on material reparation is no doubt concern that the offender may otherwise be doubly punished. Even the process of apologising could be devastating and humiliating if not handled sensitively, as when a child in Cumbria who had deceived neighbours in his local village sponsoring him for a charity event was required to visit each in turn, apologising and returning the money, a process taking a whole evening. In some such cases a general apology and return of money via a representative of the victims would have been more effective (as occurred in the South Yorkshire case where a club secretary had absconded with a collection for a lottery, an example quoted in Smith, Blagg and Derricourt, 1986).

The overhanging threat of prosecution or sentence ("bargaining in the shadow of the law" - Mnookin and Kornhauser, 1979) in any case puts a large pressure on offenders both to take part and to agree to some kind of reparation. If the British schemes were more insistent on material reparation, no doubt they would achieve it more often, as do the American schemes. Even so, one of the more dubious features of the British schemes is the way they frequently left offenders vague about the prospects of being cautioned (when this had already been decided upon) or hinted at mitigation while admitting that it could not be guaranteed. Offenders did not usually see their participation as really voluntary, a finding shared by other researchers (Coates and Gehm, 1985; Young, 1987). Schemes were obviously concerned that, were it not for such pressure, most offenders would see no reason to take part. In traditional terms, this would be so, but if reparation were accepted as a general duty that all offenders were expected to fulfil (in one of a variety of ways, not necessarily through meeting the victim), the problem would disappear. What we see too often at the moment, are, as Edelhertz (1977) observes of American schemes, *"well-choreographed and one-sided bargaining transactions in which the threat of punishment is traded off for dollars or equivalent services, with victims as only incidental parties)"*. This was particularly obvious in accounts of the rather superficial mediation often taking place in the police-based reparation schemes, but it could be a feature, too, of the court-based schemes.

There was not the same evidence of pressure on victims to take part — certainly half of those conducted by the court-based schemes were prepared to refuse the offer, and no private (ie not corporate) victim interviewed indicated that they had felt any pressure, while most of those who actually took part in a joint meeting were happy about their involvement. The same result was obtained in the study by Coates and Gehm (1985) of American VORPs. There was no evidence of the strongly 'assertive' approach to victims that Dittenhoffer and Ericson found at the Ontario VORP, whose introductory letter gave "*no indication that victims may freely choose not to participate*".

There are still questions that need answering, however. There are three main reasons why victims may take part:
(i) because they want to meet their offender;
(ii) because they want material reparation;
(iii) out of a sense of civic responsibility.

There is a possibility that the promise of mediation may be oversold when the victim's reasons are of the latter two kinds. The chances of material reparation may well be exaggerated. Such reparation when it did occur, was generally of a token kind, and greater emphasis on material recompense would have interfered with other aspects of the mediation, as well as forcing mediators into the awkward and unwelcome position of debt-enforcers (cf. the embarrassingly long period of supervision of reparation in case D, Chapter 4). The victim's sympathy may be played on in order to secure cooperation, as if the offender were really the innocent party. The gentle persuasion used by schemes, although it could not be construed as pressure, might still be objected to as an unfair extra demand to make on top of the original victimisation. It is difficult to draw the fine line between the proper provision of information and unnecessary persuasion. Although there was no evidence of such abuse, and schemes usually showed themselves sensitive to victims' needs, sometimes providing counselling or practical help, there is still a case for protecting victims from unwanted intrusions, and one might consider whether the subject of meeting the offender might be better raised by a specially trained victims support volunteer who was in a position to see the potential advantages of mediation but who held the victim's interests as paramount.

In any case, the third reason tends to predominate among current caseloads, and many victims do not seem, therefore, to be inclined to see the offer of mediation as a means of ameliorating their own problems, whereas with help and support more of them might be able to use the opportunity for their own purposes as well as for the common good. At present, the more problems the victim has, the less likely he or she is to agree to meet the offender. The higher rate of meetings at the police-based schemes occurs despite the fact that their victims have suffered less, and is presumably due to the less threatening prospect of a minor juvenile offender (one, moreover, portrayed by the scheme, no doubt, as needing help and guidance). The high rate of 'agreements' at the police-based schemes also reflected the fact that there were unlikely to be issues to be disagreed about! The agreements emerging from the court-based schemes, if fewer, were at least more substantial in terms of concrete undertakings (45%, versus 25% among the police-based schemes), many of them involving brief episodes of work, not just small monetary payments. If schemes begin to take a greater proportion of serious crimes (where the victim has been seriously affected) attention to victims' needs will be even more urgently needed.

Even if there were no unfair persuasion, the selection of cases could be construed as unfair in itself. Observations of the negotiation process at Exeter showed that there was no question of reparation being targeted at those cases where it would be of most benefit to the victim. Nor was the form of reparation (usually chosen by the scheme) selected with the victims' needs in mind. Indeed, the scheme did not really claim to be addressing victims' needs at all, or even undoing the harm of the offence. Reparation was simply a tariff option for offenders, and victims were asked to take part in order to help provide a constructive alternative to the courts for particular young offenders. Similarly, the Cumbrian scheme was established primarily with the aim of helping juvenile offenders by introducing a means of enhancing a caution. It was inherently orientated more to offenders than to victims and rarely dealt with offences serious enough to warrant intensive victim involvement. The reparation workers and probation staff involved were, however, fully aware of the problems and ambiguities of their work and approached it in a committed but self-critical way. The limitation was not so much the quality of effort as the situation in which the scheme had to operate. At

Exeter there was evidence of meetings being pre-orchestrated so as to make the maximum impact upon the offender, the mediators rehearsing victims so as to show a degree of anger, for instance, that they no longer really felt. In these cases a meeting was merely a brief climax to negotiations, not an opportunity in itself for the parties to share views and come to a greater understanding of one another. Note, in this respect, case A in Chapter 3, where the meeting at first was awkward, artificial and mechanical, and it was only the skill of the victim in dealing with young lads that made it ultimately a useful experience. The same phenomena were observed in American restitution programmes by Schneider and Schneider (1980), and Walklate (1986) in this country showed concern that victims might be in danger of being used for criminal justice ends rather than for their own benefit.

This problem did not exist to the same extent in most of the court-based schemes studied here, largely because of the emphasis placed on mediation in its own right, counteracting the pressure from the criminal justice context to use it as a means to some further end. While court-based schemes achieved a lower rate of direct mediation, this was normally of a substantial kind in terms of the amount and quality of communication between the parties. Meetings between victim and offender in the police-based schemes were usually brief and perfunctory, and not really describable as 'mediation' at all. The mediation process in the court-based schemes was, in fact, a delicate balancing of the two ideologies of reparation — as reconciliation, and as an impact on the offender. Some projects tried to introduce a counterbalance to the offender focus which resulted from their criminal justice base by visiting victims rather than offenders first (eg Leeds, N.E. Essex, the SACRO project in Scotland) but this was rarely more than a token gesture, as it happened after selection of cases not before. This selection was generally influenced by defence solicitors or probation officers interested in helping their clients avoid a custodial sentence or some other severe disposal. (This was one of the predominant reasons for referral given by probation officers in Leeds: 33 out of 53 replies.) Victims as well generally still tended to conceive the projects as something for the offender more than for themselves. In one case, the Totten scheme, there seemed to be a greater emphasis on the offender and a downplaying of the victim's role — to the extent that the reparation report to court was modelled on the traditional Social Enquiry report, giving details of the offender but none about the victim.

Nevertheless, having got to a meeting, the court-based projects seemed to carry this off quite well. There were few criticisms in interviews with the parties of the mediator's capacity to hold the ring sufficiently well for both sides to feel that they were not under threat and then to sit back and let the parties take control of the communication, intervening only when this seemed to be getting side-tracked or running into the ground. Very few instances of a meeting getting out of control were found, and in these cases the mediator quickly abandoned it. The shoplifting case in Cumbria described above that involved a vindictive victim provides an example of what can go wrong, possibly because of insufficient preparation with each party by the mediator. In three instances in Wolverhampton, however, an inexperienced volunteer mediator was perceived by the offenders as having sided with the victim and not allowing the former proper opportunity to express themselves. Such instances, however, were individual exceptions, although they emphasise the need for good training and supervision.

The lack of pressure from the mediator may have led to a good mediation experience, although it also probably contributed to the low incidence of reparation agreements. This in itself shows that material reparation was a concept imposed on the meetings because of the expectations of criminal justice agencies, rather than an aim inherent in parties' conceptions of the process. The emphasis on material agreements in American schemes may produce a different, more assertive mediation style. Those studies of the mediator's role itself that have been carried out in the United States, admittedly all in the context of divorce mediation, show a fairly assertive, interventionist style, and a correlation between such a style and ultimate success in terms of getting to a material agreement (Donohue, Allen and Burrell, 1985; Slaikeu, 1985; Kressel, 1987). It would be valuable to compare mediator styles in this country, too, to see whether some mediators are more likely to reach material agreements and whether these tend to play a more dominating role in the meeting. Although there is evidence for inter-mediator variability in the schemes studied here differences were not huge, and the numbers of cases involving direct mediation for each mediator were too small for the results to be regarded as definitive, especially as some mediators may have been selected to take the more difficult cases.

While there was little evidence, too, on the basis of our data, that the use of volunteers rather than professional workers as mediators made a lot of difference to results, it could be that a greater emphasis on volunteers in this role would help to correct the bias towards the offender in the long run. The North-East Essex scheme had made the greatest efforts to incorporate victims' interests, by its strong operational link to the local victims support scheme. Although the number of cases was small — perhaps a good indicator in itself that the scheme was trying to prioritise those cases where mediation would be most worthwhile, rather than trying to relieve the sentences of as many offenders as possible — this scheme did seem to show the best balance between the interests of different parties. All the same, it has to be admitted that the Totton scheme, which also used volunteers, was probably the least victim-orientated of the court-based schemes, so that the aims of the scheme managers are probably most important in determining predominant orientation.

Schemes showed some variation in the extent to which they informed parties of the nature of the mediation process and how it might affect criminal justice decisions. On the whole such preparation was more substantial with respect to the offender, and this balance could have been better, although the lack of social skills presented by many offenders may require more careful counselling. There will be some cases, however, where the upset of the victim is such that the balance of pre-meeting support needs to be the other way round. There was one notable case at Coventry, for instance, of a man's assault on a former cohabitee, where the mediator spent a long time with the victim attempting to relieve the latter's sense of guilt (because her boyfriend was likely to be sent to prison). Police-based schemes tended to be more perfunctory in preparation of the victim. The court-based schemes usually showed adequate preparation of the victim, although there may have been a tendency for an over-rosy picture of the likely outcome to be communicated in order to counter the initial reluctance that many potential participants will inevitably show towards a new idea that demands more involvement than is usually required of them. The results of this research will help, it is hoped, to provide schemes with more accurate information to convey to participants about the likely range of outcomes.

One area that demonstrated lack of diligence in communication across all schemes was that of follow-up after mediation. It was found in the research that either party may have needs for further information after meeting the other, and indeed their appetite for such information will have been whetted by such personal involvement. It is not fair to leave them in the dark subsequently, and in any case they may, in the event of receiving no further communication, come to revise their views of the usefulness of involvement, which does not help the schemes maintain a good reputation. More effort certainly needs to be expended in keeping parties in the picture post-mediation and providing support where necessary. A meeting should not be seen as simply the climax of the exercise, but as one, often particularly effective, component of the process of reconciliation between victim and offender and between both of them and the wider community. The interest and goodwill shown by many victims in providing a helpful and educative experience for the offender needs to be more openly acknowledged by providing feedback of the offender's subsequent progress (with the latter's permission). There is a chance here to treat those who take part as partners rather than clients in the mediation process.

The principal informing ideology of at least the court-based schemes was that much more could be achieved through a personal meeting than through formal processes without direct involvement. The research confirmed this idea, and parties responded much more positively to direct mediation. Nevertheless, a good number of cases were processed using the mediators as 'go-betweens' (35% of all cases in the police-based schemes, 21% in the court-based). The principal reason for proceeding in this way, after a meeting had been rejected (almost always by the victim), was in an attempt to aid the offender. The results were less often constructive and sometimes involved considerable effort. Schemes therefore need to re-examine whether effort should be spent on such 'lower-grade' mediation in the face of an uncommitted and unwilling victim. (Where the victim is positive in attitude, but unable — eg because of infirmity — to take part, it might be a different matter.)

Finally, one must confirm the fears of Davis, Boucherat and Watson (1987) that schemes would find it hard to resist the encroachment of traditional criminal justice aims. The police-based schemes were in any case more concerned with diversion of offenders than with restorative justice, so that they made little progress towards the latter goal, although this was associated with the particular aims of those agencies setting them up, rather than being an inherent limitation of reparation at the pre-court stage. The court-based schemes, on the other hand, did show considerable effort to maintain their original restorative aims — to the extent of putting ever decreasing emphasis on changing court decisions in favour of creating the optimum atmosphere for a successful victim/offender meeting in its own right, whatever the consequences in criminal justice terms. In doing so they were not without support among sentencers, who sometimes explicitly recognised the value of what the schemes were achieving, whether or not they took the offender's effort into account when determining sentence. Nevertheless, the effect of close liaison with the courts, and of dependence on court-related personnel for cases, was that the offenders' needs and interests tended still to be the first consideration, a fact which can only be countered by taking active efforts to represent victims' interests more strongly, perhaps by greater involvement of victims support schemes.

Ethical considerations

(a) Confidentiality

A number of issues revolve around the problem of confidentiality and the passing of information about offenders from official records to victims, and information about victims to offenders. Victims and offenders often wanted to know something about the other party before they would make a decision as to whether or not to have a mediation meeting.

At the Steering Group Meetings of the Leeds Project in March 1985 it was established that "the victim should be given relevant information about the background of the offender (with the latter's consent if it is a pre-trial situation) to ensure that consent to participation in reparation is informed consent".

The basic guidelines established for the mediators was that if the offender gave permission to the mediator for their details to be communicated to the victim then this would be done. There was no clear guideline as to what details could be given.

In practice the victim was usually told some very basic details about their offender: age, sex, approximate residential location (ie area but not street) and occupation. They might also be told that the offender had not committed that type of crime before or had never been to prison. It would be fair to say that the mediators usually played down the offender's record and encouraged the victim to recognise the remorse and sorrow that the offender had expressed.

If a victim of crime obtains the name and address of the person who committed a crime against them then there is a possibility that the victim, or another party on behalf of the victim, will carry out some sort of revenge or retaliation. This does happen already in some cases, both reported and not reported. Mediators were sensitive to the dangers of retaliation and did not give information on offenders about victims without discretion.

(b) Honesty

One of the aims of many mediation/reparation projects is to break down the stereotype of the offender: for the victim to see that the offender is really quite an ordinary person. However, by introducing an offender, with personal details, to his victim the offender's identity in the community as 'an offender' may infect be amplified or publicly announced. Although the negotiations and mediation session are conducted in private, the participants, for example the victim, may go 'public' to their neighbours, family and friends after the event. On the one hand mediation might enable victims to see offenders as less threatening than they had hitherto, and as people experiencing social and

262

personal problems, in essence as people not offenders, on the other hand, the offender's identity may be cemented to the particular crime committed.

If victims are given the full details of their offenders' criminal records then this might put them off meeting and make them doubt the sincerity of mediators' reports of remorse. One such case illustrates this point. (Featured on the BBC2 documentary Brass Tacks):

Helen and Bob were burgled by Roger and when approached by the mediation scheme they agreed to a mediation meeting. After the mediation meeting had taken place Helen and Bob talked to friends and neighbours locally about Roger whom some of them knew. They found out that he had a far worse history of crime than they had been led to believe and got a totally different picture of Roger than that given by the project's mediators. They didn't feel that they had been treated fairly by the scheme and would not have agreed to meet Roger if they had really known what he was like.

The way an offender was presented to the victim, when the victim was approached with the idea of mediation, was a crucial element in determining whether or not a victim agreed to meet. If the mediator presented the offender in too negative a way it might deter the victim from agreeing to meet. Conversely disregarding certain details of the offender's recent criminality, and underestimating the offender's capacity to renege on promises or 'fall back into a life of crime' might lead to dissatisfaction and lack of credibility among victims and the general public.

An interesting comment on a victim's perspective of 'their' offender came from one of the project staff who said that one pattern that seemed to emerge from her work with the project was that it was much more difficult to get victim and offender together if the victim already knew the offender, perhaps she said because they already know "...*he's a bad lot, no good at all etc. Whereas if the victim doesn't know the offender there isn't that knowledge and there is a certain degree of curiosity as to what they are like etc.*"

Most victims had faith in the projects' assessment of an offender's sincerity and remorse. Few victims made more than cursory enquiry into the details of an offender. How much they should know or were entitled to know was not established. This indeed is an issue within the wider context of increased information and support for victims of crime and one that is presently very much at the discretion of agencies such as the police and probation.

There is also a question as to whether offenders should be told about their victims. If reparation were to become a clear alternative to custody then such information may encourage intimidation of victims to participate in mediation and reparation.

Costs and Efficiency

One of the problems with a stress on achieving manifest 'results' and on cost-effectiveness is that it leads schemes to maximise the number of cases dealt with, often at the expense of the quality of the work done. This certainly applied to the Home Office funded schemes, that were explicitly expected to deal with at least a hundred or so cases a year. This led to an uncritical process of selection and a lot of effort 'touting' for cases, which may have wasted resources on cases where there was little to gain for either party from the beginning. The schemes cannot be evaluated as if they were solely a means of achieving criminal justice ends at lower cost: they demand an effort of users — both offenders and victims — and they must therefore provide each with major benefits.

It is important to be able to demonstrate an output that is in proportion to the economic cost, but that output must not be measured in simplistic terms such as the number of cases reaching mediation or an agreement. By having little regard to parties' needs and placing emphasis on speed and brief communications, such figures could be maximised while in fact achieving very little. The output measure that is relevant to the schemes studied here is the degree to which parties are helped to a constructive, revealing and influential experience that relieves the pain of victimisation on one side while it assists self-realisation and behavioural reform on the other. This output cannot be measured in numbers, although one can say, on the basis of various pieces of evidence presented in previous chapters, that it will tend to be higher when there is a joint meeting that is adequately managed in terms of preparation and follow-up.

Such an output does not incorporate any aspect of the ultimate criminal justice decision in the case. This is not under the control of the schemes, and thus should be taken simply as a by-product of the reparation process. It is a by-product that potentially affects the overall cost, however, and so it is better to place any economic implications of changed criminal justice decisions on the input side of the equation (effectively, in other words, as a reduction in the costs of the scheme).

This is particularly so in the case of police-based schemes, where the altered decision, if it occurs, is in advance of the mediation and not a product of it. The cost of prosecution is sufficiently substantial, if saved, to balance out the cost of a reparation scheme that was responsible for the diversion of only a few dozen cases. This means that the mere fact of diversion creates a saving, apart from any benefits of the mediation itself. The question arises, however, whether such schemes are necessary to achieve the desired level of diversion and the evidence of the research is that the reparation/mediation component was not essential in this respect. There are probably less labour-intensive, more straightforward ways of diverting more juveniles than setting up reparation schemes, and these would involve even greater savings.

If, however, more cases are diverted, more victims will lose their chance of receiving compensation via a court order. This loss in most cases where the offender is a juvenile will not be substantial — only a minority would have received compensation from a court, and this would have been unlikely to have been complete compensation. In so far as there is potential loss to the victim, and this would be more likely in the case of adult offenders were the diversion policy to be extended upwards in terms of age, a reparation scheme may provide a means of satisfying victims' needs. Even so, the research findings stress that the outcome of victim/offender mediation is less likely to be material reparation than not. Such reparation as occurs, moreover, is usually of a token kind. This finding is not necessarily to be taken as a failing of the mediation process — rather it constitutes a recognition that the suffering of victims is typically more in psychological terms that in financial ones. Such suffering is not recognised or catered for by existing criminal justice institutions and the argument for providing some facility for reconciliation between victim and offender lies in pressure to provide such a service. In order to work as a true service to victims as well as a method of making a positive impact on offenders, a scheme would, however, have to be divorced from the aim of diversion that currently dominates police-based reparation projects. Diversion could be achieved on the basis of, say, a multi-agency panel, and mediation offered in any case where the parties were willing (whether the offence was to be prosecuted or not) by an independent agency financed out of part of the savings produced by increased diversion.

When it comes to the court-based projects, potential cost savings are less prominent. If many prison sentences were avoided, there would be a substantial saving, as the cost of a local prison place in 1985-86 was taken as £11,700 per annum. Three year-long custodial sentences (or their equivalent) would, if avoided, pay for the provision of a mediation scheme, which can be expected to cost (at 1985-86 prices) between £30,000 and £40,000. The research findings were such that it was difficult to be certain about the exact effect on sentencing, but it would seem that the minor effect on custodial rates, even though apparently small (it was estimated that the three Home Office funded court-based schemes saved 22 prison sentences over two years), would have been more than sufficient to justify their cost, even without taking into account the benefits to victims, offenders, and possibly the community generally of encouraging reconciliation and reparation. A major effect seems to have been a reduction in the number of fines, thus reducing the remuneration of state coffers, but the size of the average fine is not so large that this is likely to have had more than a marginal effect on overall costs. If there was an increase in the number of probation and community service orders this would also have involved a marginal cost increase. On the other hand, another custodial term or so per year may have been saved by not having to prosecute for non-payment of a fine, which could have balanced out all the other costs. Altogether, it would seem that the court-based schemes more than paid their way. Given increasing confidence of the courts, it may be possible to increase their financial effects, but even if they were merely to break even, they would in effect be providing a service at no cost and thus be justifiable.

In the case of these schemes the criminal justice decision is not independent of the results of the mediation. Even so, the quality of victim and offender involvement is likely to be higher when the schemes are independent of too great pressure to manifest an impact on sentences. They should, therefore, be enabled to take on cases of any kind that appeared to be suitable without having to concentrate only on those where mitigation for the offender was most likely, and without having to stress material reparation, unless this was relevant to the parties themselves. A report to the court of the outcome in terms of the offenders' efforts should, however, remain an important product that sentencers in general value and which can be influential in reducing the punitiveness of the disposal in recognition of the offender's atonement.

Cost-effectiveness can be enhanced by the use of volunteer mediators instead of full-time employed staff. The necessity of more frequent training, because of greater turnover, and more provision of support and supervision, plus the need to expend resources on recruitment, all reduce the cost savings by so doing. Nevertheless, the quality of the outcome does not need to be any less when using properly trained volunteers, and the strong links so forged with the community may have other benefits for the project and for the success of its work. While the savings produced by using volunteers may be modest it may therefore be worthwhile advocating their use on these other grounds. On the other hand, it may be useful for other agencies' personnel — especially those in the probation service — to obtain direct experience of victim/offender mediation. Short-term training and placements as mediators might be appropriate for such professionals, the costs being borne by their parent agencies. This would help strengthen the links of an independent scheme with criminal justice agencies and other relevant groups, while also providing low-cost staff resources.

In terms of cost-effectiveness, therefore, the victim/offender mediation schemes were in the unusual position of providing a new, fairly labour-intensive service, at no inconsiderable cost, while being able to justify that input (and potentially produce savings above and beyond that) through an indirect effect on criminal justice decision-making, which, given the costliness of certain disposals, can have an economic influence out of proportion to the number of cases where change is effected. In so far as it is the schemes that facilitate such changes in decisions they would seem to more than justify their cost.

With respect to *efficiency* of operation, the schemes left more to be desired, but this is not surprising at such an early stage of development. The research has demonstrated more in the way of potential than in success actually realised. The following points in particular will need to be considered.

Schemes will have to ponder the value of expending resources on cases that clearly are not going to result in a direct personal meeting. The outcomes in such cases were noticeably inferior in general, and may take just as much effort in staff time. Equally, those cases that begin to involve an excessive number of preparatory contacts are more often than not ultimately unsuccessful, so that schemes may have to monitor their expenditure of effort on each case and ensure that they 'cut their losses' at a sufficiently early stage. Where complex and long-standing relationship problems were involved it would seem better to concentrate on relatively simple points of disagreement, usually pertaining to the commission of the offence, on which some kind of settlement in the short term is feasible. More fundamental reconciliation in such cases would involve longer-term counselling of each party separately, involving an escalation of effort beyond that which is economically feasible. It seems more sensible for schemes to take as their aim the facilitation of short term engagement between estranged parties in order to provide a constructive platform for the development of future relations, rather than take responsibility for trying to reconcile parties in more diffuse terms. The experience of mediation itself may provide people with the reorientation of attitudes and skills to make progress of their own accord. Ultimately that is, in any case, the only sound foundation for a successful relationship: one cannot always be seeking out a mediator to sort out every little difficulty! Schemes would thus be more efficiently employed restricting themselves to the mediation of immediate issues and the communications before and afterwards pertaining to those issues. In the same way, one can question whether the intensive counselling of offenders which was documented at the Coventry scheme — successful as it may have been in its own right, as results in terms of recidivism appeared to indicate — was a proper expenditure of the scheme's resources in relation to the basic aims. Such long-term assistance may be better provided through routine probation work, although schemes are well placed to advise on and assist the training of officers to carry out 'offence-analysis' work.

The effort involved in obtaining referrals was documented at the Coventry and Wolverhampton schemes as accounting for a major part of staff time (16% at Coventry, and 25% at Wolverhampton), seriously reducing the scope of their mediation work. This seems unsatisfactory and other means of getting referrals should be experimented with — perhaps along the lines of the Totton scheme, which wasted very little time in this respect. Greater selectivity of cases was also called for, given the large proportion that fail to move on to a completely successful conclusion: in many cases there seemed to be little to gain for all the effort. Such selection might also take the emphasis away from the attempt to get as many cases as possible and also thereby contribute to a reduction in the time spent trying to raise referrals. In the process of selection more account could be taken of victims' interests and needs, while the principle of selection that tends to operate at the moment — in terms of whether the offender is in danger of a custodial sentence — could be abandoned in favour of a general duty across all offenders to make up for their offences (materially or otherwise) whenever their victims were willing to accept this.

Another problem generally encountered was one of timing. It was expected that the schemes would contribute to faster resolution of cases by avoiding cumbersome formal processes, but all the schemes met the problem of dependence on the timing of the criminal process, with victims having largely recovered from the effects of the crime before they could be contacted. (On the other hand, the chance of meeting the offender may still come too early for the angrier victims — cf case D in Chapter 4.) Even the police-based schemes were hampered by having to wait considerable periods (weeks) for files to come through. Court-based schemes might be intervening even longer after the original crime. This appears to be a common problem among VORPs generally. Coates and Gehm (1985) cite such delay as a common complaint of both victims and offenders — typically a case would take over 5 months in America between commission and mediation. The delay in the British schemes at least seems to be much less than this. According to Bainbridge (1987) the median delay between arrest and sentence is less than two months in the West Midlands, and the court-based reparation schemes did not involve any more delay, normally, than the usual referral on conviction for social enquiry reports (ie an additional 28 days). The avoidance of further delay, however, is obtained at the expense of time for carrying out all the negotiations with both parties as well as the culminating mediation. Lack of time was a constant bugbear for all the schemes (cf case D referred to above, where it was difficult to set up mediation in just three weeks when Christmas holidays intervened). The problem was especially serious in rural areas, where visiting could be more time-consuming.

More time is available in most cases appearing at the Crown Court, but access to them depends on being able to overcome the problem of intervening before the formal plea of 'not guilty', which in one instance led to difficulties in the case of the Leeds project (see the discussion of the R. v. Clough and Moorhouse case in Chapter 4). In this respect, those schemes that divert cases from prosecution to mediation as an alternative, without having to attend further criminal justice decisions, have a distinct advantage. The Norwegian Conflict Councils, for instance, achieve resolutions within two weeks of the offender being apprehended (Hovden, 1987). This does depend, however, on the willingness, and ability, of the police force to relinquish a case as a criminal matter when it seemed better suited to mediation — a process that was tried experimentally for a year in one project in London (the Juvenile Mediation Project, see Marshall and Walpole, 1985) but which was abandoned because of too few cases. Further attempts could usefully be made to institute referrals at this early stage, given the potential benefits in time savings, and hence in the ability of schemes to be helpful to victims.

CHAPTER 7

Comparing the schemes

If the research results show anything, one of the clearest facts must be that the evaluation of an innovation such as mediation in the context of a well-entrenched tradition like that of criminal justice is no straightforward matter. Most of the quantitative indices are ambiguous. It has been shown, for instance, that it is possible for these new schemes to attract a viable number of referrals equalling or even exceeding the rates for the average American scheme that has existed for rather longer. One cannot, however, simply claim that the more referrals a scheme received the more successful it was — some schemes were poorly resourced and would have been overwhelmed by too many cases, others (like some of the police-based schemes) were bent on limiting referrals to the most borderline cases where prosecution was a distinct possibility but not inevitable, and other indices of "success" showed no direct relationship with rate of referrals (N.E. Essex, for instance, had several unique qualities and performed varied and interesting work with only a small number of cases, while among the police-based schemes the E Cumbria panel with only 12 referrals achieved the highest rates of direct mediation and of reparation, and the Sandwell scheme with only 11 was probably the most sensitive to the full possibilities of good mediation and also had a high rate of reparative agreements). Too great an emphasis on obtaining a large number of referrals may lead to inordinate amounts of time spent cajoling other agencies rather than the central task of working with victims and offenders. This was certainly a problem for the two West Midlands court-based schemes compared to Leeds.

Rates of achievement of mediation among referrals are equally ambiguous. The police-based schemes were generally able to obtain a victim-offender meeting in a higher proportion of cases than the court-based ones, but, in the farmer case, a meeting was usually all it was —

often just a quick apology and a thank you among two embarrassed and uncertain individuals. By aiming for mediation with more substance, the court-based schemes were obviously limiting themselves to fewer cases, because they were demanding more in participation from both the offender and the victim. It is worrying if mediation is achieved in too many cases, because it raises doubts about the real voluntariness of participation. Nearly all offenders agreed to mediation in the police-based schemes — but then they virtually all thought it was their only chance of avoiding prosecution (which was often untrue). The tiny number of offenders not under threat of prosecution co-operated to a much lower extent. One must question a scheme that depends on deliberate confusion of one of the parties in order to produce a willingness to be involved. The court-based schemes were usually successful with offenders, too, but not to the extent of the police-based ones, up to a quarter of offenders feeling free to turn the offer down.

Victims were less pressured to be involved, although the rate of acceptance among one of the police-based schemes appeared to be high (91% at Exeter — far above the rate at any other scheme). With this one exception, which might be explained by the fact that in this case victims were often being asked to do very little beyond 'receive' an apology or compensation, it was obvious that victims were feeling free to opt out, especially in the court-based schemes, none of which exceeded a 60% rate of acceptance by victims. Although the rate of mediation in the court-based schemes was therefore substantially lower, at least such mediation was usually a more substantial experience for both parties, lasting between one-half and two hours, while the rate of mediation was still respectable, over half of all referrals involving some negotiation, and over a third mediation.

At this early experimental stage quantity mattered less than quality and careful mediation. Rating the schemes according to quality, however, is no easy matter. If the content, substance, and full exploitation of the potential of mediation is the criterion, the court-based schemes as a whole clearly achieved much more than the police-based ones, for which actual victim-offender encounters were usually both superficial and artificial. It should be recognised, however, that the police-based schemes generally were diversion exercises rather than mediation (or reparation) projects. In diversion terms, some police-based schemes were probably effective — those in Northamptonshire and that in Exeter for example. But these were undoubtedly employing mediation to the least extent of all the schemes. It was not normally a necessary component for the achievement of diversion and there was little concept, in these schemes, of the value of mediation in terms of other ends, at least no such concept appeared in actual practice and the Northampton Juvenile Bureau explicitly rejected mediation for any other purpose. Of the police-based schemes studied, only Sandwell clearly emphasised mediation in its own right, while two of the Cumbria panels (West and, to a lesser extent, North) also showed a more careful and sensitive approach that recognised victims' interests as well as offenders'. Even these schemes, however, were inhibited by an overwhelming expectation of diversion as the main product instead of better offence-resolution, inhibited both in the number and range of cases they could work with, and in the quality of that work.

It seems that when the possibility of avoiding juvenile prosecutions presented itself, the opportunity was too much for social workers and probation officers to waste, and their energies were usually channelled not into negotiation between victim and offender but between themselves and the police representatives on the liaison panels. The most obviously successful projects were those where the police were most favourable to the same diversion aims (Exeter and Northants especially, but also West and North Cumbria panels), but this was success seen entirely in terms of diversion and the avoidance of conflict between agencies. In some cases, concern for the victim, for reparation, or for the non-material advantages of mediation, would have been strongly conducive to substantial action but the cases were resisted because they seemed to be divertible without such intervention. Occasionally such advantages were glimpsed by the police representatives but they were unable to gain ground against the dominating ideology of diversion and minimum intervention. In the court-based schemes where the potential of mediation in its own right was more powerfully promoted, it was because of the commitment of the staff (who varied in background, but tended to be probation or social work trained) to such an ideology rather than to more traditional aims. In the police-based schemes, with the sole exception of the independent community-based Sandwell project, there was no such constituency for promoting mediation as such. The social workers to whom it might have appealed in other circumstances were interested mainly in diversion; while the police officers involved, who were not committed so single-mindedly to diversion at all costs, lacked the outlook or the confidence that might have led them to see the advantages of mediation, in terms of meeting victims' needs and achieving more realistic justice through direct offender accountability, as something to promote in a general way rather than something that was relevant in just the odd case.

If mediation is to be employed in the service of such general aims, and not that of diversion (to which it does not even seem to be particularly relevant or effective), it is apparent that a base independent of criminal justice agencies is a necessary pre-condition. The only example of such an arrangement among the police-based schemes was provided by the Sandwell scheme, but it has been used in only a small trickle of cases, possibly because of lack of realisation within the referring juvenile liaison panel of the types of case which would be most relevant. Referral could be independent of any past or future decision about prosecution (and probably should be), but in that case the scheme is going to have to "sell" its services in terms of other achievements. These were all quite favourable, relative to other police-based schemes, in terms of getting to agreement, achieving reparation, and especially in obtaining other undertakings by the offender. Sandwell's preparation of cases was also more careful than all other such schemes except that in North Cumbria. The small sample of cases leaves many question-marks, but there can be little doubt that it is on the basis of the Sandwell model that pre-court mediation can be developed and its full potential assessed, not on projects run by existing criminal justice agencies.

In contrast, the court-based schemes have found themselves freer to explore the potential of mediation for serving victims' interests and those of the wider community. Diversion was not a possibility, and mitigation of sentence regarded (rightly) as at best uncertain, so that these schemes had to seek elsewhere for their main justification and could experiment with a wide range of offence types. Even the Leeds project, which (like the small Junction Project) began with a strong emphasis on diversion from custody, soon adopted more sanguine aims with realisation of the fact that initial expectations of saving a hundred prison sentences a year could not possibly be fulfilled. The project still stood out as having more serious offenders and offences than the others, but extended its early focus on the Crown Court to take on a substantial number of cases from magistrates' courts, and now is also prepared to take pre-court cases. Other schemes, starting with minor offences, have tended to extend their range to include an increasing proportion of serious offences, both Coventry and Wolverhampton having made arrangements to take Crown Court and juvenile court referrals. Coventry, in particular, has been more willing than most to take challenging cases, including nearly 30% violence offences, although Leeds still had the highest proportion of burglaries (35%), and the Junction Project — which only dealt with recidivist juveniles — had 40% violence cases. Although N.E. Essex had, overall, more minor offences, the case of domestic violence in the appendix shows that it had the capacity to succeed with potentially difficult situations. There was, interestingly, no strong relationship between seriousness of offence or offender's record and a successful outcome, although there was a tendency for violence offences to be more difficult to bring to direct mediation. There seems to be no reason to limit referrals to court-based schemes in terms of seriousness of offence — the major determinants should rather be how much there seems to be to gain from mediation, in having an impact on the offender or in helping victims, and such criteria would tend towards a focus on more serious rather than less serious crimes, although legal categories of offence are not very relevant to such determinations. Mediation is a process close to the parties, affected by their feelings, capacities and idiosyncrasies, and its success is therefore unpredictable and personal. Even the definition of what constitutes success is variable according to parties' needs, desires and preparedness.

Although the court-based schemes tended to concentrate on young adult offenders (the three Home Office funded projects had over half their offenders aged under 21) — presumably because the younger offenders were more likely to be seen as "reformable" or more acceptable to meet their victims — the research showed no relation of age to success, and therefore no reason to concentrate on the younger offender. The N. E. Essex scheme dealt with more adults (69% over 21).

The Wolverhampton scheme, in general, received the most minor referrals and it also had an unusually high number of corporate victims (55%), approaching close to the average of 60% for police-based schemes and American VORPs. This proportion is representative of the concentration of corporate bodies among victims generally, which would imply that the other schemes were tending to select private or personal victims rather than corporate ones (or to have these selected for them). Even when the other schemes took corporate victims, these were usually social agencies, local authorities, churches and so on, rather than commercial companies, whereas three-quarters of Wolverhampton's corporate victims were commercial concerns. On the whole, there was a tendency for commercial firms to be less accommodating victims, while the other corporate bodies were usually easier to deal with than personal victims (individuals and private households). This trend may have been the explanation for Wolverhampton having the highest failure rate (54% of referrals not getting anywhere) — although Leeds and N.E. Essex were not far below — and the lowest rate of agreements after direct mediation (73%, 10% lower than the other schemes). The correlation, however, was not overwhelming, and there is no reason for mediation schemes to avoid, or concentrate on, corporate victims. While personal victims may more often have emotional needs to satisfy through confronting the offender, representatives of corporate bodies were often found to be angry or upset by the crime too, and they may have other problems, such as repeated victimisation, which might be resolved through better understanding of the motivations of offenders.

Probably a more important reason for Wolverhampton's high rate of failure to get some kind of victim/offender negotiation was its apparent reluctance to carry out indirect mediation in the event of a failure to get agreement for a meeting. Only 13% of its cases were dealt with in this way. Coventry, on the other hand, carried out almost as many mediations indirectly (33%) as directly. This does not seem to have been the result of any reluctance to conduct victim/offender meetings, because Coventry's rate of 38% direct mediation was higher than any other major scheme's (the Junction Project achieved 60% over a very small number of cases). Coventry's high rate of indirect mediation was probably due partly to the fact that it was the best-resourced of all the schemes (three full-time employee mediators) for the more time-consuming work of "shuttle diplomacy".

The issue of whether victim/offender schemes should spend much of their time on work that is not preparation for a direct meeting (which, after all, is supposed to create benefits for both parties that could not be achieved in any other manner) is an important economic one. The research indicated that indirect mediation was much less likely to result in an agreement, in reparation, or in an altered sentence. There was also a decreasing chance of ultimate success the longer the negotiations took — at least after ten or so contacts with either party. It would seem, therefore, that projects should, for the sake of parsimony, concentrate on cases where a meeting of victim and offender seems likely, and only continue to work with other cases when both parties seemed keen to do so despite a reluctance to meet (or some practical obstacle). The analysis of recidivism by Judith Unell and Anna Leeming, although tentative, did suggest that individual offence-analysis work with offenders alone at Coventry seemed to produce a measurable improvement in subsequent behaviour. Even if this is so, one may still question whether a scheme instituted to carry out mediation on behalf of victims and offenders equally should spend a disproportionate amount of time with one party, when such counselling could be carried out by, say, probation officers as part of their mainstream task of helping to rehabilitate offenders.

Despite the fact that the Coventry project spent more time preparing both parties for mediation than any other scheme for which we have figures, the same project had the lowest rate of reparation agreements (direct or indirect) and the lowest rate of offender undertakings, facts which help explain why a smaller percentage of sentences appear to have changed as a result of an offender's participation in mediation at Coventry than at any other scheme. (This finding held even after allowing for the above average number of assaults in the Coventry caseload.) If the project which was one of the most thorough and "professional" in its approach failed on these indices, one must at least question whether these indices are valid measures of success. The most likely reason for Coventry's "failure" in this respect, indeed, is that the scheme itself rejected material reparation as a primary goal of its activity. More than any other scheme it was imbued with the philosophy that the central issue in mediation was the emotional exchange, the resolution of feelings, anxieties and doubts, and most of all, the creation of a relationship between the parties. Material concerns such as compensation fitted uneasily into this concept of the meeting. When they emerged they tended to be treated as symbolic, reaffirming the psychological reconciliation achieved, rather than as important entities in themselves. In this the Coventry project was very much repeating the experience of the earlier South Yorkshire Probation experiment in Rotherham and Barnsley, that eventually gave up any idea of trying to influence sentence because that introduced extraneous aims into mediation that interfered with the natural healing process.

There is a further reason why one may question effects on sentencing as a valid measure of success for these schemes. The more likely it is that offenders will "get off lightly" as a result of participation, the less likely that their involvement will be seen as genuine, and the more likely that the scheme itself will be seen primarily to be "for" the offender and not the victim. This produces an awkward dilemma for the schemes. Offenders cannot be expected to take part without some hope of material benefit, but too great a success in achieving this will sully the scheme from the victim's perspective. The research findings that suggested only a very moderate influence on sentencing were possibly the optimum that could have been wished for. There is no sign that offenders are escaping too lightly (the shift from fines may have involved a greater burden on some, even if others were released from problems of default in payment), while there is just enough possibility of mitigation to make it worthwhile for offenders to make the effort (especially if in danger of being sent to prison).

Interestingly, the estimated savings in custodial sentences were no greater for Leeds than for Coventry, despite a greater effect of the former

278

project overall on sentencing, and despite its having by far the highest proportion of reparative settlements. It was the project with one of the least serious caseloads, that at Wolverhampton, that achieved the greatest savings in imprisonment. This may have been because the Wolverhampton Magistrates' Court had the most severe sentencing record of all the courts studied when allowance for types of offence was made — which gave the project more scope for changing custodial decisions. It could also have been a result of its concentration on corporate victims, if crimes against such victims were less likely to result in custodial disposals, a factor for which we were not able to control in the research. In the latter case, the success of Wolverhampton could have been over-estimated — although there is no empirical evidence as to whether crimes against corporate bodies are treated more or less severely by the courts.

CHAPTER 8

Achievements and Difficulties

Despite the many differences between the different court-based projects on individual variables, the overall similarities in experience are more striking. Taken together they succeeded in demonstrating a number of positive achievements. Most importantly, the experiments demonstrate that victim/offender mediation can be carried out, that a good many victims welcome the opportunity to meet their offender, and that most participants were satisfied with the experience (the majority would do it again or recommend it to others). They demonstrate, too, that the community has a role to play in dealing with crime, enabling society to construct a positive experience to complement what is, perhaps inevitably, the emotively negative impact of the law alone. That experience seems to affect offenders even more than an appearance at court, and affect them in such a way as to increase their sense of responsibility rather than feeling inadequate and rejected. As far as the victims go, it was apparent that reparation in its wider sense — psychological and social, as well as material — was seen as a part of natural justice. If some were critical it was often because their expectations of receiving some returns in compensation for their suffering were heightened by participation beyond what they would ordinarily have been at the hands of normal criminal justice processes. Lastly, the schemes demonstrate that other agencies, especially sentencers, recognise the validity of what they accomplished and were willing to take it into account in making their decisions. The court-based schemes exhibited these achievements much more than the police-based ones because they had sufficient independence, practical and philosophical, to employ mediation in a truly innovative and liberating way. In doing so they have taken the first step in questioning many of the assumptions we tend to make about the nature of criminality, justice and effective social control.

If the message of these experiments is hopeful, however, it is all the more important that the failures and problems encountered among the successes should be openly faced and resolved. If these schemes demonstrate that victim/offender mediation has a future, that needs to be designed in such a way as to be more unequivocally successful.

None of the schemes studied seemed to supply a perfect model for future practice. In the rest of this chapter what appear to be the main problematic issues that need addressing will be discussed.

(i) Operational problems

(a) Referrals

Obtaining referrals was a common problem. Much time-consuming work had to be invested into publicity among relevant agencies and into the day-by-day process of persuading solicitors, police, courts, and probation officers that particular cases might be pertinent. Some schemes were affected more than others. Lack of what was deemed enough referrals led to the demise of the N.E. Essex scheme, despite several exemplary and unique features. Both Coventry and Wolverhampton felt their daily presence in court to be a substantial burden. Leeds seem to have fared most successfully in respect of referrals, but most of these only came from certain parts of their catchment area, so that the potential number of referrals was certainly far larger than the number actually received.

The number of cases where victim/offender mediation might be essayed is certainly large, given that such mediation can offer a variety of benefits depending on the individual circumstances of the case. As others come to be more fully informed about the nature of mediation, more cases will presumably be referred, but this may be a slow process. Despite these problems the level of referrals at several schemes — Coventry, Wolverhampton, Leeds, and Exeter — was at least adequate to create a viable programme. Moreover, how many referrals would be ideal? In the first place, this depends on resources available to handle them. The four above (especially the first three) were the best-resourced of all the schemes, capable of handling probably twice as many referrals as they were getting. Other schemes were running on a shoestring that prevented them placing more effort into persuading others to refer, even if they could have coped with more. Secondly, in this experimental phase of development, it is more important to proceed with care and to ensure high quality than to be too concerned with numbers. Some of the Essex cases were very good examples of what can be achieved, and they covered a wide range of types, despite the low numbers. Concern to show how many cases could be processed at this stage would inevitably have reduced the quality of performance and the usefulness of the pilot schemes for guiding future action.

It was a little unfortunate that, in order to obtain funding, some schemes had "sold" themselves on an over-estimate of the number of cases with which they could deal. The most embarrassing example was the Leeds claim to be able, potentially, to divert a hundred offenders a year from custody — obviously unrealistic, especially when it is estimated that the actual number achieved was more like seven. However realistic such prior estimates, having received money the schemes are inevitably put under considerable pressure to demonstrate quantitative, as much as or more than, qualitative achievements, a pressure that inevitably distorts their way of working. If the Coventry mediators had been content with half the number of referrals, would they have felt obliged to have spent so much time in court obtaining more, or have placed so much effort in trying to proceed even with cases that had a low probability of ultimate success? What difference would this then have made to the content and organisation of the principal mediation task, with more time available for both preparation and follow-up work?

Mediation in criminal justice is a very new idea. Many working within the system still have not even heard of it, let alone understood it. It will take time (and local experience) for referrals to be substantial from any one source. One answer in the interim is to diversify as far as possible the number of sources. If one agency will only supply one a month, six agencies will supply a sufficient number of cases for a scheme to demonstrate its effectiveness. A problem with many of the schemes studied here was their initial reliance on one source of cases. Most of them have since diversified and overcome their early problems (most notably Wolverhampton, which did not receive enough referrals for survival in the first three or four months). Having achieved an adequate flow of referrals, moreover, schemes should not be expected to expand indefinitely. More referrals may mean less successful mediation, or more wasted cases, or less selectivity and a lower cost-benefit ratio. There is danger in inexpert or unthoughtful mediation, as there is promise in the best performances. There is much to learn and, for the sake of those involved as well as the future of the innovation, proceeding with caution is better than trying to revolutionise the criminal justice system overnight.

(b) Timing

Being tied to particular stages in the criminal justice process, most of the schemes suffered from having to complete their task, sometimes involving sensitive negotiations, in a short period of time. The Tatton scheme was probably the freest of the court-based schemes in this respect, as it was able to identify cases at an earlier stage. If the operation of victim/offender mediation could be removed from any close link with the timing of other agencies' work, there would be problems with any attempt to influence the latter, but mediation would be able to proceed at its own natural pace. The influence that the experimental schemes exerted on normal criminal justice processes was, in any case, only moderate at best: to a large extent the schemes were satisfying needs that the traditional system cannot reach, rather than replacing that system. Greater independence, too, would reinforce the interests of the parties concerned relative to those of justice agencies that were found to dominate current schemes.

Independence of any particular stage of criminal justice would also resolve another timing issue: that the current point of intervention may not have been the ideal time with respect to the readiness of either party. This was especially a problem in relation to victims, who were often either too angry or not angry enough by the time the offer of mediation was presented. To exploit the benefits of mediation to the full it would be preferable for schemes to be able to adjust the timing of a meeting to the psychodynamic career of the victim. (One might also advocate a similar match to the offender's state of readiness, but it would be impossible to optimise both at once and it would seem best from every point of view to give preference to the victim.) This might mean delaying direct encounter until any formal criminal process was past, but it also implies that a scheme should obtain referrals at as early a stage as possible in order to catch those parties whose upset is likely to be short-lived.

(c) Preparation and follow-up

The best results usually followed careful preparation of both parties for mediation. An encounter between a victim and an offender is unlikely to be a situation either party is familiar with, or able to use to greatest effect, without guidance. Even if they know one another, as is often the case, the circumstances (in the "shadow" of legal process playing unfamiliar roles of "offender" and "victim") conspire against a natural, easy exchange. Both parties need prior assistance from the mediators (or other staff of the mediation scheme) to identify their principal needs and objectives and to prepare their strategy to meet these. At its worst, such preparation becomes a rehearsal with a script prepared by the mediator. Good preparation, however, does not seek to impose aims and methods but elucidates the parties' own feelings, clarifies their purposes and imparts the skills with which they may pursue them themselves. The distinction is identical to that between pedagogy or instruction (Latin derivation "build in, pile in") and education ("draw out").

The degree of preparation needed depends on the sensitivity of the case and the personal characteristics of the parties. Sometimes the victim will need a great deal of help to deal with the emotional problems arising from the crime, but offenders are often lacking the social skills that would enable them to present themselves convincingly or agreeably and may therefore require quite a lot of preparation too. Those offenders who still fail to realise the full extent of their personal responsibility may also be prepared for the process of facing up to themselves and their accountability that the meeting with the victim should complete.

A major failing of all the schemes examined was the omission of any procedure for keeping in touch with parties after mediation. There was a strong tendency for the mediators to regard their responsibilities as having ended with the facilitation of an agreement and the report back to the court or juvenile liaison panel. Their responsibility cannot end so abruptly, however. Having encouraged two people to form a relationship, however tenuous, and to share an (often emotional) experience, they cannot expect them to depart and forget the matter entirely or to have no further interest in each other. The mediators owe it to both parties to give them some news of each other. A very few may have formed a relationship of active visiting. In most cases, further direct contact will not be desired or appropriate, but there will remain some minimal degree of interest in, and commitment to, the process they have initiated together. In such cases they rely on the mediation schemes to enable them to sustain this vicarious relationship. In still other cases, mediation will have started a healing process (for victim and offender) rather than completing one, and continued support and counselling may be desirable. There will be a limit to the extent to which schemes can, or should, afford the time for post-mediation counselling, but it should not be neglected altogether, perhaps referring parties on to victims support workers or probation officers as appropriate. Mediation, obviously, can only play one small part in the total process of dealing with the causes and aftermath of crime: this makes it all the more important to exploit its benefits by further follow-up work when needed, whether further mediation or individual casework. If schemes accepted this long-term responsibility, they might also find the idea of supervising the carrying out of agreed reparation or undertakings less distasteful.

(d) Indirect mediation

The research has shown that indirect mediation is time-consuming and ultimately less often productive than a victim/offender meeting. The lack of personal contact makes it less rewarding for either party.

To some extent the poorer results may be due to self-selection of cases who are less prepared to be sympathetic or conciliatory. Whatever the reason it does not affect the message that schemes should concentrate on those cases where direct mediation is appropriate and likely. Indirect mediation should be continued only where the needs of either party are particularly pressing, and even then thought should be given to referring such parties to other agencies for whom longer term counselling is standard practice. Mediators at the Coventry project are inclined to disagree with this conclusion. They argue that their experience of indirect mediation is that it is often helpful to the parties and desired by them. They are also concerned about a joint meeting becoming a ritualistic "end in itself", without regard to the specific needs and interests of the parties. These points are well taken. There certainly are times when indirect mediation will be more suitable. The danger that concerns the researchers on the basis of the overall findings, is that indirect mediation which can be an easier, more comfortable option for the mediator, could become the norm when, in general, a joint meeting usually offers more significant achievements. The selecting of cases for different styles of work needs a great deal of care and depends on sensitive and thorough exploration of parties' needs. This is obviously a subject for more intensive research.

(e) Resources
Most of the above problems are exacerbated if a scheme lacks the time to devote to adequate preparation, follow-up and so on. Those schemes with several full-time staff were clearly more likely to carry out successful work and to survive. At a minimum two full-time co-ordinators/mediators and a full-time receptionist/secretary are necessary to provide cover at the office-base as well as adequate resources for liaison and visiting. Further mediation resources can be covered by the recruitment and training of volunteers, the return for such investment being greater the more commitment that can be generated, for instance by means of sessional payments. It needs to be stressed that victim/offender mediation, if it is to be principled and beneficial and not just a gimmick, cannot be obtained "on the cheap". At the same time, the research has shown that it is possible, at least on the basis of notional cost-savings achieved by a reduction in prison sentences, for court-based schemes to pay their way while providing services that will be beneficial for some victims and offenders.

(ii) Failure to maintain basic aims

One of the most consistent findings (which also dominated the first report from this research — Davis, Baueherat & Watson, 1987) was the difficulty schemes experienced in maintaining their underlying philosophy of restorative justice in the face of a dominating criminal justice system which persisted in its allegiance to more traditional views of crime and the legal process. This is a familiar theme. Community service orders were originally proposed as a restorative measure but have become routinised into merely one among a variety of punitive sentences. The introduction of' 'reparation schemes" with their focus on the personal involvement of victim and offender was intended, at least by their advocates, to overcome this tendency for institutionalising and converting previous reform efforts. The Home Office's discussion document (Home Office, 1986) on the possibility of a "reparation order", again confusing the innovative and the traditional, was fairly uniformly rejected by respondents involved with the new schemes, and it is plain from this research that reparation imposed as a sentence would lose its essential distinctiveness. These schemes are offering to achieve something that the criminal justice system does not even attempt. They are supplementary, rather than alternative routes to the same ends. If they might potentially replace some traditional processes in some cases, this will be on the basis that their achievements are more valued rather than because they do the same things better.

A bias towards offenders' interests was encouraged from two very different directions — from the traditional concern of criminal justice agencies with the offender rather than the victim, and from the anxiety of social workers and probation officers that offenders (especially juveniles) get a raw deal in the current system. While these two sources of influence are usually perceived as opposing forces — the one tending towards greater retribution, the other less — they share a focus on dealing with the offender and a general neglect of victims' needs. It has not been easy, therefore, for these schemes, based in criminal justice agencies, or dependent for referrals on one or other agency almost totally, to inject a different conception of handling justice that gave a central role to the victim. Even when schemes bent over backwards to promote the victim's role, as many of the court-based schemes did, they were powerless to affect the original selection of referrals that depended largely on defence solicitors or probation officers seeing advantage in it for their clients, i.e. for the offender.

It is partly this predominance of offenders' interests in selecting referrals that explains the low incidence among the caseloads of victims who had any substantial needs to resolve in terms of the aftermath of the crime they had suffered. More often they came to mediation having expurgated any emotions they had felt and prepared to help out in a process aimed, as far as they were concerned, primarily to reform the offender. There is nothing wrong with an impulse to participate on this basis (as long as schemes do not mislead as to the likely effectiveness of such measures) and the experience was one that many victims valued and sometimes found beneficial to themselves in converting a negative experience of victimisation into a constructive one of social reconciliation. What is wrong is that the benefits of mediation for easing hurt, anger or anxiety were so seldom offered to victims who still evidenced such needs. Sometimes possession of such attributes would tend to disqualify them in the eyes of the mediators as emotionally unprepared for a confrontation with their offender. There is something to such a view, and worries of victims support advocates (eg Reeves, 1984) reinforced the fear of harming victims through making demands with which they could not cope, but the answer is not to exclude them but to provide the support and preparation that would enable them to take advantage of the mediation process, to turn it to their best interests.

Similarly there was a failure in some cases to make the most of situations involving related parties, where mediation offers the chance to begin restoring a relationship or adjusting to a new relationship, over and above any individual benefits, with implications for longer term crime prevention. Some of the best examples of victim/offender mediation were carried out in such circumstances (see, eg several of the case-studies in earlier chapters and in the Appendix), and a high proportion of referrals involved prior acquaintances. Sometimes the very fact of knowing one another inhibited parties from wanting to meet, but once again thorough preparation by the mediators may have enabled more of these cases to get to direct mediation.

Both these last issues relate to a more general failure among mediators to deal with emotions rather than material negotiations. As time went by most schemes evolved from a reparation orientation to one that put more emphasis on feelings. It is not possible to carry out fruitful mediation without dealing with underlying feelings. A material agreement without this will be superficial and of little meaning to the parties. Mediators should be prepared to gain the skills necessary for ventilation and expression of grievances, not merely for their direct therapeutic benefits, but also because the ultimate settlement will have more content and value. A concern with impressing judges and other criminal justice decision-makers with "hard" reparation agreements often obscured the fact that the quality of the process before such an agreement was of far greater importance than the contract itself, which at its best encapsulates or symbolises the contributing exchange.

One final aim that has hardly been realised is that of community involvement. Although prevalent in the theoretical literature, there was little concern in practice amongst the leaders of these schemes for any degree of real input from local people. Even where volunteers were recruited, they were trained to act like professionals rather than being expected to inject local norms and definitions. With hindsight, perhaps, one can see the "community" idea as having been added artificially to the concept of victim/offender mediation, because of the concurrent growth of community mediation schemes for neighbour-hood dispute. Concepts of "community justice" appear to have no role in the "reparation" schemes. On the other hand, there is another sense of community, one not connected with neighbourhood, but connoting the feeling of being fellow citizens, of co-operation, of sharing the same society, of mutual respect and help. This formulation (which is the one contained in several theoretical texts concerning reparation — eg Zehr, 1985) corresponds well with the feelings participants in victim/offender mediation appeared to be describing in their accounts (often surprised — if pleasantly — at such developments, which violated the stereotyped expectations parties had of each other). Despite the disappointment that the schemes did not

289

receive as many "upset" victims as was anticipated, the fact that others could still enjoy such a "communitarian" experience gives hope that crime, and its aftermath, could be coped with) more than it generally is today, within the local community. Fear may keep people from intervening or taking direct action as they would have done in the past, but often that fear turns out to have been unreasonable, leading to isolation and withdrawal, especially among the old, and to a self-fulfilling prophecy that generates the ideal conditions for the growth of crime. By breaking that vicious circle, the experience of meeting offenders could help to change social attitudes to minor crime and start to provide the conditions for its control in society instead of under the heavy hand of the law.

(iii) Reparation

Throughout these experimental schemes there ran a fundamental ambivalence about the role of reparation, at least in its more material forms. Although most of the schemes were imbued with the sense that offenders owed it to their victims to make up for what they had done, there was less agreement as to how far such atonement should take the form of money or labour. In a good many cases the offender was impecunious, often already in debt, and had few skills to offer in the shape of reparative work. Even when they could offer some material reparation, victims were often found to place little importance in this, or even to find the idea of the offender working for them either onerous for themselves (implying that they would have to have the offender visit them at home, find suitable work and possibly supervise it) or undesirable in itself (as demeaning for the offender). This was less of a problem for corporate victims, but few offenders carried out reparative work for either corporate or personal victims. Work for some community cause (old people's home, church etc.) was more popular.

Negotiations about material quanta (compensation to be paid, hours to be worked) tended to be divisive and disruptive to a mediation process that was intended to bring the parties closer in terms of understanding and personal communication. Neither mediators nor parties seemed to find it easy to pass from the emotionally-charged exchange of explanations, apology and forgiveness, to an anti-climactic discussion of material things. It is interesting that calculations of this kind tended to appear more like victims determining the offender's degree of punishment, rather than the determination of what was merely the victim's due. In many cases the victim will already have replaced the stolen or damaged goods, or have suffered little tangible loss, or have been insured, so that in a sense any reparation by the offender was indeed a punishment rather than reimbursement. It was significant that victims were far happier when compensation had already been given or offered before mediation occurred.

American schemes do not seem to have encountered this problem. This may be because there are no alternatives in that country for victims to obtain compensation. When, as in Britain, compensation and community service can already be awarded by the courts, there was less urgency for schemes to make such arrangements, and thus become embroiled in unwanted problems like deciding appropriate quanta and supervising the agreed work. Again it is significant that victims who had been satisfied with mediation and had not been concerned at the time with material compensation were sometimes dissatisfied when the court failed to order compensation in their favour. Even victims, therefore, appeared to be ambivalent about the status of their "right" to material reparation, feeling it was their due but embarrassed at demanding it.

A final persistent problem was the question of voluntariness in participation. Victims clearly felt able to exercise their privilege of abstaining and mediators in general appeared to have developed a style of persuasion that was sensitive and unoppressive, although schemes should develop procedures for monitoring this process and codes of ethics to protect victims against misguided over-enthusiasm by some proponents of mediation.

On the other hand, offenders did generally seem feel a certain obligation to take part in their own interests. Sometimes, in the police-based schemes, they seemed to be deliberately misled about their chances of prosecution. If one accepts that their participation should be voluntary, any pressure is unacceptable. It can, however, be reasonably questioned whether voluntariness for the offender is really so vital. While there is no way in which one can condone deliberate deceit (and this aspect of many of the police-based schemes must be prohibited), there is no reason why one should not declare, as a matter of simple natural justice, that offenders have a duty to put right what they have taken from their victims — materially and emotionally — if it is within their powers to do so.

Here we come to a point where the experimental schemes may have gone too far in being over-ready to dismiss the material side of reparation and stressing the emotional. This shift of emphasis was needed to combat the general bias of criminal justice towards the material and its neglect of victims' complete range of needs, but it should not be taken so far that it effectively denies a victim's basic right to have the value of property stolen or destroyed returned to them. If this right is to be waived, it must be at the discretion of the victim and no-one else. It was clear from accounts of victim/offender meetings that there is among all citizens a sense that reparation was only natural and right, even if it is difficult to bring oneself to it as the one who is in the wrong.

(iv) Offender accountability

It is important to separate the ideas of mediation and reparation. Reparation, essentially, is not a matter for negotiation: it is a right that anyone would concede to be so. It may or not form part of the outcome of mediation. When it does, it is usually symbolic rather than full reimbursement. Victims may be prepared to negotiate reparation for the sake of promoting a more fruitful exchange, at least when the offender — as is usually the case — is unable to afford complete compensation, or where the victim has not suffered a significant loss in purely material terms. Others would prefer to leave the matter of compensation to the courts. If this is so the courts should be informed so that they do not neglect to consider this need when sentencing. Alternatively, and preferably, material reparation offered, or carried out before mediation (eg by handing over a payment via the scheme), enhances the offender's credibility, makes mediation easier, and avoids any negotiations about quantum. If the victim is still dissatisfied with what has been paid, it can be left to the court to adjudicate on the matter, unless it can be simply resolved at a mediation session.

This brings us to a point which goes beyond the powers of mediation schemes themselves, as it involves a principle of justice that would apply across the board, whether mediation is in view or not. Should reparation be seen as a duty of all offenders, as soon as guilt is admitted? The evidence from this research is that most people would assume it was a duty, although there is no reflection in the law of it as such, and currently no procedure for allowing it to occur. Voluntary reparation may even be discouraged as potentially prejudicing a case or because the law is intent on keeping victims and offenders apart. A scheme which can act as intermediary, however, could overcome the second objection, while the first may be seen to be infrequently applicable, and even then may be less important than the principle that offenders should be held accountable for their actions by being expected to make reparation.

When it comes down to it, the message from the mediation schemes is that offenders should be held to account personally to their victim, both for the sake of the beneficial impact it has upon themselves, and for the benefits that can accrue to victims, especially if the offender is prepared to go as far as coming face to face to apologise and provide some explanation.

There will, however, be objections to the formalisation of such a duty on the part of offenders. Traditional supporters of offenders' interests will argue that this only increases the punitive impact of society upon the offender, and that punishment is self-defeating as a means of reform. They will also argue that many offenders are unable to fulfil such an obligation.

As far as the first argument goes, one needs to distinguish between different kinds of punishment — or, rather, to see punishment as only one kind of imposition that can be placed on an offender. Such impositions may be of two basic kinds — they may be generally agreed obligations that perform a positive function in promoting reconciliation, and which the subject can identify readily as naturally due, or they may be punishments that others apply according to their own judgement of retribution, which contribute nothing to the commonweal directly but serve, in the first instance, only to cause pain or loss to the subject. A punishment is applied over and above any obligations — hence the difficulty most sentencers have in coming to terms with the idea of a compensation order as a sole penalty, because it violates the common-sense interpretation of a penalty being something more than just fulfilling one's duty.

On this view, fears of double punishment and so on should be held to be not only misguided or confused, but actually as denying the right that victims have of their suffering being made good. The fulfilment of such obligations may be a burden, but it is a positive one, that both heals and "makes sense". It does not necessarily have any bearing on a judgement about punishment, although it is likely that any court operating within a philosophy of natural justice would see the voluntary satisfaction of such obligations as a point in favour of the defendant's moral character.

Insofar as the offender cannot afford to compensate for the victim's total loss, the obligation would be correspondingly reduced — just as it is when sentencers determine the size of a compensation order. The obligation could also be altered in kind, from a financial one to one incorporating actions anyone can perform — apologising, offering some service or taking steps to keep out of further trouble, receiving and acknowledging the victim's hurt and concern.

Others may be worried that reparative obligations let the offender off too lightly. The more wealthy offender, for instance, might be seen as "buying him/herself out" of prosecution; or the offender who makes niggardly reparation could be "getting away" with the crime. These problems, however, do not exist if the distinction between obligation (offender to victim) and punishment (State to offender) is maintained. The court would have the twin duties of reviewing the fulfilment of obligations (that a reasonable effort had been made) and determining punishment (which may take into account the first and may even be set at none at all — a caution or absolute discharge — if the State's interests in the matter are absolved with the satisfaction of the victim).

The creation of a role for accountability in criminal justice could have many benefits, although it passes beyond the scope of mediation schemes themselves. It would, however, provide an excellent context within which they could operate and maximise their own peculiar contributions, capitalising on such reparation by furthering reconciliation and community understanding. The practical problems of victim/offender mediation are still substantial, but the promise of an important new contribution to the management of crime is contained within their work.

Appendix Case-studies

Case-study I

A Detective Inspector who had been dealing with this case referred it to the N.E. Essex scheme. Tom had attempted to strangle his wife. She was unconscious for a while and required hospital treatment. He was charged with attempted murder, later reduced to grievous bodily harm. He was bailed to live away from his wife until after the case had been heard in court. This was his first offence. The couple had been married for forty years, and both were in their mid-sixties.

A mediator contacted Tom and Peggy separately. Both expressed a wish to be reconciled and were keen for a meeting to take place. Tom said that he was feeling lonely and isolated away from his wife and wished to apologise to her, although he was not keen that another party should be there. However, his solicitor later phoned him and explained the purpose and nature of a meeting with a third party present and Tom then felt happier about the prospect.

It was arranged that the mediation meeting should take place in a neighbour's house (she was away at the time). The mediator accompanied Peggy. Tom arrived shortly afterwards. He immediately kissed his wife and said he was sorry. Nevertheless, the first few minutes were uncomfortable. They discussed the incident in detail, which they found difficult. Tom was very anxious to return home and make amends. Peggy was willing to have her husband home but explained that certain conditions would have to be met. Most importantly, she wanted him to stop drinking, as she considered drink was to blame for the incident, although the mediator doubted that this was the whole case. They discussed changes that Tom should make. The mediator suggested that consultation with a Marriage Guidance counsellor might help. Both parties agreed; Peggy said she had suggested it herself a year ago. The mediator brought the meeting to a close after an hour and explained what she would be writing in her report to the court.

The mediator informed the solicitors of each party about how the meeting had gone. She arranged another meeting between the husband

and wife a month later. This meeting again took place in the neighbour's house. The mediator felt that this time the atmosphere was much more relaxed. She left them alone for half an hour of privacy.

The mediator arranged a Marriage Guidance appointment for the couple and escorted Peggy to the meeting. Three days later the court altered the bail conditions and Tom moved back home. The couple attended a couple more Marriage Guidance sessions and as far as the mediator could ascertain, they were managing to repair their relationship. Tom received a conditional discharge at the court hearing — a very light sentence in view of the gravity of the attack, but one which ensured a certain degree of pressure on Tom to continue to be of good behaviour and which was sensitive to the reconciliation achieved by the mediation scheme.

Case-study II

At the Leeds Mediators Monthly Meeting issues and cases came up for discussion. Joanna and Frank, two of the mediators, described at one of these meetings a particularly powerful emotional mediation session which they had arranged. First, Joanna described to the other mediators present the background to the case: This is the mediator's account of the case:

Angus had been charged, together with a co-defendant, with two burglaries, one involving property to the value of approximately £10,000, and the other property to the value of £900. He was the "most remorseful offender" Joanna, an experienced mediator, had come across. Joanna made appointments by letter to visit the two victims. The dates suggested were not convenient so instead she popped in to see them a few days later. Mrs Carruthers was not at home, but Mrs Joseph, who had lost over 80 items and was the victim, together with her husband, of the bigger burglary, was in. Mrs Joseph welcomed Joanna in and gave her tea. Joanna recalled *"She said she was over it, but it was clear she wasn't. It was still there, 3 o'clock she wakes up in the morning, and it will be the first thing she thinks of"*. Many of the items had belonged to Mrs Joseph's deceased sister, who had died of cancer two years previously, and these items were in care ready to pass on to nieces. Mrs Joseph feared anti-semitism as a reason for why her house had been burgled. She agreed to see Angus. The project assistant arranged the meeting venue, a local village hall. Both burglaries had been committed in a prosperous leafy village a few miles out of the city where Angus lived.

It was felt by the mediators that Angus and his co-defendant had been asked to do the burglaries by a 'Mr Big' who had given them just £80-£100 each for over £10,000 worth of items.

The day came for the meeting and Joanna picked up Angus. Mr Joseph came to the meeting equipped with some notes.

Mrs Joseph confronted Angus with plenty of questions at the mediation session. *"Why my house? Had you been watching the house before?"* She asked for information about the man who set it up. She told Angus of the lack of insurance cover (only one third of the cost of items insured) and then suddenly she brought some photographs of her deceased sister out of her handbag and thrust them in front of Angus's face. "This is who you stole from!" This took Angus by surprise and brought tears to his face.

Frank said that what happened was *"something you can't get into a report"*. Joanna said that Mrs Joseph then asked about Angus. *"His mind was blown over her concern for him"*; Frank added "She wanted him to work for a Cancer Hospice". A dramatic mediation session came to an end. Joanna felt that Mrs Joseph was *"still very raw and I don't think we can leave it there"*. Joanna and Frank then stayed on for Angus to meet Mr and Mrs Carruthers at the same village hall.

Mrs Carruthers told the researcher of her experience of the reparation scheme. The crime which Mr and Mrs Carruthers suffered was one of a number committed against their property over two years. It proved to be *"an irritation on top of the others but at least all of the property had been recovered in their case"*. When asked whether they would like to meet their offender Mrs Carruthers thought it was a very worthwhile idea and wished *"to give him a second chance, find out why he had done it, and see what he was like"*. Bur Mr Carruthers didn't like the idea and he was slightly annoyed when first approached. Later Mr and Mrs Carruthers read an article about the idea of victim meeting offender in 'The

Listener' and this article helped to persuade Mr Carruthers in favour of attending the meeting. Mrs Carruthers told the researcher: *"We did feel he was genuinely sorry. 'Our' lad was more articulate than I thought he'd be, also he wasn't shifty, he looked at us directly, therefore I think he was genuinely sorry"*. She added that it must be a *"difficult thing to do for mediators — especially to decide which offenders are genuine. The mediator went to a lot of trouble. I admire her"*, Mrs Carruthers said: *"The lad had responsibility for a girl who was pregnant, therefore he needed to get a regular job, so going to prison would be very tough for her and this was the reason for him getting a job."*

Mr and Mrs Carruthers and Angus signed a Mediation Contract which stated that:

1. Angus apologises to Mr and Mrs Carruthers;
2. Mr and Mrs Carruthers feel able to accept the apology as being genuine.

There was no 'reparation' work agreement because Angus had agreed some reparation after meeting his other victim, and because Mr and Mrs Carruthers did not feel it appropriate that he do any work for them. Furthermore, Mrs Carruthers said that they *"didn't expect compensation and didn't think the Court should have awarded it in our case"*.

[Angus was sentenced to 3 months Detention Centre and no compensation was ordered.]

After the two mediation sessions the Mediators drove Angus home. On the way home, Joanna reported that Angus stated that he felt much better, that he was amazed at how he had actually coped with the situation and the attitudes of his victims left him almost speechless. That someone who he had hurt so, particularly in the case of Mrs Joseph, was able to talk to him and most of all be concerned for his welfare was the biggest shock of all. He said he had expected them to start to rant and maybe even attack him — what he had not expected was what happened and the points made had gone home the more because of it. Joanna finished by stating that "this was by far the best mediation I have been involved with so far". Angus made the point that he wished the Judge could have seen what took place. Forty hours work, for a Cancer Hospice, was agreed in the Mediation Contract between Mrs Joseph and Angus. Because he was given a custodial sentence Angus didn't immediately do this work. After his release, his girlfriend gave birth to a premature baby which died after 9 days. Because of his distress over the baby's death the mediators thought it inappropriate for Angus to carry out the voluntary work at the Hospice, so they contacted them to explain.

Bibliography

ALBERT, R & HOWARD, DA (1985) Informal dispute resolution through mediation. Mediation Quarterly, 10, 99-108.

ALPER, BS & NICOLS, IT (1981) Beyond the Courtroom. Lexington, MA: Lexington.

BAHR, SJ (1981) An evaluation of court mediation: a comparison in divorce cases with children. Journal of Family Issues, 2, 39-60.

BAINBRIDGE, DI (1987) Survey of Four Magistrates' Courts. Report to the Home Office.

BARNETT, R E (1978) Restitution: a new paradigm of criminal justice. Ethics, 87, 279-301.

BIANCHI, H (1986) Pitfalls and strategies of abolition. In Bianchi and Van Swaaningen, infra.

BIANCHI, H & VAN SWAANINGEN, R (Eds) (1986) Abolitionism: towards a non-repressive approach to crime. Amsterdam: Free University Press.

BLAGG, H (1985) Reparation and justice for juveniles. British Journal of Criminology, 25, 267-279.

BRITTAN, L (1984) Home Secretary's Speech to the Holborn Law Society, 14 March.

BUSSMAN, K-D (1987) Mediation programs as a new paradigm for a restorative justice: different experiences and models of conflict resolution programs in Canada/USA and Germany. Paper to International Seminar on Mediation, Finland, September.

CHRISTIE, N (1977) Conflicts as property. British Journal of Criminology, 17, 1-15.

CHRISTIE, N (1982) Limits to Pain. Anford: Martin Robertson.

CLARKE, R V G & CORNISH, D B (1972) The Controlled Trial in Institutional Research — paradigm or pitfall for penal evaluation? Home Office Research Study 15. London: HMSO.

COATES, RB & GEHM, J (1985) Victim Meets Offender: an evaluation of victim offender reconciliation programs. Valparaiso, IN: PACT Institute of Justice.

COHEN, A K (1955) Delinquent Boys: the culture of the gang. London: Routledge and Kegan Paul.

COHEN, S (1985) Visions of Social Control: crime, punishment and classification. London: Polity Press.

COMMITTEE ON LOCAL AUTHORITY AND ALLIED PERSONAL SOCIAL SERVICES (1968) Report (Seebohm Report). HMSO. Cmnd. 3703.

COVENTRY REPARATION SCHEME (1987) Annual Report.

CRESSEY, D R (1986) Why managers commit fraud. Australia & New Zealand Journal of Criminology, 19, 195-209.

CRIMINAL STATISTICS, 1986 (1987) London: HMSO.

DAVIS, G (1983) Conciliation and the professions. Family Law, 13, 6-13.

DAVIS, G (1985) The theft of conciliation. Probation Journal, 32, 7-10.

DAVIS, G, BOUCHERAT, J & WATSON, D (1987) A Preliminary Study of Victim Offender Mediation and Reparation Schemes in England and Wales. Research and Planning Unit Paper 42. London: Home Office.

DITTENHOFFER, T & ERICSON, R V (1983) The victim/offender reconciliation program: a message to correctional reformers. University of Toronto Law Journal, 33, 315-347.

DONOHUE, WA, ALLEN, M & BURRELL, N (1985) Communication strategies in mediation. Mediation Quarterly; 10, 75-89.

EDELHERTZ, H (1977) Legal and operational issues in the implementation of restitution within the criminal justice system. In Hudson, J & Galaway, B (Eds) Restitution and Criminal Justice. Lexington, MA: Lexington.

GALAWAY, B (1985) Preliminary experience of an urban victim offender reconciliation project. Paper to the 5th International Symposium on Victimology, Zagreb, August.

GALA WAY, B (1986) Victim-offender negotiation in an urban setting. Paper to the Annual Meeting, Academy of Criminal Justice Studies, Orlando, Florida, March.

GOTTFREDSON, MR (1984) Victims of Crime: the dimensions of risk. Home Office Research Study No. 81. London: HMSO.

GROVES, W & SAMPSON, R J (1987) Traditional contributions to radical criminology. Journal of Research in Crime and Delinquency, 24, 181-214.

GUEDALIA, L J (1979) Predicting recidivism of juvenile delinquents on restitutionary probation from selected background, subject and program variables. Rockville, Maryland: National Criminal Justice Reference Service.

HALEY, JO (1986) Comment: the implications of apology. Law and Society Review, 20, 499-507.

HARDING, J (1982) Victims and Offenders: needs and responsibilities. London: Bedford Square Press.

HARRINGTON, CB (1985) Shadow Justice: the ideology and institutionalisation of alternatives to court. London: Greenwood Press.

HEISTER, J W (1987) Property allocation in mediation: an examination of distribution relative to equality and to gender. Mediation Quarterly, 17, 97-98.

HERZ, R (1988) Juvenile mediation in West Germany. Mediation, 4: 2, 16.

HIRSCHI, T (1969) Causes of Delinquency. Berkeley: University of California Press.

HOFRICHTER, R (1980) Techniques of victim involvement in restitution. In Hudson, J & Galaway, B (Eds) Victims, Offenders and Alternative Sanctions. Lexington, MA: Lexington.

HOVDEN, K (1987) Norwegian experiences on the project "Alternatives to Imprisonment", especially on Conflict Councils. Paper to International Seminar on Mediation, Finland, September.

HUDSON, J & CHESNEY, S (1978) Research on restitution: a review and assessment. In Galaway, B & Hudson, J (Eds) Offender Restitution in Theory and Action. Lexington, MA: Lexington.

IIVARI, J (1987) Mediation as a conflict resolution: some topic issues in mediation project in Vantaa. Paper to International Seminar on Mediation, Finland, September.

IRVING, H H & BENJAMIN, M (1987) Family mediation research: critical review and future directions. In Vermont Law School Dispute

Resolution Project, The Role of Mediation on Divorce Proceedings. South Royalton, Vermont: Vermont Law School.

JAMES, S, HOSLER, S J & ALLMARSH, T (1983) Evaluating a community action scheme. Community Development Journal, 18, 20-32.

KAPARDIS, A & FARRINGTON, D (1981) An experimental study of sentencing by magistrates. Law and Human Behaviour, 5, 107-121.

KIGIN, R & NOVACK, S (1980) A rural restitution program for juvenile offenders and victims. In Hudson, J & Galaway, B (Eds) Victims, Offenders, and Alternative Sanctions. Lexington, MA: Lexington.

KNAPPER, P (1987) The development of mediation schemes in France, 1983-1987. Unpublished paper.

KRESSEL, K (1987) Research on divorce mediation: a summary and critique of the literature. In Vermont Law School Dispute Resolution Project, The Role of Mediation on Divorce Proceedings. South Royalton, Vermont: Vermont Law School.

KROHN, MD (1986) The web of conformity: a network approach to the explanation of delinquent behaviour. Social Problems, 33, 81-93.

LEEDS REPARATION PROJECT (1987) Report on Experimental Period 1 May 1985 — 30 April 1987. Leeds: West Yorkshire Probation Service.

LEFCOURT, C (1984) Women, mediation and family law. Clearing House Review, 18, 3.

MACKAY, R (1986) The place of reparation and mediation in criminal justice. Dissertation for MSc in Advanced Social Work Studies, University of Edinburgh.

MAGUIRE, M & CORBETT, C (1987) The Effects of Crime and the Work of Victims Support Schemes. Aldershot: Gower.

MARSHALL, TF (1985) Alternatives to Criminal Courts: the potential for non-judicial dispute settlement. Aldershot: Gower.

MARSHALL, TF (1988a) Out of court: more or less justice? In Matthews, R (Ed) Informal justice? London: Sage.

MARSHALL, T F (1988b) Informal Justice: The British Experience. In Matthews, R (Ed) supra.

MARSHALL, T F, FAIRHEAD, S, MURPHY, D & ILES, S (1978) Evaluation for democracy. In Social Research in the Public Sector, European Society for Opinion and Marketing Research.

MARSHALL, T F & WALPOLE, M (1985) Bringing People Together: mediation and reparation projects in Great Britain. Research and Planning Unit Paper 33. London: Home Office.

MARX, E (1976) The Social Context of Violent Behaviour. London: Routledge.

MATZA, D (1964) Delinquency and Drift. London: Wiley.

MERRY, S E (1982) Defining "success" in the neighbourhood justice movement. In Tomasic, R & Feeley, Ai! M (Eds) Neighbourhood Justice: assessment of an emerging idea. New York: Longman.

MNOOKIN, R & KORNHAUSER, L (1979) Bargaining in the shadow of the law: the case of divorce. Yale Law Journal, 88, 950-997.

MORASH, M BELKNAP, J & FERGUSON, F (1986) An empirical assessment of exemplary project publications: do they provide the necessary information for implementations? Journal Criminal Justice, 14, 509-528.

NELKEN, D (1985) Community involvement in crime control. Current Legal Problems, 38, 239-267.

NEWBURN, T (1988) The Use and Enforcement of Compensation Orders in Magistrates' Courts. Home Office Research Study. London. HMSO.

O'BRIEN, E (1986) Asking the Victim: a criminal study of the attitude of some victims of crime to reparation and the criminal justice system. Gloucestershire Probation Service.

OPCS (1982) Census 1981, Great Britain. London: HMSO.

PEARSON, J (1982) An evaluation of alternatives to court adjudication. Justice System Journal, 7, 420-444.

PEARSON, J & THOENNES, N (1985) A preliminary portrait of client reactions to three court mediation programs. Conciliation Courts Review, 23, 1-14.

RAYNOR, P (1985) Social Work, Justice and Control. Oxford: Blackwell.

REEVES, H (1984) The victim and reparation. Probation Journal, 31, 136-139.

RUTHERFORD, A (1986) Growing out of Crime: society and young people in trouble. Harmondsworth: Penguin.

SCHNEIDER, A L (1986) Restitution and recidivism rates of juvenile offenders: results from four experimental studies. Criminology, 24, 533-552. SCHNEIDER, A L &

SCHNEIDER, PR (1980) Policy expectation and program realities in juvenile restitution. In Hudson, J & Galaway, B (Eds) Victims, Offenders and Alternative Sanctions. Lexington, MA: Lexington.

SESSAR, K (1984) Public attitudes towards offender restitution in Germany: preliminary report on an empirical study conducted in Hamburg. Paper to Annual Meeting of American Society of Criminology, Cincinnati, November.

SHAPLAND, J & COHEN, D (1987) Facilities for victims: The role of the police and the courts. Criminal Law Review, 1, 28-38.

SHAPLAND, J, WILLMORE, J & DUFF, P (1985) Victims in the Criminal Justice System. Aldershot: Gower.

SHONHOLTZ, R (1984) Neighbourhood justice systems: work, structure and guiding principles. Mediation Quarterly, 5, 3-30.

SLAIKEU, KA, CULLER, R, PEARSON, J, & THOENNES, N (1985) Process and outcome in divorce mediation. Mediation Quarterly, 10, 55-74.

SMITH, D BLAGG, H & DERRICOURT, N (1985) Victim-Offender Mediation Project. Report to the Chief Officers' Group, South Yorkshire Probation Service.

SMITH, J (1986) Mediation in practice: an example of victim/offender mediation from the South Yorkshire scheme. Mediation, 2, 2, 2-4.

SUTHERLAND, E H (1939) Principles of Criminology. Philadelphia: J B Lippincott.

TARLING, R (1979) Sentencing Practice in Magistrates' Courts. Home Office Research Study 56. London: HMSO.

UMBREIT, M (1985a) Victim Offender Mediation: conflict resolution and restitution. Washington DC: US Department of Justice.

UMBREIT, M (1985b) Crime and Reconciliation: creative options for victims and offenders. Nashville: Abingdon.

VAN VOORHIS, P (1985) Restitution outcome and probationer's assessments of restitution: the effects of moral development. Criminal Justice and Behaviour, 12, 259-287.

WAGATSUMA, H & ROSETT, A (1986) The implications of apology: law and culture in Japan and the United States. Law and Society Review, 20, 461-498.

WAHRHAFTIG, P (1984) Non-professional conflict resolution. Villanova Law Review, 29, 1463-1476.

WALKER, J (1987) Divorce mediation — is it a better way? In Vermont Law School Dispute Resolution Project, The Role of Mediation in Divorce Proceedings. South Royalton, Vermont: Vermont Law School.

WALKLATE, S (1986) Reparation: a Merseyside view. British Journal Criminology, 27, 287-298.

WOLFGANG, M & FERRACUTI, F (1967) The Subculture of Violence: towards an integrated theory in criminology. London: Tavistock.

WOODWARD, K (1985) Avoiding the juvenile justice merry-go-round. Community Care, September 12, 13.

WRIGHT, M (1982) Making Good: prisons, punishment and beyond. London: Burnett Books.

WRIGHT, M (1983) Victim-Offender Reparation Agreements: a feasibility study in Coventry. Birmingham: West Midlands Probation Service.

WRIGHT, P (1986) Victims of Crime — a social work perspective. Social Work Monograph 47. Norwich: University of East Anglia.

YOUNG, R (1987) The Sandwell Mediation and Reparation Scheme: an evaluation of its development and impact. Birmingham: West Midlands Probation Service.

ZEHR, H (1983) VORP: moving towards an urban and multicultural setting. In PACT Institute of Justice, The VORP Book. Valparaiso, IN: PACT Institute of Justice.

ZEHR, H (1985) Retributive Justice, Restorative Justice. Elkhart, IN: MCC US Office of Criminal Justice.